More Than One Struggle

Fg. 175
Howard
Fuller

THE UNIVERSITY OF NORTH CAROLINA PRESS

Chapel Hill & London

MORE THAN ONE STRUGGLE

THE EVOLUTION OF
BLACK SCHOOL REFORM IN MILWAUKEE

JACK DOUGHERTY

© 2004 The University of North Carolina Press

Manufactured in the United States of America

Designed by Lou Robinson

Set in New Baskerville by Tseng Information Systems, Inc.

The paper in this book meets the guidelines for permanence and durability
of the Committee on Production Guidelines for Book Longevity of the
Council on Library Resources.

Publication of this work was aided by a generous grant from the Z. Smith
Reynolds Foundation.

The author's share of proceeds from the sale of this book will be donated to
the Wisconsin Black Historical Society/Museum.

A portion of this work previously appeared in Jack Dougherty, "'That's When We Were
Marching for Jobs': Black Teachers and the Early Civil Rights Movement in Milwaukee,"
History of Education Quarterly 38 (Summer 1998): 121–41, © History of Education
Society, reprinted with permission.

Library of Congress Cataloging-in-Publication Data
Dougherty, Jack.
More than one struggle : the evolution of black school reform in Milwaukee /
Jack Dougherty.
p. cm.
Includes bibliographical references (p.) and index.
ISBN 0-8078-2855-6 (cloth : alk. paper) — ISBN 0-8078-5524-3 (pbk. : alk. paper)
1. African Americans—Education—Wisconsin—Milwaukee—History.
2. Discrimination in education—Wisconsin—Milwaukee—History.   3. Educational
change—Wisconsin—Milwaukee—History.   4. Milwaukee (Wis.)—Race relations.
I. Title.
LC2803.M55D68 2004
371.829'96073—dc22   2003018808

cloth 08 07 06 05 04   5 4 3 2 1

paper 08 07 06 05 04   5 4 3 2 1

To all of the oral history participants,
who shared a portion of their life stories

and to Beth,
who shares life with me every day

CONTENTS

ILLUSTRATIONS, MAPS, FIGURES, AND TABLE

Illustrations

Maps

Figures

Table

ACKNOWLEDGMENTS

This book would not have been possible without the many individuals who collectively created this history of Milwaukee and shared their stories with me through decades of newsprint, archives, journals, books, videos, and interviews. Some of them kindly invited me into their homes and workplaces and allowed me to record their stories on tape or to dig through documents stored away in attics and basements. Several also listened to my first impressions and flatly told me how I had "got it all wrong," then generously took the time to redirect my thinking. While it was not possible for me to fit all of their stories into one book, I hope that people make use of the transcripts that I made of their stories and sent to them, or the ones deposited at the University of Wisconsin–Milwaukee archives and the Wisconsin Black Historical Society/Museum, to write their own histories of Milwaukee.

The research also was generously funded by several sources. Clayborn Benson of the Wisconsin Black Historical Society/Museum first offered me financial assistance to conduct the oral histories. To show my deep appreciation, the author's share of the proceeds from the sale of this book will be donated to continue his organization's work. The Spencer Foundation also provided crucial support at three stages: as the beneficiary of a mentor grant to Mary Haywood Metz in 1995, as a dissertation fellowship in 1996–97, and as a small research grant in 1998. The Colgate University Research Council paid for transcribing interviews, and the Trinity College Faculty Research Committee provided a one-year expense grant and summer stipend. Barbara Henriques in Trinity's Educational Studies Program kindly contributed funds to cover most of the photograph expenses. Finally, Mary Jo Gessler and Gail Geib hatched creative schemes to prevent the University of Wisconsin–Madison from plunging my checkbook balance deep into large negative numbers at a crucial time in this project.

Deep within the pages of this book is the profound influence of many teachers who made time to help me learn to read, listen, think, and write. At the University of Wisconsin–Madison, I thank the faculty who taught me how to ask the right questions (including my adviser Michael Fultz, Linda Gordon, Carl Kaestle, Mary Haywood Metz, and Michael Olneck), who pushed me to tell the stories (Jurgen Herbst and Tim Tyson), and who generously gave helpful feedback on my work (Jane Collins, Bill Reese, and John Witte). I also extend my deep appreciation to teachers who worked with me much earlier, including Clement Price at Rutgers University–Newark; Hugh Lacey, Lisa Smulyan, and Eva Travers at Swarthmore College; Pat Allen at Union College; and Tony Gerakopolous, Bruce Bonney, and Jay Dunn at Morrisville-Eaton High School in central New York State.

In academic conference sessions, graduate school seminars, and friendly discussions, I also had the opportunity to meet several colleagues who generously shared their comments on my research and encouraged me to rethink several assumptions: Derrick Alridge, James Anderson, Adina Back, Michael Barndt, Crystal Byndloss, Jim Carl, Donald Collins, Bill Dahlk, Michele Foster, V. P. Franklin, Eric Fure-Slocum, David Gamson, Paul Geib, Nicholas Glass, Michael Gordon, Darryl Graham, Michael Grover, Donna Harris, Ian Harris, Michael Homel, Katherine Kuntz, Catherine Lacey, David Levine, Earl Lewis, Jerome Morris, Maggie Nash, Kathy Neckerman, Adam Nelson, Bruce Nelson, Maike and Dirk Philipsen, Jerry Podair, Sonya Ramsey, John Rury, Amy Schutt, Kevin David Smith, Stephen Smith, Quintard Taylor, Margaret Tennesson, Laura Docter Thornburg, Vanessa Siddle Walker, and Polly Weiss. Special thanks go to my two outside readers, Dave Douglas and Jim Leloudis, whose comments on the final draft were especially helpful.

Several other colleagues carefully read portions of the manuscript in its later stages and offered excellent suggestions for revisions: Abigail Adams, Stefanie Chambers, Pamela Grundy, Bob Lowe, John Spencer, and Todd Vogel. When I look over the text, I realize that some of my best friends have written some of the best parts of my book.

Many outstanding archivists and librarians went beyond the call of duty to assist me with the research: Nancy Godleski at Vanderbilt and Yale Universities; James Danky and Maureen Hady at the Wisconsin Historical Society; Sarah Johnson at the *Milwaukee Journal Sentinel*; Eileen Lipinski at the Milwaukee Legislative Reference Bureau; Rose Arnold at the Wisconsin Legislative Reference Bureau; Sue Mobley and Virginia Schwartz at the Milwaukee Public Library; and Tim Ericson, Mark Vargas, and Leslie Heindrichs at the University of Wisconsin–Milwaukee Library Archives. Several undergraduate students also served as research assistants and/or commented on drafts, beginning with Jody Roy at Colgate University and Eric Lawrence, Lesley Loventhal, Jessica Martin, and students in the educational studies fall 2001 senior seminar at Trinity College.

At the University of North Carolina Press, it has been a pleasure to work with David Perry, Mark Simpson-Vos, Paula Wald, Julie Bush, and the other members of the staff. I thank Tim Tyson for sending me in their direction.

My parents, John and Linda Dougherty, and my sisters, Jill, Kris, and Ellen, have been wonderfully supportive during this long project. It's been so long, in fact, that my three children were born at various points along the way. Eli arrived just after I completed the master's paper in 1993, then Eva came to help me finish the dissertation in 1997, and Maya appeared in 2001 as a pleasant reminder to get the book done.

Finally, to my partner, Beth Rose, the real historian in the family, it still amazes me how you found the time, energy, and patience to read and edit countless drafts, provide encouragement when a boost was needed, support our family when I was unemployed, give birth to our wonderful children, care for them during my research trips, and so much more. Thank you, with love.

ABBREVIATIONS

CIO	Congress of Industrial Organizations
CORE	Congress of Racial Equality
FEPC	Fair Employment Practices Committee
MUSIC	Milwaukee United School Integration Committee
NAACP	National Association for the Advancement of Colored People
NALC	Negro American Labor Council
NCIC	Northside Community Inventory Conference
NNNPC	Near Northside Non-Partisan Conference
PACE	Parents Action Committee for Education
PTSO	Parent-Teacher-Student Organization
UCAG	United Community Action Group
YMCA	Young Men's Christian Association

More Than One Struggle

INTRODUCTION

W hen Americans learn about our history of race and education or the broader movement for civil rights, popular images of the 1954 *Brown v. Board of Education* decision become firmly planted in our minds. For instance, when visitors step into the National Civil Rights Museum in Memphis, Tennessee, one of the striking images they encounter is a wall-sized photographic mural of attorney Thurgood Marshall and his National Association for the Advancement of Colored People (NAACP) colleagues proudly beaming from the steps of the United States Supreme Court. The day is May 17th, when the high court ruled on the five Southern and border state cases and declared the legalized segregation of public schools to be unconstitutional. Images like this one appear in dozens of volumes at libraries and bookstores, on multiple websites across the expansive Internet, in history textbooks in thousands of classrooms, and on the television screens of millions of viewers. Several of these historical accounts, such as the widely acclaimed *Eyes on the Prize* documentary series, use *Brown* as a starting point to launch a story about the dawning of the modern civil rights movement. As a result, these unshakeable images of the courageous struggle for school integration have been raised to a nearly mythological status in the American public's historical memory.[1]

Popular images of the 1954 *Brown v. Board of Education* legal victory present a triumphant yet incomplete history of black education. *Left to right*: NAACP attorneys George E. C. Hayes, Thurgood Marshall, and James Nabrit. Courtesy of AP/Wide World Photos and Library of Congress, Prints and Photographs Division (LC-USZ62-111236).

These images tell a crucially important story, but there is more than one story to be told. Viewing the history of black education solely through the lens of *Brown* distorts our understanding of the past by focusing only on school integration, when in fact there have been struggles for numerous reforms: hiring black teachers; resettling migrant families; gaining better resources, including black curricula; and exercising community control. In very recent years, while some black advocates continue to press for integration, others have lobbied for Afrocentric schooling, private school vouchers, and, in some cases, partially rolling back desegregation orders to return to neighborhood schooling. At first glance, when looking back on the past from today's perspective, contemporary black struggles over race and schooling seem to have abruptly parted from the integration movement. We confront an uncomfortable gap between our understanding of the past and present, particularly at this moment when our nation commemorates the fiftieth anniversary of *Brown*.

Historians who seek to connect the popularized history of *Brown* with contemporary policy debates over race and schooling face a serious dilemma. On one hand, we should strive to make this history more relevant to people's lives. As activist-scholar Vincent Harding reminds us in *Hope and History*, activists' stories of the civil rights movement bring a special, transformative value to our present-day struggles, especially in times of despair. If we overlook stories like *Brown* (or worse yet, mistakenly assume that younger generations have already learned them), we risk losing the spiritual power of its moral victory against racism.[2] On the other hand, historians need to exercise caution against uncritical portrayals of *Brown*. The sum of black educational history cannot be cast as a one-dimensional struggle for integrated schooling. As historians Patricia Sullivan and Waldo Martin observe in *Teaching the American Civil Rights Movement*, popularized images of the struggle have inadvertently "frozen the movement in time." Yet black activism has not stood still since 1954. Thoughtful historians and educators are obligated to challenge the "conventional or master narratives of civil rights history," which tend to unfold as a straightforward journey toward justice and historical progress.[3] If we fail to challenge these celebratory accounts, then not only will we have misconstrued the past, but we also will have neglected to provide a meaningful historical basis for understanding race and education struggles in the present. Scholarship on the recent era of black freedom struggles—especially regarding education—needs an interpretive framework that satisfies both our historical and contemporary needs.

This book addresses those needs by tracing the evolution of black-led school reform efforts from the 1930s to the 1990s in one Midwestern city: Milwaukee, Wisconsin. The study defines the history of black school reform as an interconnected series of overlapping (and sometimes conflicting) group efforts to gain power over educational policy and practice for the broader goal of uplifting the race. It shares a revised interpretation of African American urban history, which holds that there were "many different civil rights *movements* rather than a single unified movement dominated by a few elite leaders" and that these movements evolved through historical shifts in national influences, local contexts, and human agency. The book also draws inspiration from some of the best recent scholarly works on Southern black experiences of schooling in the twentieth century, such as David Cecelski's *Along Freedom Road* and Vanessa Siddle Walker's *Their Highest Potential*, by exploring how similar themes played out in a Northern urban setting.[4]

The book's title, *More Than One Struggle*, operates on four levels of meaning, drawn from broader insights in the recent historiographical literature on race and civil rights. On one level, it examines continuous decades of black activism by looking at a sixty-year span rather than narrowing its scope to the rise and fall of a specific struggle. This volume presents an interwoven narrative of three successive generations of black Milwaukee activists: proponents of black teacher hiring in the 1930s, of school integration in the 1960s, and of a countermovement that gave rise to private school vouchers in the 1990s.[5]

On a second level, the book investigates activists' multiple perspectives within black-led reform organizations. Historians of gender have long argued that activists' roles within civil rights movements deserve closer study, since the official spokespeople who delivered speeches were usually men and the ordinary participants who did crucial support work were usually women. This volume contends that by studying both elite and everyday activists' perspectives, we not only expand the cast of historical actors but also reach new interpretations about why movements rose and declined during the 1960s.[6]

On a third level, it probes the contested nature of historical memory in black school reform movements. Each generation of activists created its own version of the history of prior movements, most often to add greater coherence to the struggles faced in its own period. Recognizing the role of memory in a multigenerational study helps explain how different black reformers perceived and reacted to one another.[7]

Finally, the book offers more than just another case study by exploring the degree of interaction between local and national history. To be sure, the main narrative focuses on people and events in Milwaukee, but the underlying analysis points to connections (and disconnections) between them and national civil rights organizations, federal government, mass migrations, and news media. It draws comparisons with other Northern cities at specific points to help explain why changes occurred.[8] Framing the interpretation on these four themes allows us to examine historically the relationships between past and present struggles for black education without being forced to argue that one is a direct descendant (or an abandoned stepchild) of the other.

To be sure, Milwaukee is not the most familiar stopping point on the popularized civil rights trail "from Montgomery to Memphis." Yet Milwaukee's black population, which grew from under 1,000 to over 222,000 during the twentieth century, actively participated in broader movements. Local activists attracted national headlines during the March on Washington Movement in the 1940s, school desegregation and fair housing protests in the 1960s, and the coalition for private school vouchers in the 1990s.[9] Black Milwaukeeans did not simply accept the nation's civil rights movement; they adapted it to fit their local conditions. Therefore, to gain a more comprehensive understanding of the black freedom struggle as a whole, we need to focus more attention on places like Milwaukee where the stories are not identical to those in the Southern states, nor in Northern cities with larger black populations (such as New York, Chicago, and Detroit), which have tended to attract the majority of historians' interests.[10]

More Than One Struggle is written as an analytical narrative. Each chapter is driven by an interpretive argument about a transitional period in Milwaukee's history, but the overall story is held together by narratives about four leading black activists and their contrasting visions of race and reform across successive generations. Another strand in this story—the *Brown* decision—touched all of their lives, but activists from various generations interpreted its meaning in different ways as they encountered changing forms of racism over time.

The book begins with William Kelley of the Milwaukee Urban League, who, beginning in the 1930s, fought to gain jobs for black teachers in the all-white public schools rather than push for school integration. Given the city's small black population, its weak economic base during the Depression, and lack of political clout, Kelley made a difficult compromise with white officials to hire black teachers in schools only with sizable numbers of black children. Later, in the wake of the 1954 *Brown* decision, when its meaning was not yet clear for Northern schools, Kelley reinterpreted this student-oriented ruling to serve Milwaukee's job-oriented civil rights movement and eventually won significant numbers of jobs for black educators by the close of the decade. But Kelley's gains came during the peak years of Southern black migration into an increasingly segregated city. The migrants' arrival heightened racial anxieties on all sides and sharply increased the number of predominantly black schools, thereby lowering the status of inner-city schoolteachers' work in white eyes. As a result, the partial success of Kelley's generation of activism also entailed serious consequences for the next.

The key figure of the second generation was Lloyd Barbee, an attorney and state NAACP activist who arrived in 1962 and soon launched Milwaukee's first sustained movement against segregated education. Barbee redefined the local meaning of *Brown*, insisting that it prohibited "Milwaukee-style" segregation as much as legalized separation in Southern and border states, and thereby joined a growing wave of Northern activism. He changed fellow Milwaukeeans from spectators to agitators in the fight for integrated education and formed a mass coalition to sponsor the largest and most confrontational black-led protests ever witnessed by the city at that time, and he filed a federal lawsuit to prove his case in court. But Barbee's activists collided head-on with Milwaukee's established black leadership from the previous generation, whose political interests and personal experiences had never led them to condemn all-black schooling as the integrationists did. By examining 1960s activists' motivations for joining (and later departing from) Barbee's coalition against segregated schooling, the reasons underlying the rise and decline of this movement become more complex than just a simple ideological shift from integration to black power.

By the 1970s, Milwaukee's black population had grown and diverged, giving rise to two strands of black education activism in two distinct neighborhoods. In the predominantly white, west-side Washington High School area, activist Marian McEvilly developed a small but influential black and white constituency to pursue school reforms that would stabilize their racially transitional neighborhood. McEvilly worked alongside Barbee during the lengthy school desegregation trial, and when the judge finally ruled in their favor, she had won election onto the white-dominated school board to negotiate the politics of desegregating schools. The most feasible plan, in McEvilly's eyes, called for the closure and conversion of the all-black North Division High School, a brand-new facility that inner-city community supporters had fought hard to win as a means for stabilizing their neighborhood. Activist Howard Fuller rallied to save the black-majority high school, bringing together a diverse coalition of integrationists, black cultural nationalists, and long-term neighborhood residents. They redefined *Brown* yet again for Milwaukee by arguing that placing the burden of desegregation on black shoulders was a form of racism in itself. By 1980, Fuller's coalition had displaced Barbee's generation as the prevailing voice of black school reform and had opened a subsequent era of activism for private school vouchers in the concluding decade of the twentieth century.

Generations of black activists did not simply grapple with each other over politics; they also struggled over historical memories of "the movement" for civil rights. In the early 1960s, during the rise of the coalition for integrated schools, Lloyd Barbee and his colleagues ignored the established leadership's role in mobilizing for black jobs in the 1940s. Similarly, when black activism split along the lines of the Washington and North Division High School movements in the 1970s, each group created its own historical interpretation of 1950s-era black schooling. One side supported the legal case that segregated schools were inferior, while the other side celebrated the positive memories of a tight-knit black community. These conflicting histories confirm that black activists not only fought to change educational policies in the present but also struggled to shape collective memories of race and reform in years past.

This study draws upon multiple sources of historical evidence: primary documents located in official archives as well as activists' attics, reports generated by white Washington bureaucrats and black Milwaukee organizations, news stories published by the white-owned and black-owned presses, and visual collections of photographs and videotapes. In addition, I conducted over sixty oral history interviews with black Milwaukee school reform activists and educators and, when possible, compared them to similar interviews conducted years earlier. To organize this story, I focused greater attention on black Milwaukeeans than on the white majority and their ethnic groups or other racial minority groups in the city. Furthermore, it concentrates on elementary and secondary education more than on early childhood and higher education. While the book examines sustained black-led efforts to influence educational policy and practice in Milwaukee, it does not attempt to chronicle every single event; the episodes are too numerous to wrap coherently into one narrative. Finally, the book highlights the politics of education and only occasionally examines the world inside black students' classrooms or the complex relationships between black parents and their children's teachers. These rich and diverse experiences do not always mirror the broader struggles surrounding them, and their history awaits to be recorded and written.

Just as important as historical source materials are the questions that historians bring to them. When first beginning this research in graduate school, I initially focused my attention on 1965, the peak year of Milwaukee's school integration movement, when defiant activists confronted racism by organizing protest marches, civil disobedience, Freedom Schools, and federal lawsuits. From my perspective as a young white student who was born that very year and had neither lived through the movement nor learned a great deal about it in my predominantly white schooling, I tried to read and understand as much as possible. Attempting to think historically, I began to look through archival documents from previous decades for earlier signs of the integration movement, but very few appeared. Puzzled, my first research question was: Why didn't black Milwaukeeans raise their voices against segregated schools before the early 1960s? Likewise, when I tried to catch up on contemporary educational policy and began reading through black Milwaukee newspapers from the late 1980s and early 1990s, I asked myself a second, related question: Why did present-day black Milwaukeeans abandon the 1960s integration movement? Over time, it gradually dawned on me that both of these initial questions were seriously flawed because of my misguided effort to connect all generations of activism directly to the integration movement of 1965. Months later, after meeting black activists from various time periods and listening carefully during interviews, I finally settled upon a richer and more historically appropriate research question for this study: How did different groups of black Milwaukee activists define struggles over race and schooling, on their own terms, from the 1930s to the 1990s?[11]

The book's conclusion, "Rethinking History and Policy in the Post-*Brown* Era," takes up these and related questions. First, it assesses how various historians have interpreted the transformation of black educational activism and policy since the 1954 decision. Second, it examines why history and policy are interdependent. Thoughtful policy-making does not occur without rich historical awareness, and conversely, the best historical writing on recent eras contributes to our understanding of how we arrived at present-day policy crises. When attempting to make sense of black educational policy since *Brown*, it becomes important to recognize that the victories, compromises, and contested memories of each generation frame the settings for future debates. By looking more closely at how sixty years of race and education played out in Milwaukee, as well as in other locations, perhaps we can make wiser decisions about education for all children in the decades to come.

1

COMPROMISING TO WIN BLACK TEACHERS' JOBS

A mid the hundreds of Southern black migrants who arrived in Milwaukee in 1928, William Kelley stood out. While most came to the city without a high school education and searching for factory or domestic work, Kelley had a college degree and had already lined up a position as the new executive director of the Milwaukee Urban League, a social service agency dedicated to resettling rural migrants into their new urban environment. Soon, these migrants would be standing in line to meet him, dressed in his three-piece suit and tie. "When a Negro comes to Milwaukee," reported the white press, "he is almost certain to seek William V. Kelley, the person who can best advise him on working opportunities and housing facilities."[1]

Kelley had been groomed for this position with the Urban League. Born and raised in Tennessee, he graduated from Fisk University, the most prestigious black liberal arts college of its time. There he met Dr. George Haynes, the first director of the National Urban League, who also led Fisk's innovative Department of Social Work. Haynes recognized the need for professionally trained black social workers to coordinate social service and philanthropic efforts in the North, since they had greater familiarity and faith in the black community than did their white counterparts. He tutored Kelley and others in the ways of the Urban League, instructing them to "leave

William Kelley, executive director of the Milwaukee Urban League, sought ways of persuading white school officials to hire black teachers during the Depression. From *Milwaukee Journal*, 26 November 1939; copyright Milwaukee Journal Sentinel, Inc.; reproduced with permission.

militancy to others" and to use the tools of "education rather than legislation." Unlike the NAACP, Urban League founders believed that they could be most effective in achieving their objectives through quiet negotiations rather than public protests, and their nonpartisan stance also qualified them to receive desperately needed charitable contributions for their nonprofit agency. League affiliates across the country also dealt with a complicated interracial dynamic: most staff and clients were black, but most board members and donors were white. The organization needed people like Kelley, who could draw upon his interpersonal experiences to navigate through both worlds. After graduating from Fisk, he had experienced the color line in different forms: as a soldier in Europe during World War I, as a factory worker in Detroit, as a college instructor in Oklahoma, and as an Urban League staff member in St. Louis.[2]

Immediately after arriving in Milwaukee, Kelley had to redouble his efforts to secure jobs for blacks because the Depression was ravaging the local economy. Milwaukee's workforce depended heavily on the iron and steel industry. The city had gained national prominence for its machinery products, such as tractors and cranes manufactured by its largest employers, the Allis-Chalmers and Harnischfeger corporations. When demand plunged for these products, the economic crisis hit Milwaukee much harder than comparable cities in the nation. Between 1929 and 1933, the total number of employed wage earners fell 44 percent, forcing white employees into stiff competition for jobs with newly arrived black migrants. As the city's

Urban League employment service director, William Kelley screened migrant applicants and made referrals to white businesses and homeowners who needed inexpensive labor and were willing to consider black employees. Known as "the Negro's best bet," Kelley's office drew nearly 6,000 job seekers in 1930, but only 10 percent found work placements through the League service. When black migrants did find employment, they typically performed the lowest-paid and most unpleasant labor, such as feeding blast furnaces in steel foundries, slaughtering animals in packinghouses, processing hides in tannery lime pits, and scrubbing toilets in white people's homes. Blacks had to settle for "the dirty work," as one recalled, "jobs that even Poles didn't want."[3]

Milwaukee had a tiny black community in the early twentieth century. By 1930, two years after Kelley's arrival, he counted only 7,500 black residents, merely 1.3 percent of the city population. Both newcomers and old-timers crowded together into an impoverished neighborhood known as the Near Northside. Only ten black families owned their own homes. The vast majority of black residents rented from absentee landlords, and observers judged more than 90 percent of the neighborhood housing stock to be in poor physical condition. White realtors attempted to segregate the growing black neighborhood. In 1924, the Milwaukee Real Estate Board considered a formal proposal to restrict the population to a "black belt" within the city, and although they eventually dropped this measure, white property owners found several ways to achieve this goal. Restrictive covenants appeared in 90 percent of the county property deeds filed between 1910 and 1940, according to one estimate. The typical language expressly prohibited the sale or occupancy of property by "any person other than of the white race." Most other whites informally agreed not to sell or rent to blacks outside of the Near Northside, maintaining the neighborhood boundaries that carved up the city into white ethnic enclaves. Together, these forces created recognizable, though unofficial, color lines. The city's central business district formed the southern edge of the Near Northside on State Street, while the eastern and western borders were marked by Third Street and Twelfth Street. The northern edge of the color line inched farther outward, beginning at Galena Street in 1928 and reaching North Avenue by the late 1930s. Over 92 percent of the city's black population was enclosed within this 120-block neighborhood.[4]

Yet while most black Milwaukeeans were residentially segregated into the Near Northside, it was not an all-black community at this time. During the 1930s, whites composed approximately 50 percent of the 120-block neighborhood. Even in the census tract with the greatest concentration of black residents, whites still numbered 33 percent of the population. Consequently, when Milwaukeeans looked to their public schools, they did not yet

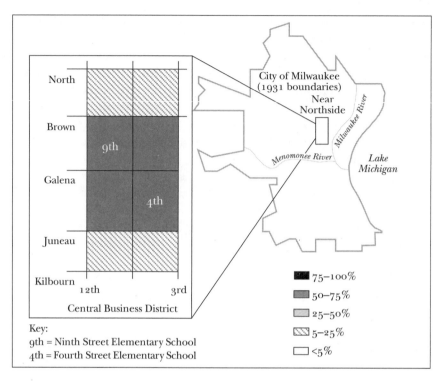

North

Brown

9th

Galena

4th

Juneau

Kilbourn
12th   3rd
Central Business District

City of Milwaukee
(1931 boundaries)
Near
Northside

Milwaukee River

Menomonee River

*Lake
Michigan*

■ 75–100%
■ 50–75%
□ 25–50%
▨ 5–25%
□ <5%

Key:
9th = Ninth Street Elementary School
4th = Fourth Street Elementary School

Black Population in Milwaukee's Near Northside during the 1930s. Although blacks were largely confined to one area in the early 1930s, they lived among significant numbers of whites, meaning that public schools were still racially mixed. Adapted from Citizen's Governmental Research Bureau, "Milwaukee's Negro Community."

see blatant patterns of racial segregation. Although nearly all black school children attended either Fourth Street or Ninth Street Elementary, both had racially mixed student bodies, enrolling between 35 to 50 percent black students in the early 1930s. Therefore, in the eyes of black community leaders like William Kelley, school segregation was not an issue. Instead, he mobilized around the fact that there had not been a single black teacher in the Milwaukee public school system when he had arrived in 1928, nor for several years later. Working together with his colleagues, Kelley defined black teachers' jobs as the city's leading black education reform issue for the next thirty years.[5]

Black teachers functioned as the levers for racial uplift during the early twentieth century. Whether one subscribed to the industrial education strategy of Booker T. Washington or the "talented tenth" approach of W. E. B. Du Bois, both relied on black teachers to advance the race. Across the South, black teachers not only provided a steady source of income for the local economy but also held respected positions as moral leaders of segregated communities. Observers consistently argued that "the genuine teacher knows that his duty is not bounded by the four walls of the classroom. He is dealing with boys and girls to be sure, but he is dealing with something more—with social conditions." Ideal Southern black teachers admonished students to continue their education within the constraints of the system and demonstrated through their own positions that schooling led to higher-status professional work. During the Great Migration of the early twentieth century, when over one million blacks left the South, one of their collective goals was to reestablish black community structures in Northern cities, in part by securing jobs for black teachers. But to do this, Kelley had to persuade white officials who ran the system to hire teachers of his race.[6]

In Milwaukee, William Kelley and his 1930s contemporaries recognized the dual purpose that schools played in their local struggles. The public schools not only were potential employers of middle-class black teachers but also served as key institutions that socialized black youth into their roles in the city's racialized labor market. Kelley heard many complaints about white teachers' low expectations for black students. One survey indicated that Milwaukee teachers and administrators believed that blacks "indirectly accept" their entry into low-level "Negro jobs" because they allegedly "feel their lot is hopeless." Vocational counselors advised black boys against training in higher-level occupations on the grounds that these jobs would not be made available to members of their race. Perhaps worse, schools taught stenography to black girls but refused to hire them as stenographers in the district's own central office. Even black students who did well academically discovered that their schooling had little relevance in Milwaukee. Three black teenage girls whose applications were rejected by a dime store were shocked to see those jobs given to white girls from the same high school. "Those other girls didn't make any better grades than we did," the black girls reported. "We used to help one of them with her algebra. If we can't even get jobs in a dime store, what's the use?" The sum of these experiences socialized black youth to believe that education did not pay, a painful lesson that Kelley sought to interrupt by introducing black teachers back into their world. Once jobs had been gained for black teachers, he believed, both their symbolic and pedagogical influence would help black students navigate their way through Northern white schools and into the workforce.[7]

During the 1930s, as the economic crisis worsened and white school officials refused to budge, Kelley proposed a compromise that led to the hiring of the first black teachers in permanent positions. Decades later, Kelley's accomplishments would be ignored by the 1960s generation of black school activists, who branded any concession to segregation as a failure to achieve true equality. Yet black school reform activists from the 1930s (like Kelley) and those from the 1960s (who rejected Kelley) had much in common: they both sought greater political influence over the white-dominated public education system in order to advance the race. This chapter lays the groundwork for later comparisons by focusing on Kelley's objectives for advancing black Milwaukee and how they were shaped by the historical context of his time.

Black Teachers and Political Power in the Urban North

Through his correspondence and annual meetings with other Urban League affiliates, William Kelley compared the status of blacks in Milwaukee with those in other Northern cities. Table 1.1 illustrates what Kelley saw shortly after his arrival in the city in the late 1920s and helps explain why black teacher employment was such a pressing issue. Cities across the North could be divided into three clusters: those where black teachers taught in all types of schools (white, black, and racially mixed), those where black teachers taught only in segregated black schools, and those that had few or no black teachers.[8]

Clearly, the size of a city's black population influenced the number of black teachers employed by its public schools, but it was not the only factor; how black communities translated their numbers into potential votes and the stance they took regarding all-black schooling mattered even more. For example, Pittsburgh's black population was nearly 55,000 in 1930, roughly comparable to Cleveland, Cincinnati, or Indianapolis. Yet Pittsburgh city schools counted no black teachers at that time. By contrast, Cleveland employed 75 black teachers in black, white, and racially mixed schools, while Cincinnati and Indianapolis employed even more black teachers (146 and 238) in racially segregated schools. In all of these cities, black communities faced some difficult decisions. How should they exercise the limited political clout available to them in the governance of public schools? Should they press for a handful of black educators in a racially mixed system, or for a greater number of black educators in a segregated system? These painful (and heavily contested) decisions, and the tense negotiations with white officials that followed, established black teacher employment as a leading education reform and civil rights issue in Northern cities during the late nineteenth and early twentieth centuries.

Across the urban North, different combinations of electoral politics and racial compromises shaped black education reform agendas in various ways. In the first cluster of cities (New York, Cleveland, and Chicago), where white politicians actively competed to win black votes, black leaders successfully negotiated to win jobs for black teachers in white, black, and racially mixed schools. New York City, for instance, gained a national reputation for not

Table 1.1: Black Teachers in Selected Northern Cities, circa 1930

City	Black Teachers	Black Population
Black teachers in all types of schools		
Chicago	300 (2.1%)	233,903 (6.9%)
Cleveland	84 (1.8%)	71,899 (8.0%)
New York	500 (1.5%)	327,706 (4.7%)
Black teachers in segregated black schools		
Cincinnati	146 (6.5%)	47,818 (10.6%)
Indianapolis	238 (12.6%)	43,967 (12.1%)
Philadelphia	295 (3.7%)	219,599 (11.3%)
Few or no black teachers		
Buffalo	4 (0.01%)	13,563 (2.4%)
Milwaukee	0 (0%)	7,501 (1.3%)
Pittsburgh	0 (0%)	54,983 (8.2%)

only hiring the largest number of black teachers but also for assigning many of them to white schools. "We are very proud of our record here, as you can imagine," NAACP leader Mary White Ovington boasted in 1920 to the Pittsburgh branch, whose city had no black teachers. The *Amsterdam News* echoed Ovington's sentiment in the black community and proclaimed in 1934 that New York City was "the only one among the larger cities of the country which accepts the Negro teacher and pupil on a basis of equality and fair play."[9]

The origins of New York City's relative success could be traced back to a long history of white politicians competing for black votes. In 1883, black New Yorkers lobbied the state legislature to allow their students the option of attending white schools without sacrificing black-run schools and thereby losing jobs for black teachers. Both Democrats and Republicans passed the bill, since Tammany Hall was fighting hard to sway black voters from the Party of Lincoln. But city school officials temporarily halted the plan by refusing to hire any new black teachers. After gaining sufficient "political assistance," the first black teacher was appointed to a predominantly white school in 1896, and the numbers of black teachers rose steadily during heated local races. Ever since that struggle, Ovington observed, "the question of race or color has not been considered in the appointment of teachers." Indeed, New York won fame as the fairest employer of black teachers, but not because city hall had suddenly become color-blind. To the contrary, black teachers secured jobs throughout much of the New York City school system due to intense white political competition to win the black vote.[10]

Black Clevelanders, despite their relatively small population, also exercised political clout to win jobs for black teachers in white schools. At least thirty-two of the city's eighty-four black teachers (38 percent) worked in all-white or predominantly white schools in 1930. Political scientist Ralph Bunche attributed these gains to black recognition of the value of "independent voting," pressuring white Republicans and Democrats to compete for black support in local and state races. During the election of 1926, one black Clevelander reported to the NAACP, "We supported Democrats and the Republicans alike, depending upon their merits." In the late 1930s, black leaders took advantage of the school board's desire to pass additional tax levies and refused to support the measure until blacks gained promotions to principalships. While blacks did not drop their concerns that whites were attempting to segregate Cleveland schools, they gained jobs for black teachers throughout the district and even won a seat for a former black teacher on the previously all-white school board.[11]

White competition for Chicago's black vote also resulted in jobs for black teachers, though with greater restrictions. Republican mayor "Big Bill" Thompson, known as "The Second Lincoln" by his supporters and "the master of Uncle Tom's cabin" by his opponents, relied upon patronage politics with black voters to hold office from 1915 to 1923, then again from 1927 to 1931. The number of black teachers increased during his administration from 40 to over 300, though only about 10 percent were in predominantly white schools in 1930. Still, these Depression-era jobs were highly sought after in a politically charged environment. Teacher candidates were required to obtain a letter of approval from a ward committeeman. One black teacher, a University of Chicago graduate, told how she relied upon black political clout to gain her job. While it was common knowledge that some white principals refused to hire black teachers, that fact did not prevent her from teaching as a substitute in an all-white school. "I didn't have any trouble at all," she explained, "because the district superintendent had been 'made,'" with the help of her relative, who was active in Thompson's Republican machine. Although the majority of the black teachers' jobs that opened up were low-status substitute or elementary school positions in segregated schools, blacks gained about 5.4 percent of the total number of school district positions (including janitor and clerical positions) in 1930, nearly matching their 6 percent proportion of the city's total population.[12]

By comparison, in the second cluster of cities (Indianapolis, Cincinnati, and Philadelphia), the politics of black teacher hiring played out quite differently. Although these three cities had higher proportions of black residents, there was less competition for their votes among the dominant white political machines. Black Indianapolis voters clung to Lincoln's party during the 1920s and early 1930s, and despite their sizable population (over 12 percent), neither Democrats nor Republicans courted them. Likewise, in Philadelphia during the 1920s, white Republican bosses considered the black vote to be safely "in the hip pocket."[13]

The result was a difficult compromise. Black communities in this second cluster of cities eventually gained significant numbers of teachers' jobs—in greater proportions than in New York or Chicago—but only upon accepting white conditions that schools would remain segregated. The source of these compromises can be traced back to the late nineteenth century. For instance, when a black Indiana state assemblyman introduced a bill to abolish school discrimination in 1897, over thirty black Indianapolis teachers rose up in opposition on the grounds that it would "remove the opportunity that colored men and women now have to strive after and obtain honorable employment in our public schools." Yet when the white Indianapolis school board overcame black opposition and segregated high schools in 1922, black support subsequently developed because jobs were promised to black teachers, who had been barred from white schools. A similar episode took place in the late nineteenth century in Ohio, where the state legislature officially banned school segregation but black Cincinnati teachers maneuvered at the local level to maintain separate schools and, by extension, their jobs. In their minds, the political equation was simple: closing all-black schools meant losing black teachers' jobs, since whites favored members of their own race as instructors for racially mixed schools.[14]

All of these cities stood far above the third cluster of cities (such as Buffalo, Pittsburgh, and Milwaukee), where black teachers had virtually no jobs, segregated or otherwise, in 1930. The determining factor was not simply the relative size of the black population but rather its degree of black political clout and whether or not the community could successfully transfer its power into a unified plan to lobby for black teacher hiring, whether in segregated or racially mixed schools. Blacks in Buffalo, for instance, struggled against internal and external barriers in their struggle to win teachers' jobs. Although a small handful of black teachers had been employed in segregated schools during the mid-nineteenth century, all of these positions had been lost when the state formally outlawed school segregation in 1881. Fifteen years later, one black college graduate obtained a teaching job in a school serving Italian immigrants, due to the assistance of a Republican candidate's political patronage, but her case was an exception. By 1925, only a half-dozen black teachers had been appointed in total over the previous three decades, mostly to low-status elementary school positions. The absence of black political power was the leading cause: established black residents continued to vote Republican in a city that became increasingly Democratic during the 1920s. Furthermore, the 1927 city redistricting plan diluted the voting strength of the predominantly black Fifth Ward. "Blacks were simply too few in number and without sufficient economic clout," observed one historian, "to force more and better political appointments from local politicians."[15]

Blacks in Pittsburgh faced even greater obstacles. Black teachers had been employed in small numbers to teach in segregated schools during the early nineteenth century, but all of these positions were lost when a state law banned all-black schools in 1881. For the next half-century, not a single black teacher was hired by the Pittsburgh public schools, despite a black population that approached 55,000. Robert Vann, editor of the black *Pittsburgh Courier* newspaper, launched a campaign to hire black teachers in 1914, arguing that the benefits that "the Negroes enjoy in Cleveland [also] must be enjoyed here." But Vann's campaign did not produce quick results, for two reasons. One factor was the political geography of Pittsburgh: since blacks lived in scattered neighborhoods, divided by hills and rivers, they had difficulty building the voting strength to control an entire city ward, in contrast to blacks who had been segregated into central-city neighborhoods in other cities. A second factor was ideological: black activists sharply disagreed about whether lobbying for black teachers' jobs would solve their community's problems or multiply them by returning to strictly segregated schools. In his 1930 study of Pittsburgh, sociologist Ira De A. Reid noted that discussions on the topic of black teachers "caused emphatic differences of opinion" among black committee members.[16]

Heated debate on the value of segregated versus racially mixed schooling also filled the pages of the presses. In 1929, L. A. Pechstein at the University of Cincinnati compiled findings from his doctoral students' research on Northern and border states and argued that "greater inspiration . . . and greater educational achievement are possible for negroes in separate public schools than in mixed schools." According to a survey conducted by one of his students, Jennie Porter, comparable Northern cities with mixed and separate schools (or separate schools exclusively) had higher black student enrollments and black graduation rates than did cities with only mixed schools. The surprising difference could be explained by the vital role of black teachers in segregated Northern schools, claimed Porter, the principal of a black Cincinnati school. Without the "self-sacrificing efficient colored teacher of colored youth, we would face positive disaster," she argued. "These teachers have in their ranks some of the best trained men and women in the world." Black Americans needed to face up to a great paradox, Porter concluded. Due to organizations such as the NAACP, "We oppose segregation in the schools. [Yet] we honor and appreciate the colored teacher in the colored school."[17]

In defense of the NAACP, *Crisis* editor W. E. B. Du Bois blasted Pechstein's article for overlooking the broader purpose of public schooling. "The human contact which comes through democratic education of all the youth of a great country" outweighs the right of any group, whether Catholic, Jewish, or African American, to educate its children in cultural isolation, he wrote in 1929. But over the next six years, Du Bois shifted his thinking on this issue. He fought with NAACP president Walter White on the organization's decision to pursue racial integration above all other agendas and eventually left his position as editor of the *Crisis*. In 1935, Du Bois rattled many nerves by writing a new article titled with the rhetorical question "Does the Negro Need Separate Schools?" in a special issue of the *Journal of Negro Education*, whose editorial policy spoke in favor of integration. Du Bois did not provide a simple answer to his rhetorical question. "No general and inflexible rule can be laid down" to cover the wide range of circumstances, he argued, noting that while some black students met acceptance, "there are many public school systems in the North where Negroes are admitted and tolerated, but they are not educated; they are crucified." Polarizing the debate between segregated and mixed schools was a mistake, Du Bois observed. "What [the Negro] needs is Education. What he must remember is that there is no magic, either in mixed schools or in segregated schools. A mixed school with poor and unsympathetic teachers, with hostile public opinion, and no teaching of truth concerning black folk, is bad. A segregated school with ignorant placeholders, inadequate equipment, poor salaries, and wretched housing, is equally bad." Under ideal conditions, Du Bois noted that the mixed school provided a broader, more natural education, similar to what he had argued six years earlier. But the present-day realities were far from ideal, he conceded, and concluded that if black schools instilled a stronger sense of humanity within the race, then they would "outweigh all that the mixed school can offer."[18]

Du Bois's recognition of multiple perspectives on black education at the national level mirrors the diversity of school reform struggles observed in Northern communities. Significant variations in the political context of black teacher employment throughout the North caused activists to define local struggles for racial uplift in different ways. In cities like New York, where blacks successfully exchanged their votes to win the most equal hiring practices for black teachers, the struggle took a different form than in places like Indianapolis, where limited black political clout led to difficult racial compromises to preserve black teachers' jobs in segregated schools. Yet both of these struggles, concerning jobs measured in the hundreds, appeared quite distant in the eyes of black Milwaukeeans at the time, who were embarking on efforts to hire their first black teacher.

Lobbying for the First Black Teachers in Milwaukee

Black Milwaukeeans had relatively little political power when they began lobbying for black teachers' jobs in the early 1930s. In white city politics, the Socialist Party had dominated elections through the twenty-four-year reign of Mayor Daniel Hoan (1916–40). Hoan's telling of a racist "darky story" at a major convention, while atypical of his daily behavior, nevertheless demonstrated that the Socialist mayor did not need black votes to stay in office. But one exception to the Socialist Party's traditional dominance briefly arose in the city alderman election of 1932. The opportunity was seized upon by J. Anthony Josey, a "dyed-in-the-wool" black Republican who published the state's only black weekly newspaper, the *Wisconsin Enterprise-Blade*. Josey arranged for the first hiring of black teachers in Milwaukee in 1931, based on his patronage connections with a white politician who challenged the Socialists. Although a growing number of black residents had graduated from Milwaukee State Teachers College, none had yet broken into the city's public school labor market. Josey and his assistant, Bernice Lindsay, approached one black graduate, Susie Bazzelle from the class of 1931, who was contemplating a move to another city to find work as a teacher. "Why should you be going somewhere else to get a position," they asked Bazzelle, "when we should be getting it right here in Milwaukee?" She agreed, so Josey and Lindsay took her case to Samuel Soref, the white city councilman for the Sixth Ward on the Near Northside, where most black Milwaukeeans lived.[19]

Although Councilman Soref was the incumbent, he needed black votes to retain his seat in the upcoming election, since he had previously defeated his Socialist opponent by only forty votes. Furthermore, the field was crowded in the approaching spring primary with several candidates, including two African Americans: attorney George Hamilton and businessman Clarence Johnson. After meeting with Josey, Alderman Soref quietly arranged for two black teachers to be hired through his brother, a member of the Milwaukee school board. Both Susie Bazzelle and another recent graduate, Millie White, were told to report to Fourth Street Elementary, where they began teaching as day-to-day substitutes, a common practice for teachers awaiting eligibility for full-time permanent openings. To return the favor, Josey's newspaper gave Soref a front-page endorsement, noting "for the benefit of the colored voters in the Sixth Ward, that Alderman Soref is directly responsible for two colored girls teaching in the Public Schools of Milwaukee." Josey sharply criticized the Socialists for denying city jobs to blacks, and also Milwaukee's branch of the Universal Negro Improvement Association for refusing to allow Soref to speak to their membership "because they do not want the masses to know the number of colored workers that Soref has placed with the city." After the votes were counted, Soref won both the primary and the election by healthy margins.[20]

Encouraged by the political climate, black community leaders took bolder, more public steps to win support for hiring black teachers, but the approach quickly backfired. P. J. Gilmer, a black physician and Urban League member, approached the Milwaukee school board in late 1932 and

Susie Bazzelle (left) and Millie White (right), the city's first two black teachers, were hired through political patronage. From *Echo* yearbook, Milwaukee State Teachers College, 1931; courtesy of University of Wisconsin–Milwaukee Archives.

urged them to approve a resolution that would authorize the administration "to give consideration to persons of the colored race" when hiring teachers. He presented his best arguments to an unfriendly white audience that generally viewed his race as inferior. (The board stenographer made a verbatim transcript of comments spoken by everyone at the meeting except Gilmer, whose speech was merely paraphrased and whose title was demoted from "Dr." to "Mr.") At first, Gilmer spoke from the position of black entitlement, arguing that the community deserved proportional representation in the public school system, equivalent to 1 percent of the 2,400 total teaching positions. But then he shifted rhetorically, delivering a broader appeal to his white audience. Gilmer observed that in the Milwaukee public schools, black children "maintained an [academic] average well up with the other nationalities" during their elementary years but fell behind upon reaching the age of fourteen or fifteen. Once students became aware of the dismal realities of black employment, "they didn't seem to be able to see just what they were going to be able to do" with a high school education, since black adults rarely found jobs that matched their skills. "When useful citizens [are] lost," Gilmer warned, all of Milwaukee loses. The school board should hire black teachers, he argued, so that black youth can "see evidence where their own schoolmates and playmates have arisen and have been accepted into positions of worth and honor." Gilmer concluded by contrasting Milwaukee to Cleveland, where black teachers had been employed for over thirty years, even to teach high school subjects such as Latin and chemistry, and added that perhaps black Milwaukeeans needed to "add a little pressure" to achieve comparable results.[21]

Gilmer's remarks provoked an angry response from white Milwaukee officials. "Pressure by you colored people has never helped the colored candidates and never will," retorted school superintendent Milton Potter. He denounced city aldermen (like Samuel Soref) who sought "to prostitute the colored race for the sole purpose of garnering votes" and acknowledged that he had authorized the hiring of two black teachers during the previous election year but had done so discreetly in order to avoid raising the race issue in public view. (That very evening, more than one school board member expressed surprise in learning that they currently employed two black teachers, since the topic had never come up before.) In Superintendent Potter's view, it was essential to keep politics out of the schools, and he insisted that the Milwaukee system had "never drawn any color line" and hired teachers based solely on merit. But the words and actions of Potter and other white school officials in 1932 painted a very different picture, illustrating just how deep racial politics were embedded in the so-called color-blind hiring process. Another school board member claimed that no previous black teachers had been hired because none were qualified, adding, "If you knew enough about the colored population here you would know why." (Gilmer responded by listing recent black graduates from Milwaukee State Teachers College but was ignored.) Likewise, board president Elizabeth Mehan supported Superintendent Potter's decision to hire qualified black teachers "in a quiet way, so it will not be glaringly noticeable," and told Gilmer that it would be preferable to employ blacks "without having it look like a sore thumb, to have some of your color on our teaching staff."[22]

Thus, black Milwaukee's first campaign to hire teachers quickly ended in defeat. The school board eventually voted down Gilmer's resolution to "give consideration to persons of the colored race." In a further setback, both black teachers lost their positions at Fourth Street Elementary School by the mid-1930s. Administrators dismissed Susie Bazzelle on grounds that she was an inadequate disciplinarian, and Millie White's full-time job was demoted to sporadic, part-time substitute work. There would be no more patronage jobs from Alderman Soref. He switched party affiliations and was endorsed by the Socialists in the 1936 elections, thereby eliminating his need to court black votes to maintain power in the Sixth Ward.[23]

With few alternatives, prospective black teachers filed into the central school office each week during the mid-1930s and sat on the "substitute bench," waiting to be called. When part-time work was available, school administrators usually assigned them only to schools with significant numbers of black students, including Fourth Street and Ninth Street Elementary and Roosevelt Junior High School. John J. Williams, a black graduate of Milwaukee State Teachers College, remembered the harsh realities of job discrimination on the bench. Despite his high school teaching credentials, he was never sent to substitute at any of Milwaukee's high schools, which were still predominantly white. "I recall specifically one case in which I, as a history teacher, was the only one qualified to go to Washington High School." But the personnel administrator refused to send Williams, stating, "I'm sorry, I can't use you." When he asked why not, she offered a candid reply: "You're a Negro and the principal will not accept you." Only twice in two years did administrators depart from their usual practice and send Williams to substitute at a predominantly white elementary school, but not once was he sent to a high school, the setting for which he was trained.[24]

PROPOSING A DELICATE COMPROMISE

At the close of the 1930s, William Kelley had learned some hard lessons about what was (and was not) possible to accomplish during the Depression. The Milwaukee Urban League had failed to secure a viable economic base for blacks in the city. At the close of the decade, Milwaukee's black unemployment rate reached 50 percent, compared to 17 percent for the city's white population and rates around 20–25 percent for blacks in Chicago and New York. More than 33 percent of black Milwaukeeans lived on government relief, compared to 2 percent for whites. Only sixty-one black residents in the entire city were engaged in middle-class professional work. In the Milwaukee public schools, black college graduates were attempting to break into the teacher market during a particularly lean period. Although Milwaukee's black population continued to rise, sparking political pressure to hire black teachers, pupil enrollments dropped by 20,000 between 1933 and 1947, reducing the total number of teaching positions by nearly 300 during this time.[25]

Kelley realized that blacks had little hope in joining with Milwaukee's white unions in the 1930s. In cities like Chicago and Detroit, black and white workers formed labor alliances through the interracial Congress of Industrial Organizations (CIO), but such coalitions did not succeed in Milwaukee. White labor unions for the Schlitz and Pabst Breweries, located in the Sixth Ward, refused Kelley's request to hire black workers in 1933. A year later, blacks became the target of white violence during labor unrest. When white workers at the Wehr Steel Foundry formed an American Federation of Labor local in 1934, they staged a walkout but did so without informing the small number of black workers still inside the plant, who suddenly found themselves cast in the role of "scabs" and facing an angry white crowd outside. When police arrived at the scene, they joined forces with white unionists and attacked blacks, "overturning an automobile filled with Negro workers." Kelley's Urban League investigated reports that one of the union's chief demands was to dismiss black workers from the plant. But when the National Urban League forwarded this news to the National Labor Relations Board, they declined to intervene, citing the lack of jurisdiction on this issue. Even federal authority would not force Milwaukee labor to cooperate with Kelley at this time.[26]

Black Milwaukeeans failed also in their attempts to establish a political base in the city during the 1930s. James Dorsey, a bright young black lawyer and Democratic politician who migrated to the city from Montana, served as president of the Milwaukee NAACP chapter. However, Dorsey decided that the city's black population was too small and impoverished to support both the Urban League and the NAACP, so he effectively shut down the latter by refusing to call meetings or raise funds. (J. Anthony Josey, only partly in jest, offered a free subscription to the *Wisconsin Enterprise-Blade* to anyone who could prove that the Milwaukee NAACP chapter was still in existence.) By 1936, James Dorsey had built a stronger political movement when he campaigned for the Sixth Ward city council seat and nearly tied the incumbent, Sam Soref, in the spring primary. Although Dorsey was the first black city candidate to win the endorsement of the *Milwaukee Journal* (a white daily newspaper) on the basis of his criticism of the Socialist Party machine, he lost the general election in what was described as "one of the bitterest campaigns in years." Despite a black population that rose to nearly 9,000 (or 1.5 percent of Milwaukee's population) in the 1940 census, no black held elected office in local government nor any regular teaching position in the city school system.[27]

Given these circumstances of political and economic isolation, William Kelley turned to a strategy of negotiation and compromise. His decade of experience in working with the Urban League's board, which included black professionals and leading white industrial executives, gave him experience in racial dialogue and making deals. Kelley's position continually required him to convince prospective white employers that it was in their own best interests to hire black workers. When he looked to the Milwaukee public school system, he saw it as another prospective white employer. And through Kelley's frequent correspondence and annual meetings with Urban League affiliates, he recognized that Milwaukee was far behind in its num-

James Dorsey, attorney and Milwaukee NAACP president, led civil rights campaigns for jobs from the 1930s through the 1950s. From *Milwaukee Journal*, 3 December 1952; copyright Milwaukee Journal Sentinel, Inc.; reproduced with permission.

ber of black teachers and picked up some ideas for what to do about the problem.

At the end of the school year in 1939, Kelley orchestrated a second attempt to publicly lobby the Milwaukee school board for black teachers' jobs and found more success than he had during the previous attempt seven years earlier. In his opening speech, Kelley began by conceding to board members that "there was a time when it was said, perhaps with a degree of truth, that we didn't have Negro people who were qualified to teach." But the teaching pool had changed, he argued, listing thirteen local black college graduates (some with master's degrees) who had applied to work in the city schools but had been denied the opportunity. In the meantime, Kelley added, the black student population at Fourth Street Elementary School had risen from 68 to 90 percent over the past decade, without any increase in the number of black teachers. Both white and black allies supported Kelley's speech. George Teeter, a professor at Milwaukee State Teachers College and president of the city's Inter-Racial Council, pointed to the "prejudice on the part of white folks" against having "Negroes teach our children" as the root of the black teacher unemployment problem. P. J. Gilmer, the black physician who had addressed the school board years earlier, vividly described cases where white teachers in predominantly black schools felt that they were "wasting their efforts on the colored children" and demonstrated insulting behavior toward them. "We are not asking for favors now," Kelley asserted. "Out of fairness to the people living in [the Sixth Ward] there should be more Negroes teaching school."[28]

These words sparked one of most candid discussions of race ever heard in a Milwaukee public forum at that time. Some white school officials responded frankly to the charges of racism. "I think everyone knows," acknowledged board member Albert Boyer, that in predominantly black schools, "we have some teachers who are dissatisfied whereas a qualified Negro would probably be very happy under similar conditions and do much better work." Another school board member, Willard Bowman, agreed, adding that since white teachers could work anywhere in the city system, the board should "give the colored person a fair deal" by hiring teachers of their race in proportion to the population. Specifically, he proposed designating the Ninth Street School as a training facility for black teachers, since it already had an overwhelmingly black student population. The plan would bring Milwaukee in line with cities such as Philadelphia and Indianapolis, which hired large numbers of black teachers and assigned them to segregated schools.

Superintendent Milton Potter strongly objected to Bowman's proposal. "We can't have colored schools in this state," he exclaimed, "thank God!" In truth, Wisconsin statutes were silent on the topic of segregated schools at that time, but Potter refused to allow his school system to be dragged into a lengthy court battle to resolve the matter. He reminded the board that in several other Northern states, attorneys had taken legal action against schools that placed only black teachers in black schools. Adding to Potter's objection, several board members raised concerns about setting aside a school for blacks, since Germans, Greeks, and Italians might begin to demand equal treatment for their groups. Arguments for both sides went on and on.[29]

Kelley sought to clarify his position on this very delicate racial compromise. "I would like to make myself very clear," he began. "I feel the most ideal, democratic way is that anyone, if they are qualified, should be allowed to teach anywhere. But if we can't teach anywhere, then for goodness' sake, let us teach where it is said we might teach," Kelley argued. "We are not asking for teachers to teach only in the Fourth and Ninth Street Schools, but if you will not tolerate them teaching anywhere else, then let them teach there." He chose his words carefully for this very public forum. While Kelley did not support segregated hiring in principle, he proposed that the community would accept jobs for black teachers with the understanding that they would be offered only in predominantly black schools. The harsh economic and political realities in black Milwaukee persuaded Kelley to cede ground on this issue, something that subsequent generations of civil rights activists would never understand.[30]

That evening in 1939, Kelley brokered a racial compromise that would last into the mid-1950s. The school board implicitly agreed to hire black teachers with the understanding that it would assign them only to predominantly black elementary schools. Superintendent Potter, who objected to an explicit agreement, nevertheless affirmed the tacit understanding by announcing that "one of [Kelley's] candidates" would soon be employed to work as a substitute at either Fourth Street or Ninth Street School. The terms of the compromise allowed the Milwaukee public school system to continue its official policy of merit-based and color-blind hiring to avoid legal and ethnic troubles. The next day's newspaper featured Potter's quote that there would be "no Negro schools" in the city, avoiding a public relations controversy over the question of segregation in a progressive Northern school district. But everyone present at the school board meeting that night recognized that race had shaped the district's behind-the-scenes negotiations and unofficial practices. Within one year, Milwaukee employed three black teachers (including two with master's degrees), and all worked at the two predominantly black elementary schools.[31]

FACING LIMITS ON TEACHERS' JOBS

Although black teachers gained a small foothold in the Milwaukee school system, they continued to confront barriers to full recognition in the 1940s. For example, after Grant Gordon graduated from Milwaukee State Teachers College in 1940, he interviewed for a teaching position in the city's school system, only to be told blatantly to "go back South." The school administrator assumed that Gordon was a Southern migrant searching for work in the North, but Gordon was a Southerner only by birth; he had been raised in the nearby city of Beloit (on the Illinois-Wisconsin border) ever since infancy and had lived in Milwaukee while attending college. Nevertheless, the comment did not totally surprise him. In the South, his parents had both been educators, but after moving to Beloit, they could not find work in their chosen field. After his outright rejection, Gordon served his country during

World War II and rose to the rank of lieutenant. Upon his return to Milwaukee, he applied a second time and finally received a teaching position at Fourth Street Elementary School in 1946. "There were only five or six black teachers in the whole system," Gordon recalled, and none dared to speak out. "Coming back from the service and then going into teaching was a matter of getting a job, number one, as far as I was concerned."[32]

Another black teacher, Ruby Young, confronted barriers of gender and marital status on top of racial discrimination. Before coming to Milwaukee in 1946, she had gained experience as a Jeanes teacher, supervising black instructors in segregated Alabama schools, and had earned a master's degree from Teachers College of Columbia University in New York City. Young settled down with her husband in Milwaukee after the war, where she hit two job ceilings. First, as a black teacher, her employment was limited to the two predominantly black elementary schools, Fourth Street and Ninth Street. Second, the district refused to grant permanent positions to married women teachers, only offering them work as day-to-day substitutes. School officials based their Depression-era policy on the principle of a family wage, arguing that married women were already supported by their husband's earnings, although this was often not the case for black families. The action greatly reduced labor costs for the district because married women like Ruby Young were paid far less than men with comparable experience and credentials. She worked as a substitute earning $5.50 per day for one year at Fourth Street, then another year at Ninth Street.

One day she went directly to the central administration office and demanded to see the rule against married female teachers, where she was told that it was an unwritten policy. "Well, I won't be available for work next year," Young replied. For the next two years she shifted to the social work profession, then learned that the school board had rescinded its ban on married women in permanent positions. Young was eager to return to the classroom, but the administration stalled on her application, forcing her to wait. "In September I wasn't called, and I wondered why, and October came and I think I was called in the latter part of October [or] the first of November," Young recalled, realizing that it was the administration's way of letting her "sweat it out" after raising her voice two years earlier. When the call finally came, Ruby Young was reassigned to the predominantly black classrooms at Ninth Street Elementary.[33]

Local college administrators acted in ways that supported the city's restrictions on black teachers. John H. Jackson was the only black student in the secondary school teacher education program at Milwaukee State Teachers College in the early 1940s. This was not by accident but due to what he described as "an understanding within the club." Both the dean and the school placement officer had called Jackson into their offices to discourage him from pursuing a high school teaching career, since Milwaukee did not hire blacks for those positions. They even offered him a scholarship to study social work at Atlanta University, a historically black institution, but he insisted on staying in Milwaukee. His grades were too high for the administration to flunk him out of the program; nevertheless, the policy of active discouragement continued. Jackson recalled that "I was rushing down the hall one day and [the school placement officer] stopped me, just out of the blue, and he said, 'You know, Jackson, I just feel so sorry for you.' And I said, 'Why, why?' And he said, 'Because you are so active and have so much energy, and what are you going to do when you graduate?' And I said [laughing], 'I hope I'm going to teach,' and he just shook his head and walked away. But that was the psychology, that was the atmosphere that we had to deal with."[34]

The "gentlemen's agreement" not to hire blacks as high school teachers evolved for several reasons in the 1940s. First, high school teachers held higher-status and better-paid jobs in school buildings that were still almost all-white in Milwaukee, and they were reluctant to surrender these prized positions. Second, many whites believed that blacks did not possess the intellectual skills necessary to instruct the city's academically rigorous high schools. Finally, high schools provided the setting for a significant amount of interaction between adults and adolescents, and some saw the ban as a white effort to stop interracial social, or even sexual, contact. Black Milwaukeeans began speaking out in public against the ban in the mid-1940s. John Williams, a former black substitute teacher and editor of the black weekly *Milwaukee Globe*, told an Urban League forum that "we have Negro doctors, lawyers, and social workers, but our only Negro teachers are in the primary schools. Roosevelt Junior High School is 43 percent colored but it has no Negro teachers."[35]

Eventually, the Milwaukee public school system hired John Jackson in 1946 but assigned him to teach seventh grade at Fourth Street Elementary rather than place him in a junior or senior high school, which were all predominantly white. For the next decade, he found it nearly impossible to transfer into the upper grades. After gaining five years of teaching experience and earning a master's degree in psychology from the University of Chicago, his request to transfer to either of the two high schools with some black enrollment was denied. Instead, the administration transferred him to Roosevelt Junior High School in 1951, which had recently become more than 50 percent black. At the central office, an administrator sat Jackson down and told him that "no Negro teacher should want to teach anywhere else until every classroom with a single black child had a Negro teacher." School officials attempted to cast the job barrier in its most positive light by portraying it as a policy designed for the benefit of black children. Despite Jackson's initiative and advanced graduate work toward a doctorate, administrators denied his request for transfer to a high school position for another four years.[36]

After Geraldine Gilmer Goens graduated from Milwaukee State Teachers College in 1950, she heard the same reasons why she should teach in a black school. But Goens was the daughter of P. J. Gilmer, the long-term Urban League member who had lobbied the school board to hire black teachers in the early 1930s, and she also represented a younger generation of black Milwaukeeans who were growing in confidence and were willing to speak their mind. One day an administrator told her, "I think you probably could teach colored children better than white children. Wouldn't you be an inspiration to them?" Goens replied, "Well, I really don't know. I've never taught any colored children. . . . I spent my whole practicum in white schools." Since there were only a handful of public schools where black teachers could gain experience, Goens had done her practice teaching at the campus training school with the children of white professors. Despite her creative argument, Goens was assigned to substitute as a kindergarten teacher at the predominantly black Fourth Street Elementary School. Months later, when another administrator called to offer her a first grade teaching position, Goens flatly told her no, since she had been trained to teach kindergarten, and offered a counterproposal. "I said, 'Why don't you move some of these white teachers [who have only two-year college degrees] out of the black schools? . . . Because you're not going to put me in a white school, I know that.'" Shocked by what Geraldine Goens had dared to say, the white supervisor was speechless on the other end of the phone line. But a kindergarten teaching position soon opened up for her at the predominantly black Ninth Street School, perhaps due to the combination of her family influence and her own self-confidence. Nevertheless, Goens clearly recognized that the system had unjustly restricted her options for employment.[37]

As young black Milwaukeeans confronted the racial barriers imposed by the 1939 compromise brokered by William Kelley, they grew more likely to challenge these restrictions, though only on an individual basis. Korean War veteran Bob Harris Jr. returned to his hometown in 1951 with worldly experience, a dream of teaching and coaching high school students, and financial support through the GI Bill, yet he encountered the familiar policy of active discouragement upon enrolling at Milwaukee State Teachers College. "I want to major in secondary education," Harris told the administrator, who replied, "I don't think you'll be able to do that. Why don't you try elementary education?" Harris knew this pattern well. Years earlier, a Milwaukee high school guidance counselor had tried to steer him into vocational education classes until Harris's father intervened to have him placed in the college prep track instead. So in his current dispute with Milwaukee

State Teachers College, Harris brought in the campus director of veterans' programs to advocate on his behalf and settled for a dual certification program in upper-elementary and secondary education. Yet in the end, Harris was forced to take the only position that Milwaukee public schools would offer him: teaching fifth grade at Fifth Street Elementary, a school that had just enrolled a majority of black students.[38]

On rare occasions when black teachers did break through racial barriers, they did so under conditions tightly controlled by white school administrators. The story of Milwaukee's first permanent black high school teacher illustrates the point. In 1951, the principal of Lincoln High School, which had a 15 percent black student population, asked the new superintendent to send him a "colored man." It was a remarkable request, since at that time the only black teachers in permanent positions above the elementary level were three home economics instructors at Roosevelt Junior High School, where the black students composed half of the enrollment. Superintendent Harold Vincent complied and hand-picked Thomas Cheeks, an experienced black male teacher who had previously chaired a high school social studies department in Indiana. The affair was handled very delicately. At first, school officials assigned Cheeks to the Lincoln Junior High School for one semester, then moved him up to teach at the senior high level the following fall. They warned Cheeks not to publicize his transfer until the school issued a public announcement, one month after the fact. Administrators saw the move as a crucial test of white parents' tolerance of black high school teachers, and their efforts to control the event apparently succeeded. Cheeks did not recall any controversy over his appointment, and the principal proudly noted that he had heard "not one murmur of comment." Other black teachers gossiped that Thomas Cheeks was hand-picked by the administration as a safe racial pioneer whose presence would not disrupt the existing racial order. His very light skin complexion may have reduced white anxiety. Superintendent Vincent soon developed a very close relationship with Cheeks, trusting him as his ambassador in dealing with Milwaukee's black community. Nevertheless, Cheeks's ascension did not radically alter the system; no additional black teachers gained transfers to the high schools for another two years. While black Milwaukeeans had attained sufficient clout to secure some positions, they still were not moving ahead in the system.[39]

BUILDING LOCAL STRENGTH FROM FEDERAL POWER

William Kelley's reluctant compromise on segregated black teacher hiring fit the context of 1939, when black Milwaukeeans were desperate for jobs.

Clearly, the restriction that black teachers could work only in black neighborhood schools was not ideal, but neither was it uncommon in Northern cities like Indianapolis and Cincinnati. At least Milwaukee would no longer be known as a city without a single black teacher. Kelley and the black community had reason to celebrate: the number of black teachers rose from zero to nine by 1950 and doubled again four years later.[40]

But black Milwaukeeans soon sensed that they had won a hollow victory. The lean Depression years had yielded to a postwar economic boom. Public school enrollments (which had fallen steadily since 1933) began to climb once again in 1948, and the Milwaukee school board increased the total instructional staff by 481 positions (21 percent) from 1949 to 1953. Yet young black teachers questioned whether they were receiving their fair share of these jobs. Black educators with advanced degrees (like John H. Jackson) or experience in white schools (like Geraldine Gilmer Goens) or veteran status (like Bob Harris) grew impatient with the unwritten rules that severely restricted the positions for which they could apply and reasonably expect to obtain. Blacks in Philadelphia, whose teachers had previously worked only in segregated schools, had gained sufficient political muscle to eliminate the hiring color line. Thus it became clearer to black Milwaukeeans that the compromise of the late 1930s did not neatly fit the context of the early 1950s.[41]

Kelley heard their complaints and resolved to do something. But the challenge was to find an effective way to strengthen the black community's weak bargaining position with respect to the dominant power of white Milwaukee. Kelley had learned an important lesson in the pre-war years about drawing upon the power of the federal government to support his local struggles for civil rights. In 1941, he had organized the Milwaukee committee of the March on Washington Movement, a campaign led by black labor leader A. Philip Randolph to bring 100,000 blacks to the nation's capital and persuade President Franklin Roosevelt to integrate black workers into the defense industry. The new director of the National Urban League, Lester Granger, bent the old rule against leaving "militancy to others" and urged local affiliates to support Randolph. Given the distance between Milwaukee and Washington, D.C., Kelley and his NAACP colleague attorney James Dorsey prepared to hold a march in their own city.[42]

Although Randolph called off the national protest after Roosevelt agreed to establish the Fair Employment Practices Committee (FEPC), the Milwaukee committee decided to continue onward with their own march. On Saturday, 28 June 1941, approximately 350 black Milwaukeeans marched through downtown streets, carrying flags and placards to protest job discrimination. "We want the right to work for democracy as well as the right to fight and die for democracy," Dorsey declared to the crowd. Decades later, he recalled that "there were no unpleasant incidents, and the protestation was effective." Kelley stayed out of the headlines, most likely to protect the Milwaukee Urban League's nonpartisan reputation among white donors. But his behind-the-scenes organizing brought together Milwaukee's first black-led planned march for civil rights.[43]

Although the march energized local activists, the real power came from the FEPC into the hiring practices of Milwaukee's powerful white industries. As millions of dollars worth of defense contracts rolled into the city, Kelley and Dorsey documented black workers' charges of job discrimination against five of Milwaukee's largest industries and presented their case during two days of FEPC public hearings in Chicago in 1942. Representatives of the A. O. Smith Corporation, which manufactured military vehicles, stubbornly replied that they "never did and didn't intend to employ" black workers. "I know nothing about discrimination," argued John Heil, the Republican governor of Wisconsin and the executive vice president of the Heil Company. He claimed that "there never have been any colored individuals applying for work at our plant," but the FEPC considered the evidence and ruled against all five industries, ordering them to halt job discrimination. Challenging such powerful whites was risky. One week after the ruling, Dorsey suddenly lost his position on the Milwaukee County draft board, upon orders directly issued by Governor Heil. But overall, the strategy worked. Together, the five plants hired 1,262 additional black workers over the next two years, increasing the proportion of black workers (2.5 percent) to match their estimated share of the city's population.[44]

If the power of the federal government could pressure Milwaukee's industries to hire black workers, Kelley wondered, could it also be harnessed to pressure the public schools to employ black teachers? During the 1940s, the connection between the politics of Washington, D.C., and Milwaukee schools was not obvious. Although black organizations had some success in forcing the Roosevelt administration to act against discrimination in federally sponsored employment contracts and public housing, the federal government had relatively little stake in local school districts and thus had no leverage. But that picture soon changed in the 1950s as the U.S. Supreme Court took up the case of school segregation in *Brown v. Board*. For Kelley, the ruling opened up a new opportunity: perhaps he could redirect the authority of the federal government to crack open job barriers for black teachers in Milwaukee.[45]

2

REDEFINING THE LOCAL MEANING

OF *BROWN V. BOARD*

In October 1953, just months before the nation turned its attention to the U.S. Supreme Court's *Brown v. Board* decision, the newly revived Milwaukee NAACP chapter launched a school reform movement of its own. Black leaders expressed confidence that their rising population of nearly 40,000 (5 percent of the city total) and increased voting strength would bring greater political power, and they called a meeting with white officials to voice their complaints. A new generation of black NAACP activists sharply questioned the 1939 compromise with the Milwaukee school board: that black teachers would be hired but assigned only to predominantly black neighborhood schools. They opposed the segregative hiring restriction and called for opening up job opportunities for black teachers throughout the entire city school system. The tone of their public complaint made it clear that patience was running out.

"Is it a mere coincidence," asked Vel Phillips, a rising black female lawyer and future city council member, "that there are so many Negro teachers at Roosevelt [Junior High School], at Ninth Street, at Fourth Street?" Restricting black teachers to predominantly black schools not only reduced the total number of job opportunities but also stigmatized those jobs. Other speakers supported Phillips and charged that school administrators "punished" white teachers they did not favor by transferring them to black neighborhood schools. In their eyes, the pattern was clear: previous generations of black migrants had been given "the dirty work" in Milwaukee's steel foundries, packinghouses, and tanneries, and now black teachers were being assigned to the inner-city schools that whites deemed least desirable.[1]

School officials denied the existence of "dumping grounds" for teachers. Board member Elizabeth Holmes acknowledged that the "so-called salt mines" had existed years ago, when teachers had considered a transfer to one of them as a disciplinary measure, but all that had changed since the arrival of the new school superintendent, Harold Vincent, in 1950. One of Vincent's assistants, Dr. Elden Bond, agreed with Holmes and claimed that the Milwaukee public schools did not keep any "race records," so personnel policies were blind to color. Teachers were simply assigned to schools close to their homes, he asserted, and since most blacks lived in the Near Northside, it was no surprise that they were largely assigned to Fourth Street, Ninth Street, and Roosevelt Junior High. Based on his personal experience, Bond added, many black teachers preferred schools with predominantly black student populations.[2]

Although Vel Phillips continued to question these claims, James Dorsey, a senior member of the NAACP chapter, stood up to refocus the meeting. "I'm not so concerned where Negro teachers teach in the system," he declared, affirming the terms of the 1939 compromise. Instead, Dorsey asked whether Milwaukee schools adequately prepared black youth to compete in the labor market for high-quality jobs rather than for "the dirty work" handed down to them. Henry Reuss, a school board member and future Democratic congressman, echoed Dorsey's concerns and many black leaders' views that some high school counselors "discouraged Negro youths who aspired to advanced education." Even Vel Phillips, who had launched the attack on black teacher placement that evening, paused for a moment to lend support to Dorsey's agenda, recalling her student days at Roosevelt Junior High School when a faculty adviser had told her that "Negro women were best prepared to train for cooks and maids and not to take college courses." Fortunately for Phillips, she had ignored this advice, won a scholarship to attend Howard University in Washington, D.C., then returned to become the first black female graduate of the University of Wisconsin Law School. Still, her memories of confronting racial job barriers in Milwaukee's public schools remained most vivid in her mind.[3]

Newspapers described this 1953 meeting as "one of the frankest public discussions of race relations in the schools ever held in Milwaukee." But it was equally significant for the topic that was not raised. On the eve of the *Brown v. Board* decision, no one in the audience posed a question about black student segregation in Milwaukee. No one mentioned that four elementary schools—Fourth Street, Ninth Street, Garfield, and Lee—had black student populations of more than 90 percent or that others were quickly following this trend. No one suggested that the racial composition of these schools would in some way harm the students who attended them.[4]

As news of the *Brown* decision spread across the nation in May 1954, Milwaukee's black community leaders began to reconstruct its meaning to fit their local context. In particular, William Kelley of the Urban League told Milwaukee school officials that the decision required equal employment opportunities for black teachers. In truth, the Supreme Court decision said nothing of the sort. It only overturned legalized student segregation in Southern and border states and was silent about the plight of black teachers. But the intense national publicity on black education offered Kelley the political pressure he needed to renegotiate the 1939 compromise on teacher hiring. Kelley therefore modified the meaning of *Brown* in Milwaukee by focusing on his true agenda, the expansion of job opportunities for blacks in the white economy.

SCHOOL SEGREGATION IN THE URBAN NORTH

When sociologist Gunnar Myrdal published *An American Dilemma* in 1944, the most widely acclaimed study of segregation of its time, he focused almost exclusively on Southern and border states. In the North, he contended, "Negroes have practically the entire educational system flung open to them without much discrimination." Myrdal was wrong. Materials collected by his research assistant, Doxey Wilkerson, provided ample evidence of segregated schools in the North. Quite understandably, Myrdal devoted his attention and energy to the South, where segregation was most intense, but his hasty dismissal of its presence elsewhere has contributed to the false historical memory of racial equality in Northern education.[5]

Although most Northern states legally abolished segregated education during the late nineteenth century, or maintained silence on the issue, segregation continued to be the policy and practice of many local districts. In fact, the number of Northern schools segregated by local officials (not simply by residential patterns) actually increased between 1910 and 1940. The most publicized cases arose in a belt of five states: New Jersey, Pennsylvania, Ohio, Indiana, and Illinois. For instance, a 1925 survey of southern New Jersey revealed the existence of racially designated elementary schools in every town with a significant black population, stretching from the southern tip of Cape May to the midstate town of Princeton. Subsequent reports filed in New Jersey during the late 1930s and 1940s indicated that the problem had grown more acute and had begun to influence school board policy

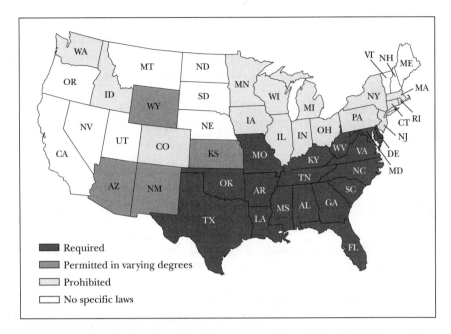

Status of School Segregation Law prior to *Brown*, 1954. Adapted from the *Crisis*, June–July 1954, 343.

on race in the northern part of the state. In Pennsylvania, several towns outside of Philadelphia maintained segregated elementary schools into the late 1940s. Black children in Morton and West Chester walked past white-designated schools on their way to black-designated schools every morning. Even the borough of Swarthmore, with its strong Quaker influence, assigned a black teacher to a segregated elementary classroom until 1939. At the far extreme was Indiana, the only Northern state that legally permitted local governments to set their own school segregation policies, until 1949, when the state abolished all officially sanctioned segregation.[6]

National NAACP legal director Thurgood Marshall announced a public campaign against Northern school segregation in 1947, encouraging black citizens to demand enforcement of existing statutes that prohibited its practice. But Marshall soon became frustrated with the widely divergent levels of black community support for his campaign. On one hand, he found support in New Jersey, where black voters held some leverage in state government and organized political actions to combat school segregation. On the other hand, in Pennsylvania, Marshall failed to locate either a black plaintiff or a black lawyer who was willing to risk helping him file a case in court. Similarly, some NAACP chapters in Ohio and Illinois actively supported all-black schools. Community support for black teachers, combined with the lack of political clout to overrule white racism, undermined efforts to combat segregation. Anguished by the mixed results of his Northern campaign, Thurgood Marshall wrote that "I am beginning to doubt that our branch officers are fully indoctrinated on the policy of the NAACP in being opposed to segregation."[7]

In 1954, Marshall's victory against legalized Southern segregation in *Brown v. Board* renewed his hopes. In some Northern cities, particularly where black political clout had already made gains for black teachers, local activists drew upon the momentum of *Brown* to energize their preexisting movements for school desegregation. In New York City, where Marshall's expert witness, Dr. Kenneth Clark, had spoken out against segregated schooling a few months before the Supreme Court's decision, *Brown* emboldened local NAACP organizers like Milton Galamison to challenge city school authorities and demand desegregated schools. Similarly, the *Crisis* magazine of the NAACP reported that branches in Philadelphia and Chester, Pennsylvania, launched renewed desegregation protests in the fall of 1954. In both Chicago and Detroit, where activists had criticized school gerrymandering in the late 1940s, the *Brown* decision reignited their protests. The Chicago NAACP, in particular, began compiling data for a hard-hitting 1957 report titled "De Facto Segregation in Chicago Public Schools," which documented that 87 percent of the city's black students were enrolled in schools that were at least 90 percent black. This marked an important shift, from challenging de jure segregation by law to de facto segregation by residence, since legal interpretations of *Brown* in the urban North would not be clear for another two decades. But obstacles such as this did not prevent activists from raising school integration as a moral and political issue in selected Northern cities.[8]

Black Milwaukeeans certainly heard about Northern campaigns against school segregation from their neighbors in Chicago. At the annual Milwaukee NAACP membership meeting in 1952, Chicago NAACP president George Leighton told the audience that any segregated school was discriminatory, "even if Negro children were assigned to a gold-plated school with diamond doorknobs." If black and white children remained racially isolated from one another, he reasoned, then they would fail to live and work together as adults. The principle applied in both the North and the South, Leighton concluded.[9]

Yet when *Brown* hit the headlines, black Milwaukee leaders interpreted the decision in a very different context, one that distanced the ruling from their local struggles for civil rights. Milwaukee NAACP president and attorney Dale Phillips (husband of Vel Phillips) spoke to white reporters after the *Brown* decision and proclaimed that it would help America "clean up a large section of its own back yard," signifying the South. But his comments did not suggest any hint of segregation in the "front yards" of Northern

PUNCHING—AMERICAN STYLE

UNANIMOUS SUPREME COURT VOTE AGAINST SEGREGATION

COMMIE PROPAGANDIST

Milwaukee's white daily press celebrated the *Brown* decision in this cartoon as a knockout punch against Communism, with a small figure representing black education standing quietly in the background. From *Milwaukee Sentinel*, 21 May 1954; copyright Milwaukee Journal Sentinel, Inc.; reproduced with permission.

schools, such as Milwaukee, where the racial isolation of black students was quickly rising. Similarly, attorney James Dorsey did not connect the ruling to Milwaukee schools but rather placed its significance in the realm of international affairs. In his vigilant effort to counter any charges that the NAACP was un-American, he consciously embraced the Cold War rhetoric of the day. Dorsey declared *Brown* to be a "tremendous blow to communism" since Soviets could no longer denounce American democracy by pointing out the contradictions of segregated Southern schools. The white daily newspapers supported Dorsey's sentiment with a political cartoon of Uncle Sam delivering a knockout punch to Communist propagandists in the foreground with a small black schoolboy standing passively in the background. It left no doubt what mattered most about the Court's decision, particularly in Wisconsin, the home state of anti-Communist senator Joe McCarthy.[10]

Even Milwaukee's youngest generation of black political leaders did not initially connect the *Brown* ruling to the changing racial composition of the city's schools. Cecil Brown Jr., one of the few black students to attend North Division High School when it was predominantly white in the 1940s, was elected to the Wisconsin State Assembly from the predominantly black Sixth Ward in 1954. Although he later became a prominent school integration activist, Cecil Brown did not perceive Milwaukee schools to be segregated in the 1950s. "I'm not aware of anybody, including myself, who was fully knowledgeable about what was happening in Milwaukee at the time of the

[*Brown*] decision," he reflected. His only memories of black activism in Milwaukee schools during this period focused on the discriminatory placement of black teachers. "Now that should have awakened me, but it didn't," Brown explained, "because there were other things that seemed to be more pressing," such as winning better-quality jobs for blacks in all sectors of the labor market.[11]

Looking at Black Schooling through Different Eyes

Black Milwaukeeans did not associate *Brown* with their own school system in the mid-1950s for several reasons. One factor was the absence of highly visible examples of clearly segregated schools. Although four elementary schools recently had become predominantly black, several other schools (especially the prominent Lincoln and North Division High Schools) were approximately 50 percent black and therefore racially integrated in the eyes of most observers. In addition, some black families participated in Milwaukee's free transfer system to enroll their children in predominantly white schools. The bureaucratic process required families to supply a valid reason to transfer, demonstrate the availability of space in the receiving school, and obtain signatures from both principals. The process required knowledge and access, and some black families navigated their way through the system.[12]

But a second reason why black Milwaukeeans did not pursue *Brown* in the mid-1950s was that the community's senior leadership did not embrace the same concept of integration as did national race leaders of that time. Lester Granger, executive director of the National Urban League, published an essay titled "Does the Negro Want Integration?" in 1951, in which he observed generational differences among blacks in the usage of the words "interracial" and "integration," a newly popularized term. Granger defined "interracial" as a stance in opposition to racial segregation yet one that continued to tolerate voluntary forms of racial congregation. In other words, "interracial" meant that blacks should have open access to the white economy and politics yet may continue to form their own racially separate communities of association. By contrast, Granger argued that "integration" represented a new philosophical stance. It challenged traditional patterns of black self-segregated community life by requiring a spiritual commitment from blacks to "reacculturate" themselves to white society. Although black Americans were readily adopting "integration" into their vocabularies, Granger cautioned against merely substituting the new word for the old. "Many of us have failed to adjust our ideas correspondingly," he concluded;

noting that it was "the exceptionally rare colored American over forty years of age who is able to assume his full share of responsibility for integration" since members of this older generation had grown accustomed to self-segregated black cultural institutions.[13]

In Milwaukee, the tension within Granger's definition could be applied to black community leaders such as William Kelley. On one hand, Kelley clearly identified with the goals of an interracial world more than an integrated one. In his view, the struggle to advance black Milwaukee focused on gaining access to white-controlled economic markets and political machines, not on acculturation into white society. Strategies for racial solidarity were central to Kelley's work in Milwaukee's black community. Shortly after becoming executive director in 1928, Kelley had opened the Milwaukee Urban League Community Center, which quickly became the city's focal point for black culture. The murals, dramatic performances, and music classes all "pointed up race pride," and the library held the city's most extensive collection of books by and about black Americans, providing many their first encounter with Negro history, a subject virtually ignored in the public libraries and schools at that time. For a brief moment, political controversy erupted around the center in 1932. Black Republican J. Anthony Josey blasted Kelley as an "Uncle Tom" for promoting segregation through the center, but prominent black supporters came to Kelley's defense, replying that the charge did not fit the "spirited Racial Consciousness" that he demonstrated through the center's cultural programs. Kelley carefully explained the subtle distinctions to a white reporter. "Milwaukee Negroes do not want to be segregated. They want the privileges of schools, libraries, churches, and other things white folks enjoy, but just like the Polish, German, Italian and other groups with a common background and sympathies, they want a place where they can gather for their own profit and amusement."[14]

Kelley argued for greater black access to white privileges without reacculturation into white society, and his life choices illustrate how he walked that fine distinction. Despite his cultural advocacy for Milwaukee's black community, Kelley successfully broke the city's residential "color line" in the 1930s. He escaped the substandard housing conditions in the Near Northside and purchased a home in an all-white neighborhood many blocks north, near Capitol Drive. Kelley's four children did not attend predominantly black central-city schools but were among the first blacks to graduate from the virtually all-white LaFollette Elementary School and Rufus King High School. Despite the family's upward class mobility, the Kelleys did not meld into white society. All four children attended the all-black Fisk University in Tennessee, their father's alma mater, rather than follow their high school classmates to one of Wisconsin's predominantly white colleges. Therefore, in Granger's terms, Kelley lived more of an interracial existence than an integrated one.[15]

The story of Ardie Halyard, another established black Milwaukee leader of the 1950s, illustrates a similar pattern of racial activism and identification. Halyard moved to Milwaukee with her husband, Wilbur, in 1923, at a time when white realtors openly discussed strategies to restrict the city's black population. The Halyards responded by scraping together funds to begin the Columbia Savings and Loan Association, the first black-run organization of its kind in the state. Over time, this institution, which had been created as an expression of racial solidarity, enabled some black Milwaukeeans to finance their own access into the white-dominated real estate market. By the late 1950s, Columbia Savings and Loan had helped over 400 blacks to purchase homes, many of them bypassing the dismal supply of central-city housing and moving into higher-quality properties in white neighborhoods. Among them were the Halyards, who also broke the color line when they bought property in a white neighborhood. Yet their move did not necessarily mean that they had reacculturated to white society. "I've never felt that I wanted to join any of the churches . . . here in my neighborhood," Ardie Halyard explained to an interviewer in 1978. Although she accepted the presence of racially mixed houses of worship, Halyard cautioned that if whites overwhelmed a black congregation, then "we don't have an opportunity for leadership and learning to lead . . . [and] that would be objectionable." In her view, strong black-run community organizations were fundamental to the advancement of the race. In 1951, Halyard revived the inactive Milwaukee NAACP chapter by launching a campaign that increased dues-paying membership from 39 to 1,416 people. Two years later, she coordinated branches from across the state to sponsor the first Wisconsin NAACP conference. As Milwaukee NAACP president, Halyard publicly challenged job barriers, housing discrimination, and the lack of black representation in city government, all in support of increasing black access to white-dominated markets and politics.[16]

On school reform, Halyard stood behind the national NAACP drive for integrated education, but on the local level she continued working to improve conditions in black Milwaukee schools. At her invitation, a Chicago NAACP field secretary visited to help kick off the Milwaukee NAACP membership campaign in 1951; he publicly announced that his organization was fighting not only Southern segregation but also "gerrymandering of Northern school districts that keeps Negro children in exclusively Negro schools." But Halyard never took up this issue during the 1950s. Instead, as Milwaukee NAACP president, she sought to improve conditions in predominantly black schools by investigating numerous charges that black students were

Ardie Halyard, Milwaukee NAACP president and co-founder of Columbia Savings and Loan, simultaneously worked for integration and racial solidarity in the early 1950s. From *Milwaukee Journal*, 3 December 1952; copyright Milwaukee Journal Sentinel, Inc.; reproduced with permission.

being mistreated by white teachers. At Fourth Street Elementary, she identified a teacher who made "disparaging remarks about the children's clothing" and engaged in "name-calling" that made "children feel 'different' and inferior." At Lincoln High School, Halyard objected to the suspension of a black male student after determining that a cafeteria incident had been caused by a white assistant principal who had threatened to dismiss black teens who socialized with whites of the opposite sex. Indeed, while Thurgood Marshall argued for school desegregation in 1954, Ardie Halyard was busy planning Milwaukee's first major campaign for the United Negro College Fund. She solicited contributions from nearly 90 alumni in Milwaukee who had attended historically black colleges and universities such as Fisk, Spelman, Dillard, Xavier, and her alma mater, Atlanta University, where black teachers and relatives had paid to send her after her mother had died decades ago.[17]

The life stories of Ardie Halyard and William Kelley illustrate how struggles for civil rights and racial solidarity were perfectly compatible in the eyes of established black Milwaukeeans during the 1950s. As long-term leaders of the Milwaukee NAACP and the Milwaukee Urban League, both represented organizations that stood at the forefront of national movements for racial integration. But Halyard and Kelley interpreted these integration movements through an interracial lens, to use Granger's terms. They campaigned (and personally strived) for increased black access to the white economy and political structures yet maintained strong commitments to racial solidarity through black community organizations and historically black educational institutions. From their perspective, there was no cause for alarm when a handful of Milwaukee elementary schools became predominantly black in 1954, since Halyard and Kelley did not equate racial composition with inferior quality. To them, the struggle for *Brown* was all about increasing access, not about racial acculturation.

Redefining *Brown* to Fit the Local Context

In the months following the *Brown* decision, the Milwaukee NAACP did little to act on the ruling other than raise funds for the national organization. Gloster Current, the national NAACP director of branches, wrote to the Milwaukee chapter to remind them that "our recent victory in the Supreme Court's decision" made this particular time "especially appropriate to approach those members who did not re-enroll in the Association, as well as increasing the membership drive." Fund-raising soon became the "backbone of the organization" for the Milwaukee NAACP chapter. The national office sent a staff member to launch the 1955 membership drive, timed to begin on May 17th (the anniversary of the *Brown* decision), and soon counted on Northern branches to cover losses in the South, where NAACP activity was under fire by white segregationists. In 1957, the Milwaukee branch pledged to raise its own quota plus that of the branch in Tuscaloosa, Alabama, which had been banned by the state government. Milwaukee NAACP workers coordinated 300 volunteers to sign up over 3,300 individuals who purchased $2 to $10 memberships, raising approximately $20,000 in dues. But these funds largely supported the national organization, not a local agenda for school integration.[18]

In this political vacuum, William Kelley saw an opportunity for the Milwaukee Urban League to draw upon the momentum of *Brown*, though he recognized the need to exercise caution. At the national level, the Urban League was not quick to endorse the NAACP's *Brown* litigation. League director Lester Granger supported President Eisenhower and the Republican Party during the 1950s, which maintained a gradualist approach on civil rights. After considerable discussion at the National Urban League conference in September 1954, delegates voted to endorse the NAACP litigation, but Granger initially withheld his support. He reminded the delegates, many who came from the North (44 out of 55 affiliates), that the Urban League's primary mission was to resettle black migrants and that the delegates should protect the jobs of black teachers, who were the means to achieve this end. Although Granger did not endorse the "separate but equal" view of *Brown* opponents, he expressed concern about the most appropriate way for the Urban League to oppose Northern de facto segregation without jeopardizing its funding sources or some of its more positive relationships with Northern school boards. Kelley recognized these dangers in his own context. The Milwaukee Urban League depended upon the financial support of annual giving campaigns to the Milwaukee Community Chest, so he needed to be careful not to upset donations from wealthy whites who saw no reason for racial activism in their Northern city. Still, Kelley worried that the absence of political action would contribute to the "alleged charge that the National Urban League did not cooperate with the NAACP," so he resolved to try something.[19]

Since the Milwaukee NAACP had not defined what *Brown* meant in the local context, Kelley stepped in to harness its powerful symbolic value and renegotiate the compromise he had reluctantly accepted fifteen years before. He launched an extensive lobbying campaign, which an observer described as one of the Milwaukee Urban League's most focused efforts during the late 1950s. Kelley sought to persuade Superintendent Harold Vincent that the spirit of *Brown* obligated the school system to take positive action on black teacher assignments, even though the justices made no ruling on this employment issue. Kelley acknowledged the conventional wisdom that the Supreme Court decision applied only to the South. "Certainly this is where the thunder will be loudest," he wrote to Vincent, "but the real application of the decision, in our judgment, is largely one of degree." He urged the superintendent to take advantage of the political climate and strategically place a few highly qualified "pioneer" black teachers in white neighborhood schools, where their outstanding personal qualities would calm anxious whites. Superintendent Vincent initially responded by interviewing a candidate that Kelley recommended, perhaps only as a courtesy, but did nothing else.[20]

Undaunted, Kelley tried a second, more assertive approach. One of his few weapons was the threat of adverse national publicity for Milwaukee's prized public school system, which had received some recognition as a progressive urban school district. He informed Superintendent Vincent that the National Urban League had requested reports from all branches, particularly those in the North, on their local school districts' compliance with *Brown*, to be published in a national magazine. Kelley included an advance copy of his own report, which criticized Milwaukee for having fewer than forty-five black teachers, "all of whom are employed in schools having a sizable Negro enrollment." In order to meet the requirements of *Brown*, he recommended that black teachers be placed "in high schools in the outlying and fringe areas of our city." This pressure tactic was, at first, a risky deception. A few days earlier, Kelley had sent a confidential memo to Lester Granger in New York City, admitting that he had stretched the truth. The national office had never requested such a report from its branches, but Kelley hoped that the threat of one would prompt Milwaukee school officials to "straighten up and fly right." He asked for support, which Granger readily offered, since he envisioned the National Urban League playing a more prominent and influential role in civil rights than did his predecessors.[21]

Kelley took the initiative by sending his own survey to Northern Urban League affiliates, asking them to report the number of black teachers in their city, their grade level and geographical placements, and whether any policy changes had arisen in the wake of the *Brown* decision. On one level, the results confirmed what he already knew: Milwaukee fell far behind other cities concerning its relative share of black teachers. But on another level, they highlighted that black teacher placement was a hot-button issue across most Northern states. Even in large cities, the number who had been assigned to predominantly white schools was very small: Chicago placed 18 out of 1,550, Detroit 15 out of 885, and Indianapolis 3 out of 400. League affiliates reported that "more Negro teachers could be placed outside the Negro area" and that they had struggled to "try to bring about a more general distribution." Kelley was encouraged to pursue *Brown* as a lobbying tool on this issue, especially when the Chicago branch wrote that the "Supreme Court decision and other factors have put more pressure on the school board to re-examine their policies" for placing black personnel.[22]

Although Lester Granger agreed to join in the lobbying effort, he expressed a much stronger concern about student segregation than did Kelley. For instance, Granger urged Superintendent Vincent to consider how racial isolation cut off some children from "easy intercultural exchange" with the rest of the city, adding that "the Negro school child is robbed of the opportunity to get to know pupils of other racial extractions . . . to such an extent [that he] tends to become withdrawn and set in a racial-cultural caste which serves to hinder him still further in his efforts toward community adjustment." But Kelley never raised this concern. Although he argued that academic standards and expectations had been lowered in predominantly black schools, he never claimed that their racial composition had an isolating, harmful effect on black children. Instead, Kelley continued to emphasize that *Brown* meant fairer employment opportunities for black teachers. "A racially integrated school system envisions more than the acceptance of Negro pupils in schools having a predominant white pupil enrollment," he wrote. "We have requested and insisted that there be a wider distribution of qualified Negro teachers through the entire system than is now the case." One difference between Granger and Kelley was the former's preference for integration over interracialism. Another was their different local contexts. At Granger's National Urban League headquarters in New York City, 2,500 black teachers enjoyed one of the fairest hiring and placement systems through the country, and civil rights activists had focused their attention on integrating the high concentrations of black schoolchildren. But at Kelley's small office in Milwaukee, the struggle still focused on gaining these jobs for black teachers.[23]

Kelley continued to pressure the school system. A newly organized city agency, the Milwaukee Commission on Human Rights, met with Superintendent Vincent in early 1955, and Corneff Taylor, its black executive director and a personal friend of Kelley's, pointed out that only two of the city's forty-five black teachers at that time were assigned to schools outside of the black neighborhood. Vincent replied that he was unaware of the gravity of the situation. Kelley organized a delegation of white civic leaders and businessmen from the Milwaukee Urban League who believed that school officials recognized the problem "in private, if not officially" and were prepared to discuss the matter "openly and sympathetically, without need for accusations, threats, etc." One of them, Roy Wilson, urged the superintendent to consider the "current nation-wide trends toward integration" and the positive steps that could be taken on school personnel issues. Vincent responded that the current hiring system was fair and that the present distribution of black teachers was accidental, yet he offered to discuss the matter with school board members. During this period, Kelley cheerfully reported that one more black teacher, Emma Mae Bowers, had been reassigned to Thirty-fifth Street Elementary School, "where there are no Negro pupils." Furthermore, he added with a small note of glee, friends had privately told him that "the Urban League had become a 'dirty word' in the Superintendent's Office."[24]

COUNTING THE RESULTS

Kelley's three decades of lobbying finally began to pay off, with staggering results. Milwaukee school officials began hiring black teachers in record numbers, with totals leaping from 45 in 1954, to 191 in 1960, to 439 by 1965. The elusive goal of the 1930s, when black activists had called for their teachers to be hired in proportion to their share of the city's population, was finally in reach. Black teachers were now employed at disproportionately higher rates than the city's total black population. In 1960, the assistant superintendent of personnel proudly announced the hiring of 500 new teachers, of whom 10 percent were black, a rate greater than the 8.4 percent black population in the city. In addition, the administration began to distribute black teachers more widely across the city, particularly in white neighborhoods. In 1960, 10 out of 191 black teachers (5 percent) worked in virtually all-white elementary schools. By 1965, that number rose to 43 out of 439 (10 percent) and included both elementary and high schools in predominantly white neighborhoods.[25]

Compared to other sectors of Milwaukee's labor market, Kelley and his colleagues had good reason to celebrate their success on black teacher employment. Wesley Scott, hired to assist Kelley at the Urban League in 1958, recalled the sparse numbers of blacks working in the commercial and industrial sectors at that time. "There was only one black [bank] teller in town. There was only a couple of salespeople. The Boston Store had one, a woman. . . . There were no middle managers, none whatsoever. And we had individuals who worked in some of the major plants who were foremen, supervisors, but none in a management position." In the civil service, the police department employed only 22 black officers (1 percent), and the fire department included only 5 (less than 0.5 percent) in 1960. Blacks seeking work in the building trades also faced tremendous barriers. In 1957, when attorney James Dorsey sued the bricklayers' union for refusing to accept a black transfer from an out-of-town local, the Wisconsin State Supreme Court ruled against him, concluding that unions were voluntary organizations that had the right to exclude members based upon race. In light of the negative publicity this decision raised for Wisconsin, Dorsey and newly elected black state assemblyman Isaac Coggs pushed a stronger fair employment bill through the legislature, but local patterns of white union membership prevailed. In 1960, for example, the plumbers' union counted only two blacks among its 900 journeymen (0.2 percent), both of whom had been trained in locals outside of Milwaukee. By comparison, teaching became a significant route for black entry into middle-class professional work, particularly for women, who made up approximately 70 percent of those hired. The only other standard occupational category with comparable black employment rates was nursing, another traditionally female profession.[26]

By temporarily shifting the historical spotlight away from the familiar story of Thurgood Marshall's courtroom battles for *Brown*, we learn more about how local black communities gave new meaning to the decision within the context of their own struggles. While Kelley and his supporters failed to gain significant numbers of black teachers' jobs during the 1930s, they achieved tremendous success during the 1950s, for multiple reasons. One clear influence was the timing of demographic change. In contrast to failed efforts during the Depression era, Kelley's successful lobbying took place during the extraordinary growth period of the postwar era. During the 1950s, the baby boom and Milwaukee's ambitious land annexation program swelled public school enrollments by 52 percent to over 100,000 students. Strong majorities of voters approved three bond issues to build twenty-five new schools, and the school board increased the size of the instructional staff by nearly 1,600 new positions. But demographic change alone does not explain how Milwaukee's racial barriers on teacher hiring were broken. The sudden leap in black teacher hiring in 1955 can be traced to Kelley's creative application of the *Brown* decision in lobbying Milwaukee school officials.[27]

Yet when Kelley finally won his prize—jobs for hundreds of black teachers—the racial context of Milwaukee's schools dramatically changed. The vast majority of newly hired black teachers were assigned to teach in central-city schools, with increasing proportions of black students. During the 1950s, Milwaukee's black school-age population rose over 300 percent, to more than 20,000 students, nearly one-fifth of the city's total student enrollment. Schools that previously had been racially mixed were soon becoming virtually all-black, greatly increasing the number that had existed at the beginning of the decade. Troubling questions began to rise about the quality of education in these schools, and it became harder for people of Kelley's generation to maintain their views on the positive aspects of black education amid a rising movement for integrated education. These demographic and cultural changes would soon alter the racial politics of school reform in Milwaukee.[28]

During the late 1950s, when Southern schools erupted in scenes of violence over school desegregation, white Milwaukeeans tended to view the absence of conflict over their schools as a sign of Northern racial progress. But white racial anxieties lurked not far from the surface. In 1958, the weekly magazine *U.S. News and World Report* published a four-page feature article titled "I Spent Four Years in an Integrated High School." Written by an anonymous white female graduate of North Division High, the article revealed one insider's view of racial change in the Milwaukee school as it shifted from a white-majority to a black-majority student body over four years. The author declared there to be "little, if any, tension between the races" at her school, and subsequent local newspaper editorials emphasized that "tolerance and good neighborliness" were more prevalent in Milwaukee "than in most American cities."[29]

Yet the body of the young author's article gave a somewhat contradictory message by clearly pointing out several examples of heightened racial anxiety at the school. Most white teachers were "constantly leaning over backward to prove they weren't prejudiced," she wrote, while another "disliked Negroes intensely and made no effort to hide her feelings." During sports tournaments at other Wisconsin schools, "we all knew that we were being watched closely because we were largely a colored school." Certainly, the most controversial section dealt with the taboo subject of "mixed dating." Every white girl she knew "had a secret crush on one of the colored boys," and while only a few dared to dance with them at school functions, several girls began to secretly date, despite the "probable hysterical reaction of [their] parents if they found out." This trend about heightened white fears of interracial sexuality paralleled one of Kelley's own observations based on his many public speaking engagements in Wisconsin. Before the *Brown* decision, white audiences continually asked him, "How do Negroes feel about Communism?" But after 1954, he quietly reported that "interracial marriage" was the hot topic, leading him to conclude that perhaps the Supreme Court ruling had "given rise to the revival of this apprehension by white people." Just as black activists constructed their own interpretation of *Brown* to suit their local struggle, they now faced new challenges created when that same decision was reinterpreted in the white mind.[30]

3

CALMING THE "MIGRANT CRISIS" THROUGH

COMPENSATORY EDUCATION

In many ways, white racial anxieties had risen well before the *U.S. News and World Report* article. City newspapers broke the story in late 1952: the South's "Negro problem" had finally worked its way North to Milwaukee. Three white Milwaukeeans had been murdered by a recent black migrant to the city; the man had a history of mental instability. In the aftermath, police chief John Polcyn requested that the city council appropriate funds for thirty-eight additional police officers, the majority to be assigned to the Sixth Ward, home of the city's rapidly growing black population. Chief Polcyn claimed that 80 percent of all major crimes took place in this Near Northside area of the city, adding that in twenty recent homicide cases, "thirteen of the killers were Negroes." Police inspector Hubert Dax agreed with the chief that Southern black migrants were linked to the disproportionate rate of crime but pressed for a broader solution than simply expanding the size of the police force. "We've got to get to these people as soon as they arrive," Inspector Dax urged, "and let them know this is a law-abiding community. Education is badly needed." But what kind of education, and how it would be delivered, was left unclear.[1]

To solve the "migrant crisis" of the 1950s, white Milwaukee officials turned to community-based and school-based education, but these programs could not do it alone. Established black community leaders, whose social class status and civil rights were jeopardized by white fears of a black migrant invasion, cooperated with whites and implemented a program of "cultural adjustment." Although white and black leaders initially recognized the structural causes behind their urban crisis, intense levels of white anxiety did not permit sufficient time to act upon them. Instead, established blacks accepted the implication that the migrants' own behavior was the cause and created educational reforms that sought to improve the migrants' character and comportment, thereby transforming them into respectable city residents and (at least in theory) relieving the crisis. In doing so, Milwaukee's white and black leaders of the 1950s continued in the tradition of mid-nineteenth-century urban reformers who called upon moral education rather than structural change to resolve the social turmoil of their own time.[2]

This chapter expands the book's analysis of black education reform in two ways. First, it steps beyond the boundary of institutionalized schooling to consider community-based adult education. By examining how established black organizations attempted to settle Southern migrants through cultural adjustment in the 1950s, we gain a more comprehensive picture of the origins of compensatory education for black schoolchildren in the 1960s. Second, the chapter draws upon recent historical reinterpretations of the mythical "Golden Age" of the black community to underscore tensions between Milwaukee's established black residents and newly arrived migrants during this period. When anxious white Milwaukeeans blamed the migrants for all of the city's troubles in the 1950s, established upper-class black community leaders rose to their defense, but they also distanced themselves from the lower-class newcomers. While established blacks engaged in the work of racial uplift, they did so partly due to their negative assessment of migrant family culture and their fears of white retaliation against the entire race. Over the course of the decade, black organizations' efforts to acculturate newcomers provided the model that Milwaukee school officials called "compensatory education," which many established blacks supported despite its problematic implications.[3]

Defending yet Distancing the Migrants

In most Northern cities, the peak years of black migration came in the years immediately following World War I. Between 1910 and 1920, the number of blacks sharply increased in large Midwestern cities such as Chicago (up by 124,000, or 148 percent), Detroit (up by 35,000, or 611 percent), and Cleveland (up by 26,000, or 308 percent). But relatively few migrants ven-

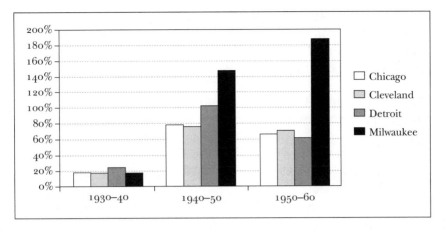

Black Population Growth Rates for Selected Midwestern Cities, 1930–1960. *Source*: U.S. Census Bureau, *Census of Population and Housing*, 1930–60.

tured to Milwaukee, another ninety miles north of Chicago, leading to a relatively smaller increase in the black population (only 1,250) during the same period. Even by 1930, Milwaukee's black residents comprised only 1 percent of the city's total population, compared to an average of 8 percent in Chicago, Detroit, and Cleveland.

Milwaukee's black population finally exploded in the 1950s, due to what local historians have dubbed the "Late Great Migration." The city's postwar manufacturing boom and improved transportation system led thousands of black migrants from Mississippi, Arkansas, and Alabama to bypass Chicago's overcrowded slums and venture farther north. Milwaukee's black population rose 187 percent (from 21,772 to 62,458) during the 1950s, the highest rate of increase for any major U.S. city during that decade. No longer a forgotten fraction, the black community now comprised over 8 percent of the city's total population. This sudden demographic shift also forced white Milwaukeeans to confront racial issues that they had previously viewed from a comfortable distance. Tensions surrounding increased black migration had sparked deadly race riots in cities such as Chicago in 1919 and Detroit in 1943, heightening concerns throughout the Midwest. White Milwaukeeans feared they might be next.[4]

Black population increases alone did not fuel white racial anxiety. What mattered more was how public officials and the mass media acted upon local events involving black migrants and whether they portrayed them as impending signs of urban chaos and disorder. In Milwaukee, white fears linking race and crime soared again in 1957 when police suspected a "gang of Negro rapists" in recent attacks on four white women. Authorities launched a crackdown in the Near Northside that "pitched an otherwise calm community into turmoil." Police squads swarmed the streets in a massive man-hunt and picked up over 260 black men for questioning, arresting many who simply appeared "suspicious" or "could give no satisfactory explana-tion for being on the street in the early morning." Although Chief Polcyn pledged to make Milwaukee's streets "safe for women" once again, his ac-tions caused a "feeling of terror" in the black community, including many who had previously heard the rhetoric of defending white women as a jus-tification for lynching in the South. One outside observer commented that Milwaukee's two daily newspapers, the *Sentinel* and the *Journal*, appeared to be competing with one another in using "scare headlines" in this racially charged environment.[5]

Milwaukee's established black citizens, particularly the men, were swal-lowed up in the wave of white anxiety over migrants and crime. Black at-torney Dale Phillips, a member of the Milwaukee NAACP delegation that met with Chief Polcyn, complained that "law-abiding citizens" were mis-takenly arrested and urged the police to exercise "more discrimination" in their roundups. A new black-owned newspaper, the *Milwaukee Defender*, offered reward money and pleaded with readers "to help us so that many will not have to bear and share the blame." The police department's indiscrimi-nate roundups of black men illustrated that in the white mind, race was a totalizing category. When one black resident engaged in criminal activity, white Milwaukeeans failed to distinguish between upper-class and lower-class, old-timer and newcomer, and as a result, all members of the race suf-fered the consequences. Shortly afterward, Chief Polcyn narrowed the man-hunts so that only those black men who actually fit the physical description of the perpetrators were sought, rather than all men in the black community at large. But he issued a stern warning to the NAACP leaders. "Law-abiding Negroes" must "accept more responsibility" for their people "by forcing the lawless to behave or leave Milwaukee." Black Milwaukeeans must "act as a police force of your own," he cautioned. "Be your brother's keeper. Watch what your brother is doing."[6]

Milwaukee's established blacks had heard these words before, and they strongly objected to the insinuation. "The Negro does not feel it is his re-sponsibility to be responsible for every other Negro," declared Ardie Hal-yard, the Milwaukee NAACP president, in her testimony before the Metro-politan Crime Commission after a similar incident in 1952. William Kelley, executive director of the Milwaukee Urban League, agreed with her com-ments. "Milwaukee is the only city in which I have lived where Negroes are not permitted to stratify themselves as other people do," noted Kelley, re-ferring to the city's racially restricted housing patterns. "The good, bad, and indifferent all share the same barrel" in the black community, he ex-plained, although middle-class white Milwaukeeans were free to move to the suburbs.[7]

The words of Halyard and Kelley, two long-standing leaders of Milwaukee's black community, revealed how they viewed themselves with respect to the newly arrived migrants and how they wished to be viewed through the eyes of whites. On one hand, Halyard and Kelley defended the newcomers. Both had migrated to Milwaukee during the tense period of the 1920s and spent much of their careers coordinating the efforts of the Milwaukee NAACP and the Urban League to give assistance to new arrivals. They also recognized underlying structural causes of the city's mislabeled "Negro problem," which had more to do with white racism. During her testimony before the all-white Metropolitan Crime Commission, Halyard argued that the city's crisis could not be solved without greater black representation in city government. "Since 80 percent of the crime in Milwaukee is supposed to be in the Sixth Ward," she reasoned, "Negroes should be on the commission."[8]

On the other hand, established black residents claimed the right to distance themselves from the migrants. The Milwaukee NAACP criticized white media coverage of the crisis and passed a resolution that warned, "This crime wave is not a racial problem. . . . All efforts to inject the racial angle into it should be discouraged." They pointed to the unfair practice of "race labeling" by white newspapers, which typically identified the race of criminals who were black but not the race or ethnicity of those who were white. Milwaukee's established black middle class desperately sought to avoid the stigma that linked them to the disreputable behavior of lower-class migrants and worried that the crisis might push whites to the extremes of law and order, eliminating some of the hard-fought gains they had made in civil rights.[9]

Intraracial distinctions of social class, complexion, and residential seniority have deep roots in African American history, surfacing especially during heightened periods of migration into previously settled Northern communities. At various times between the 1920s and 1940s, successive generations of black Milwaukee's "old-timers" sharply criticized the behavior of the most recent migrants for lowering the status of the entire race. Setting themselves apart from one another fostered conflicts, which stalled attempts to build a more unified black political base. Historians and sociologists have observed similar distinctions between "old settlers" and "newcomers" in comparable cities. According to W. E. B. Du Bois, black community stratification in Philadelphia often depended upon moral categories, such as "respectability," more than on income or occupation. In addition, E. Franklin Frazier noted the relationship between black social class position and racial ideology. Although higher-status blacks sometimes professed "considerable race pride" and affiliated with racial uplift organizations such as the NAACP and the Urban League, they were "eager not to be identified with the poor, crude, and ignorant members of the 'race.'"[10]

The Milwaukee NAACP's agenda in the early 1950s illustrates the importance of racial identity issues to the established black community as they attempted to distinguish themselves from the stereotypical images of lower-class Southern blacks. When the national NAACP passed a resolution against the *Amos 'n' Andy* television show in 1951, the Milwaukee chapter quickly jumped on board and gained national recognition for its protest against the program's depiction of blacks as "amoral, semiliterate, lazy, stupid, scheming and dishonest." They successfully pressured the local television station to drop the show, even though its national sponsor was Blatz Brewery, based in Milwaukee. The national NAACP praised the work of the Milwaukee branch, holding it up as "an inspiration to all our branches to move ahead in the fight against misrepresentation of the Negro."[11] Months later, the Milwaukee NAACP lodged another protest against demeaning black caricatures in advertisements for Borden Ice Cream. Company officials were puzzled, noting that their ads appeared in movie theaters across the country, but the only city where blacks had raised objections was Milwaukee.[12]

Milwaukee NAACP members also complained when their own organization made errors that threatened to lower their image in the eyes of whites. Millie White French, one of Milwaukee's first black teachers and an NAACP lifetime member, criticized the national office for sending a woefully inadequate black speaker to address the local chapter. "[The speaker] was very disappointing. In fact, to be truthful, she was awful," French wrote. "She caused many of us much embarrassment. We had a mixed audience, and believe me she did our organization much harm." The tensions of the 1950s migrant crisis heightened the sensitivity of established black Milwaukeeans to negative stereotypes in the eyes of whites.[13]

Some established blacks took on the role of cultural translators for the migrant community, which allowed them to interpret the migrants' behavior to white audiences yet still remain apart from it. In 1959, for example, white newspapers published a controversial set of statistics that identified black residents to be responsible for 43 percent of major crimes during the first half of that year, although they made up less than 8 percent of the population. But Stanley Hebert, the only black employee in the city attorney's office, explained these figures to white audiences by pointing to the disproportionately high levels of police patrols on Walnut Street, where many underemployed black men spent their days and nights for lack of anywhere else to go. In addition, Hebert noted that out of all of the major crime subcategories, the greatest proportion of black offenses were simply weapons charges. Carrying a weapon for personal protection was perfectly normal in the violent South, he explained. Furthermore, migrants were unaccustomed to Milwaukee's strict law enforcement, Hebert argued, since Southern police often ignored violent acts as long as blacks did them to one another.[14]

William Kelley was one of the few established blacks who publicly recognized the irony in the ways that his community treated migrants. Many
of the "old-timers" who saw newcomers as a poor social risk "were themselves so judged just a few years ago," during the 1920s and 1930s, when
they first migrated to the city and clashed with earlier generations of established black residents. Perhaps Kelley's contemporaries also reflected on
this dynamic as they passed around copies of *Black Bourgeoisie,* E. Franklin
Frazier's stinging indictment of upper-class blacks and their world of make-
believe. If these intraracial tensions had remained within the confines of
a segregated black community, they would not have seemed so important,
but this was not the case. Social distinctions between established blacks and
newly arrived migrants increased in direct response to white Milwaukee's
anxiety about race and crime. As Kelley described, this was the phenome-
non that most disturbed the "so-called old-timers": if one migrant broke the
law, the entire black community "becomes stigmatized." The fate of Milwaukee's established blacks, for better or worse, was irrevocably linked to the
migrant.[15]

Devising a Strategy for the Inner Core

While Milwaukee's daily newspapers trumpeted sensational headlines about
blacks and crime, a small number of white city leaders demonstrated a more
sophisticated understanding of the structural causes behind the "migrant
crisis." Mayor Frank Zeidler, the last Socialist to govern the city, had witnessed many changes as a long-term Northside resident and drew upon his
ideological framework to analyze them. In 1954, Mayor Zeidler defined the
problem not simply as a "migrant crisis" but more broadly as a conflict between blacks, whites, and dollars. Northern industry had produced machinery that displaced Southern black migrants from their agricultural jobs, and
when they came searching for a better life in Northern cities, they were
forced to live in slums because they "are not welcome anywhere else." He
bluntly acknowledged that "white people, for the most part, do not like to
live in Negro neighborhoods" and sharply criticized realtors and absentee
landlords who made lucrative profits from the crisis by frightening whites to
sell cheaply through blockbusting tactics and charging high rents to blacks
for substandard housing. From Zeidler's perspective, the roots of Milwaukee's racial crisis could be traced back to racism and greed.[16]

But as a politician seeking reelection, Zeidler was vulnerable. In the 1956
mayoral race, rumors blanketed the city that he was a "nigger lover" who
posted billboards across the South to encourage blacks to migrate to Milwaukee. Although Zeidler overcame that particular obstacle, white racial
anxieties continued to mount in the year leading up to the 1960 election.

One summer evening, while the mayor and his wife were driving to their Northside neighborhood home, he reported that they "literally 'ran into' a Negro mob scene." The disturbance erupted when police officers intervened during a fight between three black girls, one armed with a knife. After authorities made an arrest, two black men reportedly incited the crowd to force the girls' release, leading to the white media's vivid description of a "mob scene in which Negroes jeered police and tried to prevent arrests." Mayor Zeidler's firsthand view and rising city tensions prompted him to create a biracial panel of local experts to address the problem.[17]

By its very name, the "Mayor's Study Committee on Social Problems in the Inner Core Area" defined the city's turmoil as rooted within the inner city and carefully mapped out its geographic boundaries. During the 1930s, most white Milwaukeeans conceived of the "Negro district" as a 120-block area. But in 1960, the Mayor's Study Committee expanded white perceptions of these boundaries to the north and west by officially designating a 400-block "Inner Core" area and directly linking it to the racial crisis in the city. The truth was more complicated. Indeed, over 90 percent of Milwaukee's black residents lived within these newly designated inner-city boundaries. But it was not an all-black neighborhood, since nearly 40 percent of the Inner Core residents were white, according to the 1960 census. Over the course of the following decade, thousands of whites did flee the area, perhaps in part due to the report signaling that they were now living on the "wrong side" of Milwaukee's expanding color line.[18]

Although Mayor Zeidler previously recognized the issue as a citywide reaction to changes brought on by the increase in Southern migrants, white anxiety pressured him and his committee to define it simply as an inner-city crisis. Indeed, some portions of the lengthy report did touch on broader structural issues, such as mortgage lenders who typically refused loan applications for property located within the inner city. But in their final recommendations, the Mayor's Study Committee strongly emphasized the need to reorient and acculturate Southern black migrants so that they would maintain cleaner homes, search for job opportunities, and improve themselves in ways that would increase their chances for acceptance into mainstream Milwaukee life. As historian William Thompson observed, the Mayor's Study Committee implied that the root causes of the problem "emanated from the Core alone and could be dealt with by measures limited to the Core." Indeed, changing the behaviors of inner-city black migrants would be an easier task than overturning deeply held racism within the outlying all-white neighborhoods and suburbs.[19]

The strategy of "cultural adjustment" featured prominently in the minds of the leading white and black citizens serving on the Mayor's Study Committee. Surveys of newly arrived black families noted that they migrated most

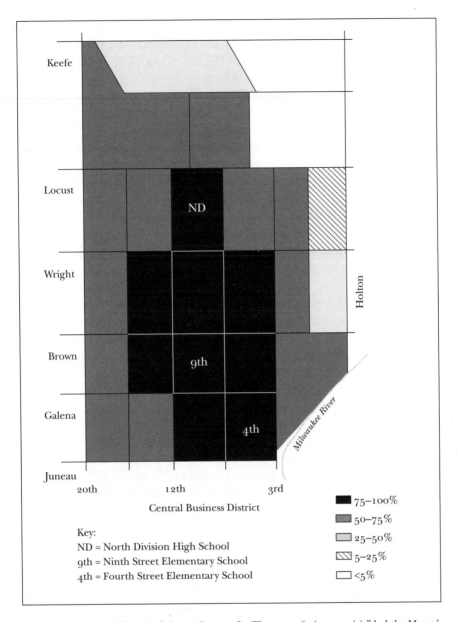

Black Population in Milwaukee's Inner Core, 1960. The 1950s "migrant crisis" led the Mayor's Study Committee to designate boundaries of a troubled Inner Core and target black cultural deprivation within it, although significant numbers of whites still lived in the area. Adapted from U.S. Census Bureau, *Census of Population and Housing*, 1960.

often from Mississippi, Arkansas, and Alabama, which, in the eyes of the committee, represented areas "in which the motivation for economic and cultural advancement has been quite limited." Although inner-city residents had access to adequate public school facilities in Milwaukee, the committee wrote that "there is a great need to increase the motivation of individuals to avail themselves of the existing opportunity." School welfare counselors also reported a highly disproportionate number of students from "problem families" with "personality and/or behavior disorders." On these grounds, Mayor Zeidler justified the committee's proposal to spend additional city funds to "remedy educational and cultural deficiencies" among Milwaukee's newest migrants before they "threaten the security of the community." A similar argument would be nationally popularized one year later by James Bryant Conant, whose influential book, *Slums and Suburbs*, warned that "we are allowing social dynamite to accumulate in our large cities."[20]

But rather than proposing bold political measures to eliminate institutional racism (among mortgage lenders and others), the Mayor's Study Committee called for remolding the behavior of black migrants through education. In doing so, they continued a pervasive American belief in acculturation as a reform strategy. Earlier in the twentieth century, Milwaukee leaders addressed "the foreign family" problem through a nationally recognized program of neighborhood social centers that sought to acculturate newcomers. In the same way that Americanization programs remolded southern European immigrants in the pre-war era, the Mayor's Study Committee believed that urbanization programs could redesign Southern black migrants in the postwar era. These beliefs perpetuated the logic of ethnic succession, expressed in the scholarly literature of that time by Harvard historian Oscar Handlin. According to Handlin's interpretation, just as European immigrants had adapted to urban American culture and pulled themselves out of the ghetto in the early twentieth century, so would black and Puerto Rican migrants adapt and pull themselves out of Northern ghettos in the latter part of the century. Yet this formula did not fully consider the powerful economic and political forces that contained black Milwaukeeans within the inner city; it simply sought to adjust the migrants to them.[21]

CRITICIZING YET COOPERATING WITH CULTURAL ADJUSTMENT

Several leading black ministers sharply criticized the Mayor's Study Committee soon after its formation had been announced. Rev. E. B. Phillips of the influential Greater Galilee Baptist Church joined two of his colleagues to denounce the scapegoating of the migrants. "For anyone to conclude that most of our disaster arises from newcomers is baseless and without foundation," they declared in a public letter to the press. Instead, the ministers charged that the fundamental cause of recent street disturbances was the brutality of the Milwaukee Police Department.[22]

Although established blacks distanced themselves from migrant crime, they often recognized that street uprisings served as a form of mass resistance to police brutality. Looking through their perspective opens a different interpretation of events that the white media typically depicted as angry "Negro mob scenes." For example, during a 1955 incident that the white press described as mob violence against police, several prominent Milwaukee NAACP members offered their own interpretation to reporters, explaining that black migrants had "attempted to 'rescue' a woman from arresting police." One year later, the white press carried another story, focusing on two police officers surrounded by a crowd of 400 black teenagers who were stoning their car. A Milwaukee police inspector spoke with reporters and sharply criticized a black minister who had been at the scene and "could have helped if he had the right attitude." Instead, the black minister focused on the black teenage boy who was being questioned by police inside the car and busily wrote down badge numbers to document what he perceived as a case of police misconduct.[23]

Black community outrage against police brutality peaked in 1958 when officials lied about the shooting of a black citizen named Daniel Bell. Two white officers pursued Bell for a traffic violation and then fatally shot him in the back. But the police changed their stories about crucial facts in the case. They later claimed that Bell had lunged at them with a knife, but neither officer had mentioned a knife in his initial written report, nor did this explain how Bell had been shot in the back. Despite these blatant contradictions, the district attorney and a jury panel determined that the white officers were innocent.

The Bell shooting brought together black Milwaukeeans for a debate about what to do. Speaking to a crowd of 450 at Mount Zion Baptist Church, Assemblyman Isaac Coggs, the city's lone black representative at the state capital, drew loud applause for criticizing the police department. "There is no difference between shooting Dan Bell in the back than killing Emmett Till in Mississippi," he declared. In the black-owned *Milwaukee Defender*, one letter to the editor read, "Hats off to Ike Coggs for not pussyfooting. . . . Almost everyone is saying it was 'down right murder.'" Following his lead, Rev. R. L. Lathan from New Hope Baptist Church announced plans to hold a "Prayer of Protest" march against police brutality. But other black leaders called upon the audience to cooperate with law enforcement rather than to criticize it. Attorney James Dorsey, the former Milwaukee NAACP president and fair employment advocate, told the crowd that Bell's tragic clash with the police signaled that "Negroes [should] be a little more respectful of law and authority." A second *Milwaukee Defender* letter also cautioned that "one of the things we have to learn before we start yelling 'police brutality' [is that] we must teach our children to respect the law and quit fighting the police." Days later, under pressure from fellow black ministers and white city officials, Reverend Lathan called off plans for the protest march.[24]

Despite their awareness of the deeper roots of the problem, Milwaukee's established black leaders cooperated with the strategy of cultural adjustment more often than they criticized it during the 1950s. White leaders faced significant pressure to quell migrant violence, and adjusting the behavior of Southern newcomers arose as the most politically expedient solution. In turn, white leaders pressured established blacks to carry out their strategy, since whites could not do it alone. Milwaukee's black leadership did not hesitate for long in joining the struggle to acculturate the migrants. Given the severity of the racial crisis and the lack of white political will to address broader structural issues, established blacks worked hard to achieve the limited success that was attainable under these conditions. Furthermore, the extensive network of Milwaukee's black civic and religious organizations was best positioned to support resettlement work.

Although black Milwaukeeans held few positions of power in white society, their leadership flourished through dozens of black civic and religious organizations in the 1950s. Although some occasionally voiced protest against racism, most engaged in the task of self-improvement and cultural adjustment. Black women's clubs in Milwaukee, in particular, drew upon their community resources to settle Southern migrants in ways more consistent with established cultural norms. When women from the prestigious Mary Church Terrell Club gathered together in early 1959, they discussed one of their most important "housekeeping jobs," the integration of Southern black newcomers into Northern city life. During a conference sponsored by the Mayor's Study Committee in 1960, the clubwomen urged greater moral training for families, since education at home "counts the most," and concluded with a call for more volunteers to reach out to families who had not yet been assisted by social welfare agencies. As one of three local affiliates of the National Association of Colored Women's Clubs, the organization had a long history of programs for self-improvement of its members as well as of charity work for newcomers.[25]

The *Milwaukee Defender* briefly joined the protest over the Daniel Bell shooting but devoted much of its agenda to cultural adjustment for migrants. Publisher Mary Ellen Shadd, concerned that black Milwaukee's moral standards had deteriorated, wrote editorials against the "profane, vulgar and indecent language which people who lay claim to respectability must endure if they walk the streets of the Near Northside, or ride the No. 20 bus." Shadd also sponsored a "Better Living Show" with thirty public and private welfare agencies to help reorient female "Negro Newcomers" of the city. "We're going to urbanize them," she explained. "We're going to show them the ideal Negro mother" and introduce migrant women to the basic rights and responsibilities of life in the city.[26]

The Milwaukee Urban League, well known for its employment service, expanded its programs for acculturating Southern migrants, specifically in family and community life. In the late 1950s, the League distributed brochures, such as *You and Milwaukee*, which advised newcomers to "think first" before complaining about mistreatment from whites, since "many times it will be because of what you are doing." In addition to providing information about locating jobs and schools, it urged migrants to become good neighbors in Milwaukee and to "keep your home clean; keep your children clean; keep yourself clean." Lucinda Gordon, who designed the brochures and directed the League's Community Organization Department, graduated from the Smith College of Social Work and was married to Grant Gordon, one of the city's early black schoolteachers. Previously, she had served as the executive secretary of the Milwaukee NAACP, but the promise of a more stable salary drew her to the Urban League, where she organized dozens of block clubs and home self-improvement programs to make inner-city neighborhoods more attractive.[27]

Although established black Milwaukeeans recognized the deeper roots of the crisis, many also shared the same negative assessment of black migrant family culture as did most whites. After the street disturbances of 1959, reporters interviewed Corneff Taylor, a respected black official and trained sociologist, whom Zeidler had appointed to serve as executive secretary of the Milwaukee Commission on Human Rights and eventually to the Study Committee. Taylor pointed to substandard housing and the lack of black representation in government as the roots of the problem, but he also added that "complete family disorganization [in the inner city] . . . brought about by broken homes" played a significant role.

Taylor's close friend at the Urban League, William Kelley, agreed with his assessment and argued that black teachers were best suited to restore the breakdown in black migrant families. Kelley was keenly aware of black teachers' traditional roles in reinforcing cultural norms and high standards in Southern communities. In his view, most Southern migrants came from "a culture where the teacher knows the parents of most of the children and cooperates to see that the youngsters stay in line." Gaining jobs for black teachers affected far more than the individuals earning the paychecks, Kelley recognized. Teachers played a key role in racial uplift, serving as cultural role models for the community and encouraging migrant students and their families to better themselves.[28]

One black teacher who fulfilled this role was Sarah Scott, known as

"Mother Sarah" to her students at Lincoln High School. In 1953, she became the second person to break the barrier against black teachers at the high school level. Many cherished her "no-nonsense" attitude on discipline, which she may have acquired as a student at the highly acclaimed all-black Dunbar High School in Little Rock, Arkansas, during the 1930s and further developed as an educator and wife of a black minister in Milwaukee. During a Northside community meeting held after the 1959 disturbances, Sarah Scott sharply criticized parents whose "kids come to school sleepy, because they were up all night." She gave a rendition of her daily conversation with these wayward students.

> *Teacher*: Where were you?
> *Student*: On the street.
> *Teacher*: Where were your parents?
> *Student*: I don't know.

"Sometimes," she noted sarcastically, "I think if we'd call a meeting of these parents in a tavern we would have a better turnout." To be sure, not everyone could publicly criticize black families in the same way that Scott did. At another community meeting two years earlier, the audience "began to grumble" when Robert Taylor, a black Republican candidate for county supervisor, declared that blacks had brought troubles upon themselves by neglecting their own children. By contrast, respected teachers like Scott earned the trust of a black community as it faced difficult times.[29]

Even Rev. E. B. Phillips, the black minister who had sharply criticized the formation of the Mayor's Study Committee for promoting the belief that "our disaster arises from newcomers," simultaneously embraced the strategy of cultural adjustment. Speaking before the same Northside community meeting with teacher Sarah Scott in 1959, one day before issuing his public letter, he conceded that "it's not enough to run to the newspapers. . . . We cannot excuse ourselves by sitting at home and criticizing." Phillips urged his audience to tend to the needs within their own neighborhood. "We should work out a program to teach newcomers to the community our way of life." By initially challenging white racism, yet eventually cooperating with white leaders, established black Milwaukeeans created programs to acculturate migrants in their community, developing a model that Milwaukee school officials would soon adapt and implement under a new name: compensatory education.[30]

From Cultural Adjustment to Compensatory Education

In the late 1950s, the Milwaukee public schools stood at the forefront of a new national movement for compensatory education. At first, classroom educators responded to the growing presence of Southern black migrant children who arrived with less-developed academic skills by designing more individualized curricula to match the perceived abilities of different groups of students. Soon, Milwaukee superintendent Harold Vincent formalized and expanded these efforts as part of a broader collaboration with major urban school districts across the North. With intellectual support from the nation's leading academics and financial support from the Ford Foundation, they laid the groundwork for a strategy that would eventually be adopted by the federal government in its grand-scale effort to eliminate poverty through public education: Title I of the Elementary and Secondary Education Act of 1965. In Milwaukee, during the early years of compensatory education in the late 1950s, the agendas of established black leaders and white school officials coincided on these programs, drawing praise from both sides for addressing the urgent needs of their changing city. But over the course of the 1960s, the negative presumptions of "cultural deprivation" and racial inferiority embedded within these programs and their long-term consequences for the black community as a whole began to outweigh their merits and eventually shifted political coalitions on race and school reform.[31]

Compensatory education was not the first time that Milwaukee schools used cultural adjustment strategies to respond to social change. During the Progressive Era, Milwaukee school officials responded to the diverse working-class populations of native-born and European immigrant children by creating special tracks for presumably lower-ability students. Milwaukee trade schools were opened in the first decade of the twentieth century, the first continuation school was formed in 1912, and elementary-level classes designated "Special B" and "Special C" were in place in various schools by the late 1920s. By the 1950s, when Milwaukee educators began experimenting with special classes for the children of Southern black newcomers, they adopted models based on approaches learned from previous decades.[32]

Some of the early proposals for compensatory education in the 1950s arose with the heightened white anxiety over black migration and sensationalized crime news. In 1953, Mayor Zeidler suggested using Milwaukee's public and vocational schools to address cultural deficiencies, low skills, and criminal behavior among Southern newcomers. He proposed that a series of "community adjustment courses" could instruct migrants in "etiquette for ladies and gentlemen, social manners, accepted customs in the city," city functions, and healthy living standards. For migrants with few vocational skills, particularly young women, Zeidler recommended additional courses "in home making and home crafts . . . how to make simple and wholesome meals, how to make simple furniture and decorations, how to mend and repair clothes." As an incentive, the mayor proposed that when police arrested migrants for juvenile delinquency and other crimes, city judges could offer them the option of taking these classes rather than send them to jail. Compensatory programs were designed not only to educate black migrants but also to preserve whites' sense of security during the urban crisis.[33]

When Milwaukee public schools adopted compensatory education programs for the postwar era, a distinction was initially made between the children of established blacks and those of the newcomers. At the Booker T. Washington Young Men's Christian Association (YMCA) branch in 1948, a gathering of parents whose children attended the predominantly black Fourth Street Elementary School heard their principal announce that children of migrants who had arrived during World War II had not kept up with black children who had previously resided in the city. Thus, Fourth Street would establish two special classrooms to be "concerned entirely with the readjustment of Southern Negro pupils to the educational requirements of Northern schools." This distinction arose again during a black community meeting on education in 1953, when white school board member Elizabeth Holmes told the audience that migrant students had attended "inferior schools" in the South, making it difficult to bring them "up to Wisconsin standards" without placing them in grade levels behind their age group. In the growing number of predominantly black elementary schools in the early 1950s, this tracking policy was designed to educate underprepared migrant children without holding back the children of long-term black residents.[34]

Teachers at the predominantly black Lloyd Street School found it "virtually impossible" to instruct reading groups made up of both "migrant children" and regular students in 1956. They received permission from administrators to create a smaller, new Special B class of only twenty-five migrant students from grades four through six who had IQ scores between 70 and 80. In his graduate school thesis on the experiment, one classroom teacher observed that many students were "woefully shy and backward because of the great awe the big city invoked in them." He borrowed primary level materials to design a curriculum on the home-school-community relationship, with field trips around the neighborhood. Children learned "acceptable behavior patterns" both in and outside of school as well as personal hygiene, standards of dress, and the proper use of "modern lavatory conveniences." Without any note of irony, the vice principal observed that creating a separate migrant classroom was the school's way of "integrating Southern Negroes into our school" without lowering the standards for everyone. By integration, he meant educating Southern black children and Northern black children in the same building: a 90 percent black school.[35]

Beginning in 1956, the Milwaukee public schools began to participate with other leading districts, like Chicago and Detroit, in the Great Cities School Improvement Program to formalize and expand their curricular innovations. Three years later, Milwaukee received a Ford Foundation grant to develop a pilot program for "in-migrant" students. Six orientation centers were established in the inner city to acculturate selected migrant children to their new community before they were placed in a regular school. At first, these programs were very small and experimental, serving only 250 students during the first year and a half in operation. But within five years, the concept of compensatory education became adopted by the entire district as an appropriate educational response to Milwaukee's "Negro problem."[36]

The rise of compensatory education marked a significant change in the relationship between established black Milwaukeeans and white school officials. Prior to 1960, black leaders like William Kelley and James Dorsey had battled with school administrators to hire black teachers and to stop discouraging black youth from entering higher-skilled occupations. In particular, the Milwaukee Urban League had worked independently from the school district to launch its Vocational Opportunity Campaign speaker series and the "Tomorrow's Scientists and Technicians" after-school club. But by 1960, Urban League board members decided that these efforts were insufficient since they were not integral to the organizational life of the schools. The League shifted its policy and decided to "cooperate actively with the Milwaukee School System" on programs for migrant youth, perhaps due to the school district's recent willingness to hire black teachers.[37]

Compensatory education made sense from the Urban League's perspective, since migrants from the agricultural South needed more advanced skills to compete for better jobs in Milwaukee's industrial and clerical workforce. In the early 1960s, William Kelley's assistant, Wesley Scott, pointed out that the League had received more than a dozen requests from local firms to hire secretaries but had no job applicants sufficiently trained to fill them. The stark reality of many migrants' limited educational backgrounds, readily apparent on job application forms in the League office, shaped League personnel's stance on educational issues. Years later, Scott recalled, "I'll never forget. . . . We had a question, 'What kind of work can you do?' And this individual had written down, 'Anykind,' [spelled] i-n-n-i-e-k-i-n-e. Okay? These are the kinds of things that dictated our position in terms of compensatory education." Given the scale of the problem, the mounting pressures to act quickly, and the limited organizational resources available, the Urban League decided to cooperate with the Milwaukee public schools.[38]

In their first joint venture, the League and the school district cosponsored the "Youth Incentive Project" in 1963, financed with $50,000 from city industries. Their objective was to help black students build stronger connections between school and work. Counselors selected a control group of black teens who had "no apparent reason to study, learn and get a good education" because they saw so few job opportunities open to blacks from their racially isolated neighborhoods. Project staff introduced them to successful black employees to discuss career opportunities, tutored them in the academic subjects necessary for those professions, and arranged job interviews for summer employment. In addition, the project sought to adjust black student "attitudes and habits" to assist them in "entering our complex society as useful citizens." Home visits were designed "to bring about the change in attitudes of disinterested and uninformed parents" who often "do not understand, or have little appreciation for" the vocational aspirations of their children. Staff also led youth discussions on topics such as "The Meaning of Law and Order" and guided field trips to museums, operas, symphonies, and other centers of elite white culture. In contrast to the 1930s, when the Urban League Community Center nurtured stronger ties inside the black neighborhood, particularly through black history, the Youth Incentive Project of the 1960s sought to build bridges to the outer world. No one objected to the term "compensatory education," Wesley Scott recalls. "We used it with alacrity. You know, there was no point of hesitation, as far as we were concerned."[39]

But compensatory education soon gained many negative connotations, particularly when national publicity for Milwaukee's programs incorporated overtly negative portrayals of black migrant family culture. A *New York Times* article described compensatory education students as "children who come to school with only a soda for breakfast. Some don't know their birthdays. . . . The idea of percent is a mystery, even with reference to baseball, because many don't know about baseball." A *Milwaukee Journal* reporter observed orientation classes for Southern migrants at Palmer Street School and wondered in amazement over children who seemed to enjoy school more than spending time with their own families. "[But] it's not hard to understand when you see the homes . . . problems of health, of undernourishment, of homes where there is no father or where both parents work." Journalists also puzzled over the case of an anonymous twelve-year-old Arkansas boy, who had lived in eleven different homes and attended six different schools since arriving in Milwaukee, leaving him two years behind his grade reading level. "How do you educate a child born in the rural South, whose parents are separated, who has no books in his home, when he becomes a pupil in a large city school system?" they wondered.[40]

Compensatory education gained widespread acceptance among Milwaukee school officials because it placed the blame for black student academic failure squarely on the shoulders of culturally deprived families rather than on educators. Speaking with a reporter, Assistant Superintendent Dwight Teel compared two different families with preschool children. On a trip to the grocery store, a "typical child" might "see a product and call it the wrong name, and the mother, in a pleasant tone, will say, 'No, it's not soup, it's soap,'" Teel explained. "But in a number of homes of deprived children, there isn't this learning experience." Other compensatory education advocates extended their analysis beyond motherhood, pointing to a perceived "lack of motivation among young Negroes to train themselves for job opportunities." According to the *New York Times*, examples were plentiful in Milwaukee. "A brewery here had six white-collar jobs and made it clear it would welcome Negro applicants. None came. . . . [Also] a young Negro woman [who] trained to teach didn't look for work in education but became a maid." Within the white media, the explanation of cultural deficiencies and laziness among Southern black migrants was now being interpreted to apply to the race as a whole.[41]

Mayor Frank Zeidler lost his 1960 reelection bid to Democratic challenger Henry Maier, who demonstrated little interest in the problems of the inner city. But cultural deprivation theory remained strong within the new administration. In 1963, Maier's appointees on the Milwaukee Commission on Community Relations published *The Negro in Milwaukee: Progress and Portent* to celebrate 100 years of national emancipation and local racial progress. Yet the commission, sharing the dominant white perspective of prominent scholars of that time (such as Nathan Glazer and Daniel Patrick Moynihan), diagnosed black migrant culture in pathological terms: "We must also realize that Negroes of low-income, still unaccustomed to life in a Northern city, *do not have a long heritage of culture and an ethical tradition* on which to build to build their lives. They seem to lack a sense of family intimacy and interdependence; as a result, their families often do not instill into children good behavior patterns and ideals. Not everybody is fortunate enough to be born into families with these principles. In time, of course, Negroes will learn them." The commission's language extended the educational challenges facing low-income migrant families to a cultural pathology of the race as a whole. (In an act of resistance, most likely years later, an anonymous reader at the Milwaukee Public Library underlined the passage above and scribbled "NO!" in the margin.)[42]

In the late 1960s and 1970s, critics would look back upon this era and denounce compensatory education for perpetuating the racist myth of cultural deprivation among black families. Indeed, the Milwaukee case study adds fuel to those charges. White policy-makers and educational practitioners affirmed their own sense of racial superiority through the safety of compensatory programs designed for children of the other race. But these critics, often writing from a national perspective, have overlooked an important dimension of the local history of compensatory education: the complex role of established black leaders and teachers. During the 1950s, faced with increasing white anxiety over the rising migrant population and crime, established black Milwaukeeans cooperated to support and direct programs for cultural adjustment. Although black leaders recognized deeper causes behind the migrant street uprisings, they made the politically expedient decision to reach out and acculturate Southern newcomers using the tools at hand, such as the Milwaukee Urban League and the network of black civic and religious organizations. Over time, as cultural adjustment strategies were adopted by the public schools, established blacks extended their support to compensatory education. Yet this solution would soon be challenged by a new generation of black Milwaukeeans who promoted an entirely different reform strategy in the 1960s: the racial integration of public schools.[43]

4

CONFRONTING ESTABLISHED BLACKS

AND WHITES ON SEGREGATION

In 1963, Lloyd Barbee stepped up to the podium of the Milwaukee Junior Bar Association and shocked his white audience. The thirty-eight-year-old black attorney was president of the Wisconsin NAACP but a relative newcomer to Milwaukee, having moved there from Madison. The white lawyers who had invited Barbee to speak at the luncheon meeting expected to hear him represent the national NAACP's perspective on recent atrocities in the South, where the Birmingham police recently had attacked young nonviolent civil rights marchers with dogs and high-pressure hoses. But Barbee had something different in mind. He took a bold step and turned everyone's attention to civil rights struggles in the North, in their very own city.

Barbee launched Milwaukee's first sustained public challenge to segregated schools. "If the *Brown* decision means anything," he called out to his audience, "it means that school segregation is unconstitutional wherever it exists, north or south." Although *Brown* originally banned only legalized segregation in Southern and border states, Barbee redefined its meaning for Milwaukee, as William Kelley had a decade earlier, though the focus was now exclusively on student segregation. Barbee charged that Milwaukee public schools were in violation of the Supreme Court ruling that segregation was inherently unequal, citing as proof the rising number of predomi-

Lloyd Barbee (center), Wisconsin NAACP president and civil rights attorney, launched Milwaukee's campaign for integrated schools. Courtesy of Marilyn Morheuser Papers, in author's possession.

nantly black schools and the long-standing practice of assigning the vast majority of black teachers to work in them. To end racial segregation, Barbee announced that the Wisconsin NAACP would request the intervention of the State Superintendent of Public Instruction to order the Milwaukee school board to desegregate on the same grounds that other top school officials had recently used in New York, New Jersey, and California. Both state and local school officials had a duty "to act affirmatively" to eliminate segregation, regardless of its origins. If school officials failed to respond, Barbee warned, his organization was ready to wage both a legal battle in the courtroom and mass protests in the streets, such as picketing, sit-ins, or school boycotts. A new civil rights movement was gearing up for a fight.[1]

Barbee's confrontation provoked a sharp response from white Milwaukee authorities. School board president Lorraine Radtke, an advocate of compensatory education for the inner city, strongly disagreed with his charge that Milwaukee schools were segregated. "There is segregation by geography, perhaps," she allowed, "but we don't have any control over that." Milwaukee's neighborhood school policy was a "normal, natural procedure," Radtke explained, and any attempt to redistribute students into racially mixed schools would unfairly force some to be bused far from their homes. The *Milwaukee Journal* editors also criticized Barbee and the Wisconsin NAACP for attempting to solve black student underachievement through expensive bus transportation. A far better approach, they argued, would be to "attack job discrimination and housing discrimination" by ensuring a fair distribution of white and black teachers and by encouraging white families to return to the inner city. Simply by responding to Barbee's speech instead of ignoring him, white Milwaukee authorities raised publicity about the question of segregated schools, giving him exactly what he needed at the very early stage of the integration campaign.[2]

Yet Barbee and his supporters did more than defy white authority; they simultaneously confronted Milwaukee's established black leadership. At one level, this chapter examines how new civil rights activists in the 1960s challenged the philosophy, tactics, and political organization of the older generation. Barbee and his followers took a courageous stand for racial integration, arguing on the grounds of social justice rather than political expediency or group entitlement. They adopted methods of public confrontation and direct-action mass protest, welcoming the participation of thousands of everyday citizens and youth in shaping governmental policy, in contrast to the backroom diplomacy between elites of the older generation. Moreover, the new civil rights activists organized themselves outside of Milwaukee's established black community networks. With support from the national NAACP in New York, Barbee and other newcomers built up the Wisconsin NAACP state chapter to maneuver around the "old guard" of the Milwaukee NAACP local chapter. By comparison, this account of the new Northern civil rights movement differs from studies of the Southern movement by sociologist Aldon Morris and others, who emphasize its indigenous origins and the role played by grass-roots community networks, especially the black church, in providing leadership and an organizational base. But in Northern cities like Milwaukee, these networks did not operate in the same way.[3]

At another level, this chapter examines how the new activists and the older black establishment differed on cultural identity and strategies for racial uplift through the schools. Although Barbee served as the black spokesman and figurehead for the new organization, its leadership included several white allies. Together, this interracial coalition focused on changing the racial composition of Milwaukee's schools as the primary means for improving educational and political equality for the black community rather than on hiring black teachers into the system as the older generation had done. Yet while Barbee and his supporters pressured white authorities to accept their interpretation of *Brown*—that all-black schools were inherently unequal wherever they existed—they indirectly confirmed the prevailing white belief that blackness was equated with inferior schooling. By doing so, the new integration activists strained their relationship with established black leaders, who generally shared a positive cultural identification with the dignified tradition of all-black schooling and the icon of the respected black community teacher. As educational researcher Michele Foster points out, "The interests of African-American students and teachers have been pitted against each other" in most school desegregation movements. The struggle to win jobs for black teachers became so entangled with the maintenance of black schooling, she argues, that "it has been difficult to attack segregated schools and at the same time to praise and respect black teachers." These tensions became very apparent in Milwaukee during the early 1960s, where the visions of black education reform by a new generation of activists collided with those of the old.[4]

Joining the Northern Integration Movement

Like most new arrivals to the city, Lloyd Barbee had originally migrated from the South to find a better life. He was born in Memphis, Tennessee, in 1925, but his mother passed away only six months later. He attended segregated schools during the Depression and graduated from Booker T. Washington High School. But Barbee was not a typical young black man. He joined the NAACP at the age of twelve, while still in grade school. After serving three years in the Navy during World War II, he returned to Memphis and earned a degree in economics from the all-black LeMoyne College in 1949. Then Barbee moved North, where he obtained a scholarship to attend the University of Wisconsin Law School in Madison, becoming one of the early racial pioneers at the virtually all-white institution. He dropped out after the first year, partly due to negative encounters with racist professors and students, and became a student activist with Americans for Democratic Action before returning in the mid-1950s to finish his law degree. Barbee continued to live in Madison but had difficulty finding a private law firm willing to hire him. He eventually found work as a legal examiner for the State Industrial Commission and as a legal consultant for the Governor's Commission on Human Rights in the late 1950s.[5]

Barbee's civil rights work focused on jobs during this period, bringing him into contact with several of Milwaukee's established blacks, such as attorney James Dorsey and state assemblyman Isaac Coggs, who were engaged in judicial and legislative battles for stronger enforcement of state fair employment laws. In the realm of public education, Barbee actively participated in the struggle to win black teachers' jobs. In 1959, he gave a speech to teachers and administrators at the predominantly white Wisconsin Education Association convention, urging them to support fair employment practices for black educators, even to the point of making racial preferences in hiring. He posed a hypothetical question to the audience, asking that if a school had a choice between hiring two equally qualified teachers of different races, "Would it not be worth something to democracy to have the Negro teaching?" It was not merely a rhetorical question. Two of Barbee's cousins in Milwaukee, Grant Gordon and Louise Gordon Rhodes, had struggled to become two of the first black teachers hired by the district in the early 1940s. Thus, Barbee's initial activism fit neatly into Milwaukee's established context of the struggle for black employment.[6]

But Barbee's personal trajectory in the civil rights movement began to shift course in the early 1960s. He gradually expanded both his definition and tactics for the struggle by broadening his focus from jobs to housing and by bolstering his governmental agenda with direct-action protest. In 1961, while still employed by the state government, he launched a thirteen-day sit-in on the floor of the State Capitol in an unsuccessful attempt to pressure the legislature to pass a fair housing bill. A year later, he clashed with the University of Wisconsin over its refusal to release a documentary film he had produced about housing discrimination in Madison. Barbee continued to rise up through the ranks of the NAACP, serving as president of the Madison branch from 1955 to 1960, then as president of the Wisconsin state branch from 1961 to 1964. Through his leadership and legal contacts, he became more aware of the changing shape of civil rights activism in other Northern cities, such as Chicago, Detroit, and New York.[7]

Barbee became intrigued by changes in the federal courts on Northern school segregation, such as the *Taylor v. New Rochelle* decision in 1961. Federal district judge Irving Kaufman ruled that this suburban New York City school board had gerrymandered neighborhood school boundaries and refused to act on citizens' multiple requests to take corrective action against racial imbalance. The ruling prevented the school board from blaming segregation solely on de facto residential patterns because it demonstrated how the board's own actions (and inactions) had reinforced and intensified racial segregation. Judge Kaufman wrote that "compliance with the [*Brown* decision] was not to be less forthright in the north than in the south" and demanded that New Rochelle submit a school desegregation plan to the court, the first ever required from a Northern school board.[8]

The *New Rochelle* decision reenergized the commitment of the national NAACP to organize isolated efforts by various branches into a Northern campaign for school integration. At the national NAACP convention in Philadelphia in 1961, executive director Roy Wilkins announced that the association would renew its demand for "desegregation of schools in Northern cities as well as the South." June Shagaloff, the newly appointed special assistant for education at the national NAACP, traveled extensively for the next two years to help coordinate a unified school integration movement in fifteen Northern and Western states. She assisted local branches on launching investigations on segregation, negotiating with school boards, preparing recommendations for reform, and filing legal protests or leading mass demonstrations if necessary. Together, they successfully pressured school boards to close segregated buildings and begin open enrollment policies in several northern New Jersey cities. Organizing efforts also took root in several communities in Long Island, and pressure on the New York State Commissioner of Education led him to declare publicly that segregated schools were undesirable and to call for their elimination by local authorities. In other areas where local school boards were unresponsive, such as Philadelphia, Gary, and Chicago, local NAACP branches filed school desegregation lawsuits and mobilized protests. By the close of 1962, Shagaloff counted legal action and activism for school segregation in sixty-nine cities and communities across the North and West. NAACP general counsel Robert Carter, who had served with Thurgood Marshall on the *Brown* case and now supervised this new legal campaign, described the North as a "crucial and critical battleground." Even black activists in Buffalo, a city that had been nearly as powerless as Milwaukee in hiring black teachers nearly thirty years earlier, had publicly challenged the Buffalo school board to provide maximum school desegregation.[9]

But there was no school integration movement in Milwaukee in 1962, a fact that troubled national NAACP leaders. Gloster Current, the national NAACP branch director, traveled to Milwaukee to speak at the local NAACP's Freedom Fund dinner, also attended by Attorney General John Reynolds, the Democratic candidate in the Wisconsin governor's race. Current declared that "under NAACP pressure, an increasing number of communities and states are beginning to take action to eliminate school discrimination in the North," yet he saw little sign of activism on this front in the city. So national NAACP officials began to hold high hopes for Lloyd Barbee. Not only was he a skilled attorney who understood the complex and evolving case law on Northern school segregation, but he was also growing a reputation as an experienced protest organizer. Robert Carter invited Barbee to attend an NAACP regional leadership conference led by himself and Shagaloff and discussed possible strategies for desegregating Wisconsin schools. At the end of one letter, Carter added this postscript: "This issue . . . [has] fund raising and membership potential, and I would suggest that you keep this in mind."

National NAACP leaders hoped that Barbee could persuade the Milwaukee NAACP branch to join in the Northern school integration movement. In the fall of 1962, Barbee left Madison and moved ninety miles east to the city of Milwaukee, bringing along a new civil rights agenda with him.[10]

FROM POWERLESSNESS TO PROTEST

Black Milwaukeeans still had relatively little traditional political power when Barbee arrived in 1962, since at least three factors worked against black representation in the city government. First, the city council redistricted wards in 1954, splitting black voters from the inner city into five separate districts and diluting what little strength they had. Although attorney Vel Phillips was elected by the Second Ward in 1956 to serve as the first black (and female) representative on the city council, she remained the only black member for nearly ten years. Second, the Milwaukee school board operated on a citywide at-large election system, making it extremely difficult for black candidates to attract sufficient numbers of white voters to win office. Both Vel Phillips and Pauline Coggs ran unsuccessful campaigns for school board in the 1950s. Although Cornelius Golightly, a philosophy professor from the University of Wisconsin–Milwaukee, became the first black school board member by winning third place in the 1961 election, observers later noted that many whites did not realize that the light-skinned professor was black. Third, while Milwaukee's black population reached over 62,000 in 1960 (8.4 percent of the city total), very little of this potential energy connected with the electoral process. Two years earlier, black politicians estimated that 30,000 black citizens were eligible to vote, but only half were registered, and the percentage who actually entered the voting booth dropped even lower. For all of these reasons, black Milwaukee became a leading example of "institutional powerlessness" during the 1960s.[11]

But outside of the traditional realm of electoral office, a new form of black political power was rising, and it would soon alter the course of civil rights activism for decades to come. In the wake of the 1958 shooting of Daniel Bell, confrontations increased between white police officers and black working-class residents of the inner city. One key event took place in July 1960, when three young black sisters were arraigned in the courtroom of Milwaukee district judge Frank Gregorski for allegedly creating a late-night street disturbance. One of the sisters began to testify that police brutality had sparked the incident, but Judge Gregorski cut her off, refusing to listen to her claim. "I don't believe that police would . . . ," he began, until an outburst of laughter from somewhere in the courtroom audience drowned him out. Angered by this public defiance of his authority, Gregorski called out to his bailiffs, "I want all the dark people brought up [to the bench]," where he promptly fined ten black spectators $100 each for contempt of court. Regardless of whether or not they had laughed at the judge, all members of the race paid the price for the crime.[12]

Both white and black newspapers covered the incident heavily and weighed in on opposite sides. On one hand, the white daily *Milwaukee Journal* supported Judge Gregorski and called his actions appropriate for the "unruly group" of blacks who had "burst out in derisive laughter" and exhibited unacceptable behavior in a Northern courtroom. While blacks may have some cause to distrust the legal system in the Jim Crow South, "*they have no such cause here,*" the editorial warned, "and this for their own good they must speedily learn." On the other hand, the black-owned *Milwaukee Defender* blasted Judge Gregorski's actions and questioned the motivations of the *Milwaukee Journal* editors, who had declared Gregorski "totally unfit to be a judge" only four months earlier, prior to city judicial elections.[13]

Established black leaders united themselves with newly arrived black migrants on this outrageous case of courtroom racism. Milwaukee NAACP leaders began a publicity campaign to condemn Gregorski's actions, since penalizing all blacks in the courtroom, regardless of guilt, threatened the entire race. Even retired detective Calvin Moody, one of the first blacks to have been hired by the police department in the 1930s, reportedly "took money out of his own pocket" to post bail for the innocent black victims.[14]

But a new black-led organization took a further step by harnessing the energy behind the migrants' street battles with police into a focused group protest action against white racism. Calvin Sherard, a thirty-four-year-old metal finisher at the American Motors plant, led eight black men and one white woman from the Crusaders Civic and Social League to march a picket line against the judge. Sherard, who had migrated to Milwaukee only five years earlier, did not fit into the city's black establishment and soon began to challenge the political dominance of the Milwaukee NAACP. Later in 1960, after the Gregorski incident had faded from the headlines, Sherard walked into a community meeting at New Hope Baptist Church and called for mass protest against the continuing problem of police brutality. "Get up off of your knees," one listener recalled Sherard announcing to the crowd. "There's a time for praying, and a time not to pray. . . . These folks out here are hurting us. Let's go march." Sherard dared to criticize the Milwaukee NAACP and other established groups "as nothing but social clubs" whose leaders used their "intellect to keep the lower Negro classes in hand." One of his colleagues, Ali Anwar, responded to the charge that Sherard's group was not sufficiently qualified to lead the black community by turning the question around to focus on the Milwaukee NAACP, asking the black audience, "What are they doing for you?"[15]

Meanwhile, some Milwaukee NAACP leaders were expressing similar doubts—though much more quietly—about the efficacy of their own organization. President Eddie Walker, who had orchestrated the public relations protest against Judge Gregorski, wrote a candid letter at the end of his two-year term to national NAACP branch director Gloster Current. Walker repeated the charge that many black Milwaukeeans viewed the local chapter as merely a "social club" run by a "few complacent professional persons" who are "not militant enough" to improve civil rights for "the average man." In Walker's opinion, the charge was partially true. As president, he had attempted to introduce new leadership to the executive committee by circumventing the traditional nomination committee and offering a petition for a new slate of candidates. His proposal sparked a "very heated board meeting" and the stiff opposition of long-term members, most likely Ardie and Wilbur Halyard, who had controlled the position of treasurer between them for more than a decade. Furthermore, a recent decline in mass membership had driven the local chapter to put more effort into soliciting $500 life-membership contributions, thus giving a small black elite much greater influence over board policy. Walker's petition for new leadership did not prevail, and he withdrew it.[16]

Although both Calvin Sherard and the Milwaukee NAACP fought to win more jobs for black Milwaukeeans, their civil rights tactics differed sharply. By 1962, Sherard's Crusaders had transformed into a local chapter of the Negro American Labor Council (NALC), affiliated with A. Philip Randolph's national organization. The Milwaukee NALC began picketing three A&P grocery stores in the inner city that served a predominantly black clientele yet hired virtually no black employees. During two straight weeks of sidewalk demonstrations, Sherard's group demanded jobs for black store clerks, butchers, and management trainees. Although the NALC chapter counted only 100 dues-paying members, its protest tactics involved mass participation from newly arrived black migrants, including sixty high school students who distributed leaflets and walked the picket line.[17]

By contrast, Milwaukee NAACP leaders took a less public stance to promote black jobs, using methods that did not include participation by everyday citizens. In the early 1960s, attorney Clarence Parrish, the new NAACP chapter president, called a series of private conferences with white retail store owners located along Upper Third Street in the inner city to request the immediate employment of black workers wherever black consumers spent their dollars. Although Parrish worded his "request" diplomatically, it was accompanied by different degrees of pressure. The presence of selected influential black ministers at these private conferences reminded white businessmen of the black establishment's power to direct consumers away from uncooperative stores. When the store owners denied having any available openings, Parrish confronted them with evidence that the NAACP had sent "testers" to their stores who had found that although job openings most certainly existed, applications from blacks were routinely rejected. Parrish reported that when store owners faced this type of pressure, "the entire picture of the conference changed" and several black sales workers were quickly hired: four at Walgreen's Drug Store, five at W. T. Grant Department Store, and twelve at Schuster's Department Store. Although NAACP efforts were less successful with the Schlitz Brewing Company (which diverted negative reaction to its dismal black hiring record by making a well-publicized donation to the Milwaukee Urban League), Parrish and his colleagues made progress against job discrimination.[18]

Judging by the number of black workers hired in 1962, the Milwaukee NAACP's quieter tactics prevailed over the public picketing led by Calvin Sherard. Although the NALC initially won agreements that A&P stores would hire more black workers in exchange for ending the demonstrations, store owners reportedly did not fulfill their obligations, complaining that low staff turnover and union seniority rules made it impossible to comply. Moreover, the NALC pickets did not seriously disrupt business, as the necessity and convenience of local supermarket shopping led many black customers to cross the picket lines. Yet the ascendancy of Sherard's NALC and its direct-action protest tactics presented a serious challenge to Milwaukee's established black political leadership. Over time, it signaled that a new style of civil rights activism was forming in the city that could potentially draw thousands of newly arrived black migrants into participatory roles in the power struggle. While the NALC did not achieve immediate success, it set the stage for a new generation of activists, such as Lloyd Barbee, to make its next move.[19]

COLLIDING VISIONS OF CIVIL RIGHTS

Before Lloyd Barbee launched Milwaukee's campaign to eliminate school segregation in July 1963, the topic of school segregation had publicly arisen only a handful of times, and then very briefly. Concerns about the racial composition of public schools fell back as secondary priorities to Milwaukee's two long-standing civil rights issue: jobs and housing. On one occasion, when lone black city council member Vel Phillips proposed a fair housing ordinance in 1962, her legislation included the statement that housing discrimination contributed to other forms of segregation, "including racial segregation in the public schools." She later clarified to the press that "school segregation does not exist by law, but it does exist in fact," yet the issue dropped from public view because her main focus was on housing, and her bill lost by a 13 to 1 vote. On a second occasion, black state assembly-man Isaac Coggs unexpectedly told fellow legislators in early 1963 that "the school segregation system in Milwaukee is no better than in Mississippi." Newspaper reporters leaped on his comment, but Coggs soon backed away from it, since it distracted attention from his primary goal of building support for a stronger fair employment agency. Later, when a fellow Democratic legislator asked whether Milwaukee's predominantly black schools offered the same educational opportunity as all-white schools, Coggs wavered by answering that the two were equal now but might not be equal at some point in the future. The topic of segregated schooling dropped from public discussion.[20]

In his role as Wisconsin NAACP president, Barbee attempted to persuade the Milwaukee NAACP branch to join the national campaign for Northern school integration. A year before moving to the city, he had given a speech at the Milwaukee NAACP branch membership drive, updating the group about new protests against de facto segregation in other Northern cities. But the audience's limited response had disappointed Barbee. "The only educational questions raised," he wrote years later, "concerned employment of more black teachers at the high school level."[21]

Barbee confronted Clarence Parrish, the Milwaukee NAACP president in 1961, about his organization's seemingly apathetic response to the Northern school integration movement. The two black lawyers clashed in an argument about civil rights goals and strategies. "Don't you know that most of our members are teachers?" Parrish reportedly told Barbee, ". . . and [Superintendent] Vincent is hiring more of us now." "That's accommodation," Barbee objected, bitterly opposing the idea of accepting student segregation in exchange for black teachers' jobs. "You're an idealist," Parrish shot back; "you should be more practical." But Barbee disagreed on principle, favoring an integrated society as a higher goal than black employment. Thus, two competing visions of civil rights for Milwaukee, shaped by different generations of racial ideology and lived experience, met in a head-on collision.[22]

In Parrish's eyes, continuing the decades-long struggle for black jobs seemed entirely appropriate, given the obstacles faced by his community. "I don't think that we have a major racial problem in Milwaukee," he explained to a white reporter in 1962, "but we have an economic problem." In his mind, the difference could be explained by comparing two different points in time. As a young boy growing up in New York City during the 1930s, Parrish had encountered overt acts of white racism, leading him to join the local NAACP at a young age. But now, as an adult black professional living in Milwaukee in the 1960s, Parrish saw a different world. Through his legal work, he had obtained the income, status, and connections to purchase a home in a predominantly white neighborhood, on the north side of

Capitol Drive, past what many perceived as the city's color line. Parrish's two daughters attended virtually all-white elementary and junior high schools yet never reported any encounter with overt racial prejudice. Thus, the Milwaukee NAACP president believed that blacks primarily needed economic opportunity, a key ingredient that allowed him to move beyond the inner city as previous generations of newcomers had done. In the realm of public schools, Parrish's plan meant continuing the struggle to hire black teachers (now numbering over 200) and win them better jobs in the system.[23]

Several black teachers who successfully gained these jobs soon joined Parrish and other members of Milwaukee's small but growing black middle class. Although fewer than ninety black families lived outside the central city in 1960, many of them were teachers. Grant Gordon (one of the first blacks hired in the 1940s and the first promoted to school principal in 1960) and his wife, Lucinda Gordon (former Milwaukee NAACP and Urban League staff member), recalled moving from the inner city to their new home in a predominantly white neighborhood on the north side of Capitol Drive in 1955. "The area was crowded, our [old] house wasn't that good, and we wanted to have a newer, better house and better surroundings, like . . . the American Dream," Grant recalled years later. "I was not moving from black people," Lucinda explained, "because the neighbors [at my old home were] an elderly white couple. I was moving to my dream of a new house with space." The Gordons skirted around housing discrimination by purchasing an empty plot of land from another black owner through a black realtor. When white neighbors found out that a black family was moving into the newly built home, "For Sale" signs quickly went up, but most went back down, Grant observed, "when they saw that they weren't going to be invaded." Only one or two white families actually moved out. Another black teacher, John H. Jackson, who had been actively discouraged from seeking a job by Milwaukee college officials in the 1940s, encountered barriers when seeking clearance to build a home in suburban Wauwatosa. Several members of the all-white town board initially refused to approve his building plans, commenting that they did not want to condone "the foisting of Negroes on families in Wauwatosa," yet after substantial legal pressure, Jackson eventually prevailed.[24]

But in Barbee's eyes, these individual black teacher success stories covered up deeper concerns about racial segregation and educational inequality. Although Milwaukee now employed greater numbers of black teachers, officials increasingly assigned them to predominantly black schools, with the rate rising from 64 percent in 1960 to 68 percent in 1965. Racially transitional schools experienced the greatest change in staffing. When nine elementary schools shifted from a partial to a predominantly black student body over the same five-year period, black teacher assignments rose from

15 to 51 percent in these schools. Milwaukee officials attempted to defend themselves from charges of discrimination by insisting that black teachers were assigned to schools near their homes (which happened to be in predominantly black areas) or by arguing that black teachers "were more comfortable" in predominantly black schools. While these claims may have been defensible in the 1940s and 1950s, they became more difficult to justify in the 1960s, when surveys reported that only 5 percent of black teachers preferred to work in predominantly black schools. Moreover, racial job ceilings held back black educators. Although Barbee's cousin Grant Gordon had been named the first black principal in 1960, the school was Garfield Elementary, with a nearly all-black student body. No other blacks were named principal for five more years.[25]

Underlying the political conflict between Barbee and Milwaukee's black establishment on the future direction of civil rights activism was a deeper cultural struggle about the contested meaning of all-black schooling and the quality of black teachers employed to work in segregated systems. Barbee had very negative impressions about many of the black teachers hired during the growth years of the late 1950s and early 1960s. "I could get along well with most of the black teachers *that were good*," Barbee confided, "because we would read some of the same books and articles, or like some of the same music . . . , [or talk about] the best way to solve the problems of race." But teachers who did not share Barbee's intellectual interests did not fare as well. In a private interview, Cornelius Golightly, the sole black school board member during the 1960s and a later Barbee supporter, described the reservations held by many integration supporters about the quality of black Milwaukee teachers. "There was a great hiring during [the late 1950s and early 1960s] of inadequate, incapable teachers," he explained. "[The school district] just went down South and . . . accepted teachers [wholesale]. After three years a lot of these teachers have tenure. They are here now to stay. And only the teachers in the integrated neighborhoods are the better Negro teachers. So that we have a whole host of Negro teachers teaching in Negro [schools] that aren't very good. This presents a great problem. The Negro community is not about to criticize Negro teachers per se."[26]

The negative comments Barbee and Golightly made about most black Milwaukee teachers reflected their personal experiences regarding the differences between segregated Southern education and integrated Northern schooling. Barbee had attended all-black schools in Tennessee before enrolling at a virtually all-white law school in Wisconsin. Likewise, Golightly had studied in segregated Mississippi public schools and the all-black Talladega College before earning his doctoral degree in philosophy at the prestigious University of Michigan. Both men encountered an entirely different world of schooling after moving from the South to the North and strongly associated educational quality with the vast resources and high expectations found at predominantly white campuses.[27]

By contrast, many of Milwaukee's established black leaders identified positively with all-black colleges and affirmed strong support for the integrity of teachers in all-black settings. Ardie Halyard, the long-standing Milwaukee NAACP leader, had graduated from Atlanta University and led local fund-raising activities for the United Negro College Fund in the years after *Brown*. Her contemporary William Kelley had graduated from Fisk University and transformed the Milwaukee Urban League into a black community education center in the 1930s. When Lloyd Barbee declared that the *Brown* decision applied to the North as well as to the South, he adopted its view that "separate schools are *inherently* unequal" and its corollary that all-black education was inferior, by definition. Barbee's perspective on the inherently low quality of black schooling provoked intraracial tensions. Wesley Scott, the Milwaukee Urban League's new director in the 1960s, recalled years later how he and others felt about the cultural implications of the school integration movement. "When you think back to who were some of the African Americans who were in leadership roles in this time . . . [there was] the guy who was going to Howard, the guys who were going to Fisk, the guys who were going to Meharry. [The school integration movement] was saying that, you know, if you went to a segregated school, your education can't be as good as an integrated one . . . and most of us were not willing to admit that, or buy into that." Perhaps Scott could see both sides more clearly than others. While he earned a graduate degree in social work from the predominantly white Ohio State University, he still positively identified with his education in segregated West Virginia public schools and the all-black Xavier College.[28]

Both Milwaukee's black establishment and Barbee's new integrationists held firmly to their own strategies for civil rights in the early 1960s. On one hand, established black leaders (like William Kelley of the Urban League and Clarence Parrish of the Milwaukee NAACP) fought for better employment and fair housing opportunities. Several of these middle-class leaders had already moved out of the inner city, and they sought policies that would open up the path that they had followed to larger numbers of black Milwaukeeans. In the realm of public schooling, their strategy entailed better jobs for black teachers and compensatory education to help Southern migrant children adjust culturally to their way of life in order to prepare them to take advantage of new opportunities. In the eyes of established black leaders like Ardie Halyard, who personally supported historically black colleges, all-black schooling was not inherently inferior as long as access to political and economic opportunities were available.

On the other hand, Barbee and his Wisconsin NAACP supporters believed that a few hundred jobs for black teachers did virtually nothing to address the overall quality of schooling for Milwaukee's black children, which plummeted as the expanding black population became increasingly segregated in the inner city and written off by the more powerful white majority. Compensatory education was a sellout, in their eyes, by forcing blacks to accept segregation in exchange for a paltry handful of additional resources. Barbee also wanted better employment and fair housing opportunities for black Milwaukeeans, but he believed that integrating schools was a necessary condition to bring about these reforms, in contrast to the established leadership position. During the early 1960s, the civil rights visions of these two black-led groups collided forcefully, perhaps more so than in other Northern cities (like New York, Chicago, and Detroit) where black teachers had secured an economic foothold in the public schools for a much longer period of time. Now that some of these gains finally had been won in Milwaukee, the demographic and political changes brought on by the 1950s "migrant crisis," the added pressure from the national NAACP on local branches, and the arrival of new black leaders like Barbee shaped the conditions for a new movement for integrated schools.

CHANGING PERCEPTIONS OF INNER-CITY SCHOOLS

In the weeks leading up to Barbee's public declaration of Milwaukee's school integration campaign in July 1963, he began investigating his case that segregated schools were educationally inferior. He led the Wisconsin NAACP education committee, which consisted of a small team of black and white professional men, most of whom, like Barbee, had recently moved to the city. Tom Jacobson (Barbee's white law partner), E. Gordon Young (another black attorney), and Morgan Gibson (a white English professor at University of Wisconsin–Milwaukee) all played leading roles. At this early stage, they had relatively little concrete data to support their argument. Although they knew that the black population had dramatically increased in the last decade and that perhaps thirteen schools now had nearly all-black student bodies, the Milwaukee school district made no racial statistics available, maintaining its official color-blind stance. As one white school board member later stated, "It's almost sacred in our democratic concept of things that we do things without reference to race, religion and all the other things." Yet underneath this policy, changes in perceptions about race and the quality of inner-city schooling were becoming quite public.[29]

The status of teachers' work in inner-city schooling had dramatically changed over the past three decades, as black teachers fought their way into the system. During the Depression years, white teachers sought full-time positions in any of Milwaukee's public schools, as evidenced by the racial and marital restrictions to protect jobs and also by the long line of candidates waiting on the substitutes' bench. For many years, the majority of Milwaukee's black students had been taught by white teachers. But in the wake of the 1950s migrant crisis, as inner-city schools became increasingly black, most white Milwaukeeans came to identify teaching in them as burdensome, undesirable work. While compensatory education programs created more jobs for black teachers, they entered into a segment of the profession whose status had declined in white eyes. Black community members publicly questioned whether inner-city schools had become "dumping grounds" or "salt mines" for unwanted teachers. Just as black workers entering the industrial and domestic sectors in the 1930s had to settle for the "dirty work" formerly done by white ethnics, the vast majority of Milwaukee's new black teachers were assigned to the "Negro schools," where many middle-class whites (and blacks) perceived the children to be culturally deprived, dirty, and difficult to handle.

White newspapers headlined the story: "Teachers Shun the Area." The white principal of Fulton Junior High School, which was 93 percent black, told a reporter about the stigma of working in his inner-city school. When the school first opened in 1961, there was a general feeling of "hysteria" due to fears about "this many in a group," referring to the high concentration of black students without directly mentioning them by race. "Teachers just don't want to teach here," he acknowledged. "They want to teach in a more normal situation. Nobody ever asked to be transferred here." Milwaukee teachers who did request transfers out of the inner city sometimes candidly recorded their reasons on the application. "Would like to get out of the colored neighborhood," wrote one on her 1960 transfer form, while others gave less racially explicit reasons to leave, such as a desire to work with a "different socioeconomic group." Indeed, several white teachers chose to remain in inner-city schools and took immense pride in their work. But their personal commitment to educating black youth could not stop changes in public perceptions of their labor. In a news story about the white female principal of Fifth Street Elementary, a virtually all-black school, the reporter wrote that "one might regard the management of a 'Negro school' as an uncommon burden for a woman who is 52." By simply praising inner-city teachers for going beyond the normal call of duty, the racial stigma about their labor was firmly planted in white Milwaukeeans' minds.[30]

Many white teachers' negative attitudes about inner-city schools were shaped by personal experiences and perceptions of race and violence, particularly within the law and order climate created by the 1950s migrant crisis. After some highly publicized reports of assaults on teachers at inner-city schools in 1962, Milwaukee schoolteachers lobbied the board to reinstate corporal punishment, which had been banned since 1937. Eileen Cantwell, a white teacher from Twenty-first Street Elementary, praised corporal punishment as a defensive measure for teachers' self-protection and challenged critics who feared it might spark "an open season on children." When Cantwell's view finally prevailed in 1963, it coincided with her rise to the presidency of the newly created Milwaukee Teachers' Education Association, soon to become one of the most powerful voices in setting city educational policy. Thus, the rise of teacher unionization in Milwaukee was partly linked to efforts to physically control newly arrived black students from the South.[31]

Following in teachers' footsteps, many white families also fled inner-city schools by applying for transfers in the late 1950s and early 1960s. Most gave nonracial reasons for leaving, or worded their explanations in discreet terms, such as the mother of a kindergartner at Fifth Street School who asked for her child "to have the advantage of being with his own kind." But other white families filed requests based on overt racial bias. For instance, one white parent complained that Hopkins Street School had "too many colored children" and insisted on a transfer, while another demanded to get out of Palmer Street School due to "colored children fighting." When district officials approved transfers like these, the impact on school populations was widely noticed. For example, although a significant number of white teenagers still lived in neighborhoods feeding into North Division High School, its student population rose to 99 percent black in 1963. Some attended parochial high schools, but the North Division principal candidly admitted to a reporter that "most whites transfer out of the district," meaning they attended a public high school in a different area. "They transfer for a lot of reasons," he continued. "Some even say it's because of the Negroes, but most aren't that frank."[32]

Immediately after Barbee's July 1963 speech to the Junior Bar Association, the Wisconsin NAACP demanded that State Superintendent Angus Rothwell officially declare that Milwaukee schools were segregated. Rothwell's response was disappointing. He determined that while Milwaukee's inner-city schools did have a preponderance of black students, the situation was "not a result of discriminatory action on the part of school boards but is the result of a residential pattern." He found no evidence that Milwaukee school officials had "considered the race of pupils" in its neighborhood school attendance policy. Barbee was frustrated by the failure to win intervention from the Democratic state administration. In 1961, Wisconsin education officials had inspected a sample of Milwaukee schools and reported that "educational opportunities offered to children attending Fifth Street Elementary, Fulton Junior High, and North Division Senior High School are shockingly inferior to those offered children attending Manitoba Elementary, Audubon Junior High, and Pulaski Senior High School." Yet in the written report, state officials failed to acknowledge the obvious difference between these groups of schools: the first three schools were virtually all-black and the latter were virtually all-white. State officials maintained an official silence on race in Milwaukee schools. While Barbee and his colleagues knew that black students were receiving a lower-quality education, no one in a position of authority would acknowledge this painful truth. So their next challenge was to make these connections in the public mind.[33]

SEPARATING INTEGRATION FROM COMPENSATORY EDUCATION

After Lloyd Barbee and the Wisconsin NAACP made public their demand for integrated schooling, the Milwaukee school board responded by creating the Special Committee on Equality of Educational Opportunity. Although the committee included some liberal-minded members, the board president chose Harold Story, a white corporate lawyer, as its chairman, and it eventually became known as the Story Committee. Story's conservative views on race and politics were widely known. When black Milwaukeeans had advocated for open housing legislation in the early 1960s, Story publicly told fellow members of the Milwaukee Catholic Interracial Council that blacks should seek housing in all-white areas only after they achieved "social compatibility" with their future neighbors. It was better to improve oneself than to rely upon the law, he advised. (Black Catholics, like attorney James Dorsey, strongly disagreed.) Story also had prior experience in combating labor activism. Fifteen years earlier, he had been the chief legal strategist at the Allis-Chalmers Manufacturing Company during the controversial United Auto Workers Local 248 strike. Story testified at a U.S. Senate committee hearing that the Local 248 labor leaders were not authentic trade unionists but rather were "conceived, born, and midwifed in the Milwaukee downtown office of the Communist Party." By attacking the strikers' leadership as radical extremists, Story divided and then conquered the union, a tactic he would soon try on Barbee.[34]

Chairman Story tightly controlled the agenda for public hearings in the fall of 1963. First, he insisted that the committee address the legality of the neighborhood school attendance policy, and he was confident of the answer. Although the 1961 *New Rochelle* decision had favored the integrationists, Story reminded Barbee that the more recent *Bell v. Gary, Indiana* decision ruled that school officials could not be held responsible for segregation caused by housing patterns. "Please bear in mind," he wrote to Barbee, that the Milwaukee school district has only an "educational responsibility" to its students and "no functional responsibility to eliminate the conditions of housing and employment which are largely the source of such handicaps." Second, Story declared, the committee would hold hearings on community recommendations for academic and administrative improvements for inner-city schools. This limited the discussion to Milwaukee's nationally recognized compensatory education programs, which aimed to counteract what he described as the "inadequate home life" of migrant families. Finally, only after these first two agenda items had been addressed, Story would allow hearings on what he labeled "the sociological" dimension, where the topic of de facto segregation might be discussed.[35]

Barbee challenged Story's agenda and the limited definition it placed on equal educational opportunity. "The aspect which you call 'sociological' is not a separate, but an inextricable part of your educational responsibility," Barbee wrote. Regardless of the cause of segregation, he asserted that the school board was obligated to become involved because of its negative impact on black students' education. In Barbee's eyes, the Story Committee was attempting to follow the same strategy used by the *Brown* defendants a decade earlier: divert the integration movement by offering additional resources to improve black schools without altering segregation. It was simply "another separate-but-equal idea," Barbee explained. "You keep them segregated, but you give them a little more money and a few more token bones." He defiantly wrote back to Story that "compensatory education, no matter how massive, cannot eliminate segregation in our public schools." To Milwaukee's black press, Barbee declared that the school board has tried "to get Negroes to settle for compensatory Negro education—only half a loaf." The black community deserved the whole loaf and would get it only through equal access to white schools.[36]

But Story knew that Milwaukee's established black community organizations had fully invested themselves in compensatory education as the lead reform strategy, and he attempted to drive a wedge between them and Barbee's nascent integrationists. Just as Story had divided and conquered the labor strike years earlier, he sought to portray Barbee as a radical extremist on the fringes of Milwaukee's black community. Story set out to pack the committee hearings with established black leaders who would speak out in favor of compensatory education, and for this sensitive task he went to the Milwaukee Urban League.

Chairman Story invited Wesley Scott, the new director of the Milwaukee Urban League, to present his organization's views on educational opportunity in September 1963. Story counted on the League's recent decision to cooperate with the Milwaukee public schools on the Youth Incentive Project, a cultural adjustment program intended to motivate and transform inner-city middle-school students into more respectable citizens and pro-

ductive workers. Scott realized that by cooperating with Story and supporting compensatory education, the Urban League might be criticized for ac-
commodating segregation. But the committee hearings also presented a
valuable forum to present the League's views on this complex racial issue,
so Scott accepted the invitation and laid out a middle ground between the
two extremes of Barbee and Story. It was a dual strategy: embrace the general principles of *Brown* while simultaneously recommending tangible ways
to improve black neighborhood schools. Years later, Scott recalled his thinking behind this dual strategy. "[Harold] 'Buck' Story was a well-intentioned
bigot and segregationist . . . and there's a way of dealing with people like
Buck Story. It's a way that most people won't accept, but you have to take
the fact that he is a bigot and you have to use that. This means sometimes
giving the appearance of agreeing with Buck, but at the same time, insert-
ing language that lets people like Buck know that you have some concerns
with what he believes, what he thinks, and what he wants."[37]

During the Urban League's first presentation to the Story Committee,
Wesley Scott introduced a group of eleven black members of parent-teacher
organizations and community groups led by Gwen Jackson, chair of the
League's Family Living Committee. Jackson followed Scott's strategy by taking a stance midway between Story and Barbee. On one hand, she supported compensatory education by calling for more guidance counseling
for migrant youth, particularly for those with parents "whose limited opportunities and deprived backgrounds make them inadequately prepared
to guide their children in important areas of educational experience." On
the other hand, Jackson inserted language charging that school officials had
neglected predominantly black schools by assigning large numbers of inex-
perienced teachers to Roosevelt Junior High and by expressing an "attitude
of indifference and a lack of interest" in the culture of neighborhood families. She noted that school administrators could have solved many of these
problems simply by promoting more qualified black educators into super-
visory positions.[38]

Although Gwen Jackson did not directly endorse Barbee's school integration agenda, she saw her proposals as complementary to his. "You have to remember," she reflected years later, "Lloyd Barbee was not over here [on one
side] and Gwen Jackson and her group were over there [on the other]. . . .
I was a member of the NAACP, [and] Lloyd and I worked together for many
years." Prior to the Story Committee hearings, Jackson advised the Milwaukee NAACP Youth Council, whose teenage members had begun to use more
assertive protest tactics than the mainstream adult branch. When a Marc's
Big Boy restaurant owner refused to hire one of the black Youth Council
members on the grounds that the youth's presence would hurt business,

Jackson helped the teens organize three days of picketing, which successfully overturned the discriminatory hiring decision. Jackson's key supporter in the protest was Tom Jacobson, Barbee's white law partner and school integration activist. Thus, Jackson did not see her recommendations to the Story Committee about improving inner-city schooling and compensatory education to be in conflict with Barbee's agenda. As she looked back, she recalled that her proposals dealt with community-level factors "which impact our young people" while Barbee addressed the "legalistic side" of the issue. The two poles of the Story-Barbee debate—compensatory education versus district-wide integration—were not mutually exclusive, at least in her eyes.[39]

Wesley Scott also introduced the Story Committee to a second Urban League organization, the Northside Community Inventory Conference (NCIC), composed of twenty-four delegates from neighborhood organizations. Clara New, the NCIC spokesperson, followed Jackson's middle-of-the-road pathway on black school reform by calling for "two simultaneous approaches." The NCIC accepted "the need for a massive program" of compensatory education, preferred by Story, but also gave its support for the "complete school integration" proposed by Barbee. "This is not an 'either/or' situation," New explained to the committee. In contrast to those who rejected compensatory education as only "half a loaf," the NCIC viewed it as an essential step—half the solution—in combination with school integration. The NCIC's dual strategy supported Barbee by voicing the general principles of *Brown*, but the group did not share his belief that all-black schools were inherently unequal. Instead, its dual strategy of reform suggested concrete ways of improving black neighborhood schools, affirming that such institutions should continue to exist. It was not the unconditional support for racial integration that Barbee had hoped for.[40]

The Milwaukee Urban League continued its struggle to improve black schooling on a separate track from that of Barbee and the Wisconsin NAACP. Given Story's personal history of segregation and anti-Communism, Wesley Scott claimed that "no direct confrontation with Buck Story would have accomplished anything." Instead, the Urban League worked gradually, through the official channels of power, to make white Milwaukeeans more aware of the problems facing African Americans in public schools. While the group's recommendations still upheld the logic of compensatory education, its underlying language criticized white school officials' neglect of predominantly black schools. Scott argued that the Urban League's efforts to communicate black criticisms to white Milwaukeeans eventually "made it possible for Lloyd Barbee to make his legal confrontation with Buck Story. A lawyer versus a lawyer. But . . . this was not something that happened overnight."[41]

In the years immediately following *Brown*, protests against school segregation arose for brief periods in various Northern towns and cities. Typically,
these short bursts of activism tended to be geographically scattered and
relatively disconnected from one another. But after black nonviolent sit-ins
arose in Greensboro, North Carolina, and other Southern cities in 1960,
the national news media began to cover black civil rights protests more
closely. News about Northern protests spread more widely among black and
white audiences. During the fall of 1963, 250 citizens of Cleveland picketed
their school board to eliminate segregated education. In Boston, 10,000
marched in the Roxbury area to protest de facto school segregation. In
nearby Chicago, local civil rights organizations challenged segregative practices and sponsored a Freedom Day boycott of city schools, with 224,000
students participating. Mass activism for school integration was growing in
cities across the North.[42]

Lloyd Barbee heard all of these reports in Milwaukee and became more
aware that his fledgling school integration movement still had not attracted
mass support. In October 1963, he was hard-pressed to deliver on his public promises about mass demonstrations, sit-ins, and boycotts made three
months earlier. Although several busloads of black and white Milwaukeeans
traveled to hear Martin Luther King at the March on Washington in August, only some felt compelled to join direct-action protests in Milwaukee. The newly organized Milwaukee chapter of the Congress of Racial
Equality (CORE) picketed against Fred Lins, a white county government official who publicly voiced racist comments. Barbee marched with them but
could count only a few dozen civil rights activists in Milwaukee at the time.
The struggle was clearly not driven by the city's black religious leadership.
Out of nearly fifty black churches in the city, only three black ministers
publicly identified themselves with the movement: Rev. B. S. Gregg of St.
Matthew Christian Methodist Episcopal, Rev. Louis Beauchamp of Antioch
Baptist Church, and Rev. Lucius Walker of the Northcott Neighborhood
House. Nor did Milwaukee's black educators flock to the movement at this
stage. Only one, a substitute teacher named Elner McCraty, participated in
these early protests. Barbee commented to white reporters that black teachers participated in scholarship fund drives and upper-middle-class cultural
programs, "but [in] working with the rank and file outside the classroom,
I think the educators are as inactive a professional group as there is in the
community." As for McCraty's role on picket lines, Barbee acknowledged,
"Some people think that's too far out. But that's the role some educators
are playing in other cities."[43]

June Shagaloff, the national NAACP organizer for the Northern school integration campaign, traveled to Milwaukee in October 1963 and attempted to rally local support. She urged a Wisconsin NAACP audience to lead the fight against "segregation, Milwaukee-style." Derrick Bell Jr., a black staff attorney for the NAACP Legal Defense Fund, joined her by calling on the Northern audience to demand their civil rights as fervently as activists were doing in the South. "Direct action can work in Memphis, Miami and Montgomery," Bell challenged the crowd, "and it can work in Milwaukee too." Despite the motivating speeches, Wisconsin NAACP organizers bemoaned what they described as "apathy, Milwaukee-style," about school integration. No more than 100 people attended their "mass meeting" that weekend, and many of these were out-of-town delegates from NAACP branches across Wisconsin. Were black Milwaukeeans seriously interested, they wondered, in the fight for integrated schools?[44]

Other integration advocates publicly conceded that Barbee's base of support was relatively thin in the fall of 1963. Cornelius Golightly, the sole black member of the school board, criticized the current policy of "massive doses of compensatory education" and urged racial integration techniques such as school pairing and zone redistricting. Yet he admitted that these innovations had limited backing from black Milwaukeeans. "Now, I would say in all fairness, in all frankness," Golightly told his fellow board members, "that it is very likely the case that the great mass of Milwaukee Negroes are not yet concerned about de facto segregation." Middle-class blacks already living outside the inner city were unlikely to press the issue, he noted, suggesting that a different set of Milwaukeeans represented the emerging movement. Golightly pointed to the new integrationists, who were concerned about school segregation "because they feel it is an injustice and that something ought to be done about it. . . . Therefore, the push comes from them." Although the numbers of people involved in this new movement were relatively small now, Golightly warned the school board that it could soon mushroom to match the crowds who demanded integration in other major Northern cities like Chicago and New York. "When you get 75,000 or 50,000 or so Milwaukee Negroes who themselves get concerned with [de facto segregation]," the professor predicted, "then you have a problem." So Barbee's task was to create this problem.[45]

Barbee and his allies lacked a clearly visible symbol of white racism to mobilize their school integration movement. Although the number of predominantly black schools was rising, statistics did not serve as the ideal culprit, since they alone did not prove that Milwaukee school officials had intentionally discriminated against the race. In other cities, such as Detroit, black activists had successfully mobilized protests when school administrators had abruptly and blatantly gerrymandered the boundaries of neighborhood schools to preserve white-majority areas. But Milwaukee school officials were much more cautious. School boundary changes were carefully documented and presented to the board on the grounds of seemingly color-blind criteria, such as school capacity, traffic routes, and industrial barriers. Based on the data available to them in 1963, Barbee and the Wisconsin NAACP did not claim that Milwaukee officials had redrawn neighborhood school boundaries based on racial reasons. In fact, Cornelius Golightly published an article in *Integrated Education*, a leading journal of the national movement, in which he claimed that Milwaukee was an "ideal case" for a de facto segregation controversy, because "no claim was made that school district lines were gerrymandered to bring about racial segregation." For a philosopher such as Golightly, the Milwaukee case posed a fascinating question: Should Northern school districts be obligated to intervene against racial imbalance? But for a movement organizer like Barbee, philosophical questions did not mobilize the masses. Blatant examples of racism did.[46]

The integrationists found some success by drawing public attention to Milwaukee's stunning practice of "intact busing." As the population of black migrant schoolchildren rose dramatically in inner-city schools during the 1950s, school officials searched for strategies to cope with overcrowding. Since redrawing neighborhood school boundaries would provoke white opposition, the board approved efforts to increase capacity in inner-city schools by converting basements and gymnasiums into instructional space or by building new classroom additions. Yet overcrowding continued and even worsened when older inner-city schools temporarily closed for remodeling. So in 1957, the Milwaukee school system began transporting entire classrooms of elementary students to nearby under-enrolled schools, where they were kept "intact" for the entire day. At the sending school each morning, students and their classroom teacher marched onto their bus and rode to the receiving school, where they were taught in their own classroom rather than mixed in with other students. In some cases, students from "intact classrooms" were also separated from the other schoolchildren for playground recess or bathroom time. By 1962, when space became even tighter, the process became more racialized. Hundreds of children from virtually all-black schools were bused across town to predominantly white schools, which had more room due to white suburbanization. But the black intact classrooms were bused back to their sending school for lunch hour, then bused again to the receiving school for afternoon instruction, then finally back to their sending school at the end of the day. The two round-trips per day not only curtailed instructional time but heightened the stigma of racial separation.[47]

Technically speaking, both black and white students were bused intact, contended Milwaukee school superintendent Harold Vincent. Increasing school enrollments and renovation projects all over the city, in both black

The *Milwaukee Star* black weekly newspaper published front-page photographs to draw the city's attention to intact busing. At the beginning of the school day, entire classrooms of black students (and their teachers) were transported from overcrowded inner-city schools to underenrolled white schools but not mixed into the regular student population. From *Milwaukee Star*, 15 February 1964; courtesy of Milwaukee Courier/Star, Inc.

and white neighborhoods, required them to transport children of both races. Intact busing was an efficient system for dealing with contractors' unpredictable schedules, Vincent argued, since it maintained continuous instruction for all children. If students from two schools were merged together and then separated again after renovations were completed during the school year, learning would be disrupted for both groups of students. Intact busing was a rational system, Vincent claimed, not a racist one.[48]

But in this case, photographs mattered as much as the facts. Intact busing created dramatic visual representations of Milwaukee-style segregation, and Barbee's supporters seized the issue. The *Milwaukee Star*, the city's leading black weekly newspaper, ran front-page photographs of black students stepping off buses and walking into their segregated classrooms in white schools, communicating a story about racism to the paper's readers more effectively than words ever could. Indeed, the *Star* itself was transformed by the growing integration movement. In July 1963, the newspaper barely mentioned Barbee's initial speech on the issue, doing so two weeks later. But soon thereafter, it became known as "the civil rights paper." The transitional figure was Marilyn Morheuser, a former white nun from the Loretto Order in St. Louis, who had joined the black paper's staff and also developed a close relationship with Barbee, becoming one of the hardest-working activists in the early school integration movement. In the fall of 1963, she planned and wrote the breakthrough stories on intact busing to focus public attention on racism and devoted extensive coverage to the growing movement as she rose to the position of managing editor. In later years, observers would point to both Barbee and Morheuser as the pivotal leaders behind Milwaukee's 1960s school integration movement.[49]

Yet while black Milwaukee parents objected to intact busing, they did not necessarily embrace integration as the best solution. CORE's national director, James Farmer, encouraged Northern chapters to seek more participation from working-class inner-city residents, and Richard McLeod, the chair of Milwaukee CORE's education committee and a white graduate student at the University of Wisconsin–Milwaukee, complied with his request. As a strong integration supporter, McLeod firmly believed that intact busing caused psychological damage to black children by separating them from the regular student body. But McLeod soon grew frustrated by the lack of black parents who shared his interpretation. At a CORE-sponsored community meeting, only one black parent actually complained that intact busing created "unfriendly attitudes toward Negro children" at the receiving school. By contrast, a greater majority of parents criticized intact busing on the grounds of "class time lost" due to long bus rides and the "inconvenience and disruption" it caused in the normal school day routine. The parents' discussion focused on demanding that the school board eliminate the noon-hour bus trip and use the money to fund a hot lunch program for students who were bused to the receiving school. But no one at the community meeting, other than McLeod, proposed that the children be integrated with the receiving school students. As a result, Milwaukee CORE's report to the Story Committee was disjointed. In the introduction and conclusion, McLeod condemned intact busing on the grounds that separating inner-city children bred attitudes of racial inferiority. But in the body of the report, he dutifully recorded black parents' simpler demand that intact busing be limited to one round-trip per day.[50]

As the Story Committee hearings continued into the late fall of 1963, black presenters continued to give mixed support both for improving black schools and for integrating black and white pupils. The Near Northside Non-Partisan Conference (NNNPC), an organization composed of black ministers and political activists who had supported the March on Washington, literally presented two separate reports on two different nights. Cecil Brown Jr., the black chair of the NNNPC education committee and a former state assemblyman, delivered the first report and strongly recommended improvements for black neighborhood schools. He described how the curricular offerings at North Division High School, which had been racially mixed when he attended in the 1940s, had deteriorated as the school became predominantly black in recent years. North Division had formerly offered four foreign languages but ceased all by 1959 and had only recently restored Spanish. Non-athletic extracurricular clubs had dropped from thirty-four to fewer than fifteen, and the student newspaper, the *North Star*, was no longer published. Brown urged the school board to improve the quality of inner-city schools but made no mention of integration in his first report.[51]

One month later, the NNNPC returned to present its second report, which blended proposals for improving black-area schools with support for integrating black students into white schools. One reason for the second report was that Chairman Story finally opened up discussion on the third agenda item, the "sociological" dimension of equal educational opportunity. But the NNNPC still did not embrace integration alone. Rev. Louis Beauchamp, the organization's president, introduced the second report by echoing previous recommendations for improving black schools. But when his colleague, Cecil Brown, stepped up to read the body of the second report, Brown departed from earlier discussions of increasing resources for inner-city schools and gave a much stronger endorsement for racial integration. In the month that had passed since the NNNPC's first presentation, Brown reported that he had uncovered additional information that led him to wonder whether Milwaukee schools were segregated due to official actions rather than simply by residential patterns. He had reviewed enrollment data from racially mixed elementary schools that fed into virtually all-black junior high schools and questioned whether school officials actively encouraged white families to transfer their children out of inner-city schools. Brown acknowledged that his evidence was incomplete, but he was sufficiently persuaded to reconsider the NNNPC's earlier proposals. Rather than calling to improve black-neighborhood schools, Brown now insisted that the school board halt intact busing, merge those students into the classrooms of the receiving schools, and create new schools and transfer policies that would promote the racial integration of students and faculty. Although Story had built a wall dividing the school integrationists from mainstream black supporters of improving neighborhood schools, cracks in that strategy became more apparent as individual leaders sought to bring their membership closer to Barbee's side.[52]

The Wisconsin NAACP finally made its presentation in December 1963, after Chairman Story had delayed the hearings to build as much support as possible for improving black education through additional compensatory resources. Yet Barbee clearly rejected Story's proposed solution. "No amount of compensatory education will repair the damage done to students and teachers by segregation," he declared. "Equal educational opportunity is impossible without racial integration." His colleagues Morgan Gibson and E. Gordon Young assisted in reading portions of the seventy-seven-page report (prepared in part by June Shagaloff), which surpassed those offered by other local black organizations in both size and scope. The Wisconsin NAACP detailed its evidence to date on inferior inner-city schools and proposed integration solutions drawn from other communities, such as the Princeton school pairing plan. Barbee's group acted far more assertively than other groups by presenting a list of demands with a specific timetable. It called for the school board to issue a policy statement on racial integration within one month, declaring it as a major factor in all new school construction, attendance zone, and student/faculty transfer decisions. Also, the Wisconsin NAACP demanded that intact busing students be fully integrated into their receiving schools immediately. Finally, it insisted that the school board submit a comprehensive plan, no later than September 1964, for integrating Milwaukee public schools at all grade levels. "If such a plan has not gone into effect by that date," they warned, "the NAACP shall embark on legal and direct action." At its conclusion, Richard McLeod from Milwaukee CORE and Cecil Brown from the NNNPC formally endorsed the Wisconsin NAACP report.[53]

But Barbee's actions that evening still did not provoke a reaction from Chairman Story, and the hearing ended without a confrontation. Instead, Story requested that Barbee and the leaders of Milwaukee CORE and the NNNPC return for a question-and-answer period at the next meeting in January 1964. Two days later, in a letter to June Shagaloff at the national NAACP, Barbee expressed his surprise at the school board's silence. "When their reaction becomes more vocal or active," he promised, "I will call you." Meanwhile, Milwaukee's integration supporters continued to build their emerging coalition in preparation for an eventual confrontation with Story. Barbee spoke again to the Milwaukee NAACP branch about his organization's commitment to hold demonstrations and boycott schools if the Story Committee did not meet its demands and secured additional support from Edward Smyth, a black realtor and the branch's new president. Milwaukee CORE contacted its Chicago chapter and requested organizers who had experience in building grass-roots support for a school boycott; it also held workshops for its members to practice persuading black parents to support school integration rather than improving black neighborhood schooling.[54]

Barbee was still waiting for a high-profile confrontation over segregation with the Milwaukee school board. The opportunity finally arose when the Story Committee reconvened in January 1964. During the first few minutes, a simple dispute arose over seating arrangements. Chairman Story opened the hearing with an unusual request. "Because this may be a long evening," he noted, "I suggest, Mr. Barbee, that you join our family at this table," in the one empty chair next to other members of the committee. But Barbee refused to be seated alone, separated from McLeod, Brown, and other members of his nascent coalition. "We will not proceed unless all members of CORE and the [NNNPC] participate," Barbee shot back. "You will not ask me any questions unless you have all three groups" sitting at the table. The

With television cameras rolling, Lloyd Barbee (far left) stormed out of the school board hearing after Chairman Harold Story (far right) attempted to isolate him from other civil rights representatives. From *Milwaukee Star*, 25 January 1964; courtesy of Milwaukee Courier/Star, Inc., and Wisconsin Historical Society, Visual Materials Archive (WHi-5763).

two attorneys, Story and Barbee, momentarily debated over how the meeting should be conducted, and when Story refused to budge, Barbee and his crowd of supporters defiantly marched out of the meeting in front of the newspaper photographers and television camera operators.[55]

Milwaukee's mass media conveyed the story of the confrontation and its symbolic politics in both pictures and words. Photographs showed a black group of school integration supporters carrying Lloyd Barbee atop their shoulders and singing "We Shall Overcome" in the hallway outside the meeting, more unified and energized than ever before. Inside, Chairman Story insisted on continuing the meeting and proceeded to question Barbee's empty chair for nearly two hours. Story's scripted questions reveal how he had planned to paint Barbee as a radical extremist with an integrationist agenda far removed from the desires of Milwaukee's established black community. "Now, if Mr. Barbee were here," he continued, "I would ask him: Wouldn't [compulsory integration] meet opposition not only from white parents but also from Negro parents? I don't think Negro parents want to be pushed around any more than any other parents."[56]

Barbee's supporters carried him aloft, cheering their confrontation with the school board.
From *Milwaukee Journal*, 22 January 1964; copyright Milwaukee Journal Sentinel, Inc.;
reproduced with permission.

But Story's plan backfired. While he correctly observed that black Milwaukeeans had differences of opinion about black education reform strategies, he seriously misunderstood the consequences of publicly attempting
to manipulate these for his own benefit. By refusing to seat a group of
mostly black citizens together and by not listening respectfully to their concerns, Story had insulted the entire black community, even those who did
not subscribe to Barbee's integrationist vision. The confrontation sparked
the beginnings of a mass movement, which the news media had visually
framed as a battle between a white giant and a black underdog. "It was all

a show anyway," Barbee told a white reporter, "since Story wanted to be scriptwriter, producer, and director." Yet Story unintentionally gave Barbee exactly what he had been waiting for—the leading role in Milwaukee's 1960s civil rights movement. Barbee announced that demonstrations against segregated schools would begin the next month and began planning for a bigger show of protest in the spring.[57]

At their next meeting, several white school board members struggled to understand what had happened and asked Cornelius Golightly, their lone black member, if the black community stood behind Barbee and the NAACP. Golightly reminded them that "if you listened very carefully to the people that came in, they talked about many things," including unmotivated teachers, a declining curriculum, and the lack of extracurricular activities in inner-city schools. "They are not the sort of issues that stir people up," he observed, but Barbee's movement was different. In recent weeks, Golightly argued, "the Negro community seems to have consolidated itself behind the NAACP on the grounds that the school board has deliberately made no positive move to concern itself" with black educational issues. While black Milwaukeeans "may not think highly of Mr. Barbee as a person . . . [or] may not think highly of the NAACP as an organization," he added, "it would be a great mistake for you ever to assume that the Negro community is not behind this demand or this effort to bring Negro children into the mainstream of American life." Whether or not the majority of black Milwaukeeans specifically supported Barbee's school integration proposals was not the point. Instead, the school board needed to understand that if they made no effort to advance the interests of black children, then a confrontation with Barbee would only serve to portray themselves as the enemy of civil rights.[58]

As Milwaukee entered into a new phase of the broader school integration movement, Martin Luther King paid a visit to encourage local civil rights efforts. "Several months ago," he told readers of the *Milwaukee Star*, "the Northern Negro arose from his apathetic slumber." Before Barbee stood up at the podium in July 1963, there had been no activism against segregated schools in the city. Now King urged Milwaukeeans to take one more bold step forward. "A school boycott," he suggested, "is a creative way to dramatize the whole issue." Local school integration supporters had already begun planning this event, which would offer thousands of black adults and youth a participatory role in Milwaukee's 1960s civil rights movement.[59]

CONTRASTING HISTORICAL MEMORIES OF
EARLY CIVIL RIGHTS ACTIVISM

Years later, as Lloyd Barbee looked back on this decade, he wrote his own history of the early school integration movement and granted several oral history interviews. In his view, Milwaukee had been "backwards" on civil rights. The city's established black leadership was bogged down by a "lethargic, apathetic sense of complacency." Their efforts to win jobs for black teachers merely sold out their community to white segregationists, he believed, and delayed the rise of the school integration movement, distancing the city far behind its Northern peers. According to Barbee's historical memory, Milwaukee's struggle for black education began in the early 1960s, when he had arrived in the city.[60]

Yet Barbee's account tells us virtually nothing about earlier struggles for black education reform. One month before Barbee launched Milwaukee's school integration campaign in 1963, the city's longtime black residents mourned the death of William Kelley, the retired Milwaukee Urban League director and organizer from an earlier era. Barbee never mentioned meeting Kelley and certainly did not know him in Kelley's prime years. From the 1930s through the 1950s, Kelley led black Milwaukee's struggle to win jobs, particularly for schoolteachers in the white-dominated school system. In Barbee's mind, these actions were simply accommodation to segregationists, but he did not comprehend the historical context in which Kelley's black education reform strategy arose. Nor did Barbee recognize his own historical connection to Kelley's struggle. Prior to the school integration demonstrations of the 1960s, Milwaukee's largest civil rights protest had been the 1941 march for defense workers' jobs, organized by Kelley and his NAACP colleague James Dorsey. "That's when we were marching for jobs," recalled longtime resident Calvin Moody. "They didn't even have the first black teacher then." Yet scarcely any mention of this nearly forgotten civil rights protest appears in Barbee's numerous interviews or in any historical account of black Milwaukee published during the "modern" civil rights period.[61]

Indeed, Kelley and Barbee led different struggles, and in different ways. The former directed the Urban League's employment services, which required businesslike negotiations with white employers and the cooperation of white board members. By contrast, the latter held a private law practice, which enabled him to speak out on causes for which he might be compensated through litigation, as long as he could build a strong base of black popular support. One focused on winning black teachers' jobs and did not perceive all-black schooling to be a major issue, while the other challenged segregative policies and practices that kept black migrant children away from better-quality white schools. By the late 1950s, as Milwaukee's expanding black population became increasingly segregated in inner-city neighborhoods and schools, it became clear that Kelley's vision of education reform was losing ground as Barbee's gained newly energized followers. But these two representatives of different generations shared one common thread: both of them organized movements to gain more power for blacks in Milwaukee's education system and did so in ways that made sense within their own historical context. Their respective struggles should not be compared head-to-head but understood through a historical lens as part of a long line of cumulative, and sometimes conflicting, movements for black education.

5

UNITING THE MOVEMENTS FOR INTEGRATION

AND BLACK POWER

They called themselves MUSIC—the Milwaukee United School Integration Committee—and nearly brought the public school system to a halt during their peak years of protest in the mid-1960s. Over a dozen black and white civil rights, religious, and political organizations joined forces in early 1964 and unanimously elected Lloyd Barbee as their chairman. MUSIC enabled thousands of citizens to step into participatory roles in the battle against school segregation, and its tactics stepped up the level of confrontation with the Milwaukee school system. In February 1964, over 300 protesters picketed the school administration building, the city's first civil rights march of this size in over two decades. Teams of nonviolent direct-action protesters began forming human chains around buses to prevent the transport of black children to isolated classrooms. By May, nearly 11,000 black and white children boycotted the city schools, with many joining hands at MUSIC's alternative Freedom Schools to raise their voices in protest for integrated education. In less than ten months, Milwaukee had been transformed from a city with no school integration movement to one that attracted thousands of supporters and national attention.[1]

Yet by late 1965, the mass movement for school integration began to decline nearly at the same pace it had arisen. MUSIC's second and third boy-

MUSIC activists engaged in civil disobedience, blocking intact busing at the peak of their movement in 1965. *Left to right*: Maxine Jeter, Juanita Adams, Mrs. Joseph White, Marilyn Morheuser, Minnie Butler, and Lloyd Barbee. From *Milwaukee Journal*, 24 May 1965; copyright Milwaukee Journal Sentinel, Inc.; reproduced with permission.

cotts attracted fewer supporters than did the first. Direct-action protests against segregated schooling trailed off. Fewer financial contributions arrived by mail. Although MUSIC did not formally disband, its level of activity dropped nearly to zero by late 1966. The speed with which these events took place, in Milwaukee and elsewhere, are puzzling. How do we explain the dramatic rise and decline of mass movements for school integration in the 1960s?

To answer this question for Milwaukee, this chapter seeks to move beyond the traditional source materials of civil rights histories, which typically rely on speeches and documents generated by official spokespeople (most often male), to investigate the stories of ordinary movement participants (most often female). In addition to carrying out much of the behind-the-scenes organizing and support work for the movement, these everyday activists sometimes participated in more than one struggle for school reform over time, occasionally in ways that conflicted with the ideology of the official integration leadership. By reconstructing black activists' oral narratives through the lenses of gender and organizational roles, we gain a clearer understanding of the multiple factors underlying the rise and decline of the school integration movement in Milwaukee, thereby questioning some conventional assumptions embedded within national civil rights history.[2]

Collectively, these activists' stories challenge the *abandonment narrative*, the traditional interpretation most commonly invoked by historians to explain the apparent rise and decline of the Northern civil rights movement during the 1960s. As a literary device, it has the virtue of simplicity, as it accounts for historical change during a complex decade by splitting it into two ideological halves. During the early 1960s, the story goes, black Americans struggled for racial integration until the frustrations of white racism led them to abandon the cause and turn instead toward black power and community control in the latter half of the decade. In fact, some historical works pinpoint the exact week of this alleged national transition. On 6 August 1965, President Lyndon Johnson signed the Voting Rights Act, marking the peak of federal civil rights legislation. Yet five days later, several historians have observed, black residents of the Watts ghetto near Los Angeles became so frustrated by racism that they rioted for several days, resulting in thirty-four deaths, 1,000 injuries, 4,000 arrests, and millions of dollars in destroyed property. According to this familiar narrative, black Americans deserted the peaceful interracial dream of Martin Luther King to follow in the violent, separatist footsteps of Malcolm X.[3]

The abandonment narrative also appears in histories of the 1960s school integration movement, at both local and national levels, written from opposite ends of the political spectrum. Historian Diane Ravitch, for example, adopts the narrative in her interpretation of the Ocean Hill–Brownsville controversy in New York City in 1968. Up to that point, many black school activists had rallied for citywide school integration plans. But "the impossibility of attaining city-wide racial balance caused many integrationists to abandon the principles of integration and common values, in favor of local control, even though local control had been the battle cry of those who fought integration." Likewise, two of her frequent critics, Robert Lowe and Harvey Kantor, draw upon the same theme in their account of the national demise of the black-liberal coalition. "Frustrated by the slow pace of desegregation and by injustices faced in schools that had accomplished it," they argue, "many African Americans abandoned the pursuit of desegregation at the very time the courts most actively pressed it."[4]

Narratives like these deserve attention because they shape our implicit historical thinking about the civil rights era. They become the familiar stories, buried within our collective memories, which we unknowingly rely upon, at times, to explain the past and present. The abandonment narrative, like most, contains a strong element of truth: racism certainly continued during the 1960s, and some black Americans became understandably frustrated at the slow pace of progress, leading several to undergo a change of heart on integration. But its characterization of the period is too static and simplistic and its transition too abrupt to fully capture the dynamic range of local black activists' experiences during the decade. A growing number of historians have criticized the conventional narrative, such as Peniel Joseph, who derisively labeled it a "neatly packaged" presentation of "history as a made-for-television movie" with simplistic binary struggles between Martin versus Malcolm and integration versus segregation.[5]

In Milwaukee, the abandonment narrative presumes a greater degree of uniformity in black opinion than the evidence warrants. It asserts that black supporters of the school integration movement were of one mind in the early 1960s, marching in unison for one purpose. In reality, Milwaukee's school integration movement did not arise as a united front but rather as a diverse coalition of participants with different motivations. While all became members of the same movement, there was not a universal ideology cohering their disparate views, experiences, and expectations. Some activists joined because of their strong commitment to building an integrated society, but others took part because they saw the integration strategy as the best path toward gaining better resources for black schooling, strengthening black cultural identity, or challenging white supremacy. Thousands of black Milwaukeeans marched together in the early 1960s under MUSIC's banner of school integration, whether that precise label fit them or not. Yet when this umbrella organization folded in the later 1960s, it did not represent as large an "abandonment" as the familiar narrative entails, since not all of the participants had embraced the same principles at the beginning. Several activists who moved from MUSIC to other school reform groups affiliated with community control or black power typically did not perceive their actions as an abandonment of previous efforts but rather as a series of uninterrupted steps in their long journeys for improving black education. Historian Clayborne Carson lends support to this reinterpretation by challenging historians who presume the existence of a neat ideological division between the two halves of the decade. "There was much continuity between the period before 1965 and the period after," he contends, suggesting that we reconceive the entire period as one "black freedom struggle" where early movements were not abandoned but instead evolved into new forms to achieve the aims that previous efforts had not fully attained. This chapter seeks to examine closely the voices and actions of six local activists who came together through MUSIC in the early 1960s, then diverged along different paths for the remainder of the decade, to better understand how they made sense of reform ideologies on their own terms within their local contexts. From this perspective, Milwaukee's struggles for school integration, community control, and black power share more commonalities than most historical accounts have previously assumed.[6]

Integration to the Core:
Juanita Adams and Arlene Johnson

Some activists remained so faithful to the cause of integration that they perceived the later movement as abandoning them rather than vice versa. When Juanita Adams returned to Milwaukee after traveling to the March on Washington in 1963, the transformative experience catapulted the twenty-two-year-old black woman into the school integration movement. "When I left [Washington], I was just on fire. . . . I saw the world as God had designed it," she recalled. "It was like a religious experience for me . . . to see all the races, black and white together with common cause." Adams had grown up in the segregated schools of Memphis. When she migrated to Milwaukee in 1959 to start a family with her new husband, she and other black Catholics joined the inner-city St. Boniface Church parish, where they encountered the Christian Family Movement, which encouraged them to find ways of living out the Scripture within their local communities. They soon found their calling in Milwaukee's emerging mass civil rights movement, where a strong spiritual commitment was almost essential, since this early generation of activists had no way of knowing whether or not their risky efforts would be successful. It took a leap of faith.[7]

Originally, Adams planned to stay home and raise money to sponsor others to make the Washington trip. But a white friend, Arlene Johnson, persuaded her to reconsider. They knew one another because both of their husbands were black auto workers at the American Motors plant and had met through Calvin Sherard's Negro American Labor Council earlier in the 1960s. Arlene Johnson was a native white Milwaukeean and had more experience than Adams in civil rights activities. She also had firsthand experience with Milwaukee's aggressive police force and its intense surveillance of interracial couples who participated in the movement. But at that time, Johnson recalled, "Juanita and I were really homebodies and mothers, you know, we were spouses. . . . We weren't able to just up and go." Johnson finally decided to call Adams and told her, "Take your bags, we're going." When Adams asked who would handle household chores in their absence, including caring for their young children, Johnson replied, "Let your husband worry about it, we're going." Together, Adams and Johnson boarded the bus. With over 100 other civil rights activists from Milwaukee, both black and white, they began a thousand-mile journey that would lead both of them to commit their lives to realizing Martin Luther King's dream of a day when black and white children would play together. "Going to Washington," for both of these young women, "was our liberation."[8]

When Adams and Johnson returned, they joined their husbands and colleagues to become co-founding members of Milwaukee CORE, a new chapter of the nonviolent interracial civil rights organization. After initial protests against blatantly racist local government officials and housing discrimination, Milwaukee CORE became attracted to the Northern school integration movement, a priority also identified by national director James Farmer. When Lloyd Barbee called for the first wave of demonstrations against intact busing in February 1964, the chapter responded. "CORE was the foot soldiers of this community," Johnson remembered. "We had the people who were willing to hit the pavement," adding that her own children "learned to walk on the picket line." Members of other organizations, such as the Milwaukee NAACP and the Urban League, were reluctant to participate in direct-action protest, but "CORE had the people and the strength." Through the efforts of Tom Jacobson, a Milwaukee CORE co-founder and Barbee's white law partner, the group joined forces with MUSIC.[9]

Women like Juanita Adams and Arlene Johnson provided the crucial support work for the school integration movement. "We went door-to-door canvassing, we did voter registration," Adams recalled, in addition to the painstaking work on educating parents, one by one, about schooling issues. Grass-roots activists often received their training at the Northcott Neighborhood House through seminars led by Rev. Lucius Walker, one of the earliest black ministers to support the cause. The gender dynamics of civil rights activism became even clearer during nonviolent protest actions. "The women did the work . . . going to jail," Johnson added, "and the men made the decisions." Photographs and arrest records published in the daily newspapers confirm the disproportionate role played by women in Milwaukee's school integration protests. When MUSIC leaders escalated the level of confrontation with school officials, groups of predominantly female activists formed human chains around school buses intended to transport intact classrooms of black children, or blocked construction equipment used for building new inner-city schools. Pregnant with her third child in December 1965, Juanita Adams physically blocked a cement truck from pouring the concrete that would later become the predominantly black MacDowell Elementary School. Some women, like Adams, were not employed full-time outside their homes and did not fear direct economic reprisals if they were temporarily jailed. But protest work was dangerous. When activists' names appeared in the newspaper, "people would call on our phone and threaten to kill us," Johnson recalled. "The neighbors on both sides and across the street of our home would come to the door and tell us, 'You guys go on and do what you have to do. We've got babysitters here for the kids.' . . . It was dangerous."[10]

Adams and Johnson defined themselves as "staunch integrationists," yet their participation in protest actions had ceased by 1966 for personal and political reasons. When Adams gave birth to her fourth child, she had even less time for activism. "I just couldn't do it any longer," she decided, after a typical schedule of four late-night strategy meetings and fund-raising sessions per week. "I've got to start taking care of my children," she recalled thinking to herself. The demands of balancing activism, work, and family also pressured Johnson. After losing one job due to protest activity, she began working at Jacobson's law firm, and in 1969 she divorced her husband. "Our marriage was sacrificed for the cause" of integration, Johnson concluded.

At the same time, Adams and Johnson felt that the black freedom struggle was moving away from their lives. First, they objected to "opportunists" who marched with the integration movement but abruptly departed when the black power movement came along. "A whole segment of foot soldiers went in that direction," Johnson explained. Second, Milwaukee experienced a widely publicized urban disturbance in 1967 when approximately 300 young black men vandalized neighborhood stores and city and state authorities responded with 4,800 National Guard troops and a strict curfew. Four people lost their lives and many more were arrested. In comparison to Newark and Detroit, the Milwaukee disturbance was on a much smaller scale (total damage was estimated at only $116,262), but Mayor Henry Maier and the newspaper headlines proclaimed it to be a major riot on the national scene. Regardless of its actual size, the circumstances surrounding the event changed the climate for some long-term integration activists. "I was committed to nonviolence," Adams asserted, "and I was scared to get in a picket line after the riots." The new faces behind the violent protest "didn't represent me any longer, and I moved into the political arena," she continued, recounting her late-1960s affiliation with the Young Democrats. "After that, we moved into Jesus," Adams explained, describing how her recent religious activities, including work at a women's shelter, brought her back full circle to the place where her civil rights activism had begun. Indeed, there were black Milwaukee activists who abandoned the school integration movement during the 1960s, but not Adams and Johnson; in their eyes, they perceived that the movement had abandoned them. "Some people might have said that we dropped out," Adams reflected thirty years later. "[But] we haven't dropped out. We have gone to a new level." [11]

From Freedom Schools to Community Schools: Mildred Harpole

Other activists joined up with MUSIC on different terms than its organizers had intended. When Mildred Harpole moved to Milwaukee, she became one of the nearly 300 black teachers employed by the public school system in the early 1960s. She was more than qualified for the position, since in addition to her teaching certification she held a law degree from Case Western Reserve University in Cleveland. Harpole found work as a substitute reading teacher at Wells Junior High School, located on the western edge of the inner city, and eventually became a full-time reading specialist. She had very few curriculum materials when the program first began, "so we could be very creative and innovative in our approach, and so I loved that," Harpole remembered. She had students from black, white, and other racial groups, but nearly all of them were poor children who lacked reading stimulation in their homes. To unlock their motivation to learn, Harpole immersed them in everyday media—newspapers, popular songs, television shows—and led them to read and discover current events, poetic structure, and plot development.[12]

Harpole's life became entwined with the school integration movement when MUSIC leaders announced a one-day boycott of public schools on 18 May 1964, the tenth anniversary of the *Brown* decision. They justified their protest on the grounds that all reasonable attempts to negotiate with school authorities had failed and invited students to attend the Freedom Schools instead. Adopting the idea from similar boycotts in Boston, Chicago, and New York, MUSIC organizers made arrangements for over thirty black churches to donate space for the day and scrambled to staff them with nearly 300 volunteer instructors, both black and white. Harpole was one of a handful of black schoolteachers to join the team. She strongly felt that the children should not lose one minute in their quest for education. "I didn't feel that it was productive for children to sit home or be on the street during the boycott," Harpole recalled. It was absolutely critical for the Freedom Schools to run parallel to the boycott. Furthermore, children had the opportunity to meet local civil rights activists and visiting national celebrities, such as comedian Dick Gregory. "They saw the pages of many of their texts in living color, so to speak," explained the reading teacher. The Freedom School concept attracted her with its supportive environment for innovative teaching, learning, and liberating thinking for black children. "I took the same concepts that I was using in the Milwaukee public schools [and brought them] to the Freedom School."[13]

Marilyn Morheuser, the former white nun who had become MUSIC's secretary, designed a curriculum to bring coherence to the Freedom Schools. When speaking to a white reporter, she stressed that the curriculum was "not a day of rebellion against the school system and authority" but rather "a positive program" that sought better schooling through integration and increased black students' pride in their history and sense of value. Yet woven into the black history lessons were themes of battles against white racism. Primary grade students heard stories about black heroes during the struggle

Students and teachers boycotted their regular schools and participated in Freedom Schools held in black churches around the city. From *Milwaukee Sentinel*, 19 October 1965; copyright Milwaukee Journal Sentinel, Inc.; reproduced with permission.

against slavery, such as Frederick Douglass, Sojourner Truth, and Harriet Tubman. Freedom songs reminded students of the need to confront white opponents of open housing. The lyrics to "The Welcome Table" included these verses:

We're gonna sit at the welcome table
We're gonna sit at the welcome table
One of these days, hallelujah,
We're gonna sit at the welcome table
Gonna sit at the welcome table, one of these days

I'm gonna live anywhere I want to . . .

I'm gonna live in South Milwaukee . . . (add Whitefish Bay, etc.)

We're gonna shake up all Milwaukee . . .

High school students engaged in more philosophical writing and discussions about defining freedom and in role-playing scenarios about taking a stand in the ensuing public debate about the boycott itself. Overall, MUSIC's Freedom Schools provided the most expansive black history curriculum since the Milwaukee Urban League's community center programs, begun by director William Kelley in the 1930s.[14]

Fierce opposition to MUSIC's school boycott came from all sides. Daily newspapers and television stations ran editorials against it, and Mayor Henry Maier urged organizers to postpone it. The auxiliary bishop of the Milwaukee Archdiocese prohibited any Catholic parishes or priests from participating. Public school officials warned that teachers and students would face disciplinary actions for joining the protest. The district attorney threatened that parents who allowed their children to boycott would be prosecuted for truancy, punishable with up to a three-month jail term. The Milwaukee Police Department "Red Squad," formally known as the Special Assignments Squad, conducted extensive surveillance on boycott organizers and intimidated black ministers who offered their churches as Freedom Schools, persuading at least three to change their minds. MUSIC also faced continual opposition from pro-segregationist groups, such as the Citizens organization, led by president John Carroll, who compiled 20,000 local signatures against racial integration in 1964. The Citizens also demonstrated to reelect Lorraine Radtke to serve a second term as school board president, holding her name alongside other signs such as "Negroes Should Only Be Athletes." In a public speech to the city's religious leaders, Radtke had described herself as "pure German" and later warned that in a "Prussian" city like Milwaukee, "Germans cannot be pushed around" or forced to accept black children in white classrooms. Radtke also publicly voiced her views on cultural deprivation, charging that newly arrived black migrant schoolchildren urinated in water fountains. Radtke and her numerous white supporters strongly disagreed with MUSIC's boycott.[15]

Even some established black Milwaukeeans opposed the school boycott strategy. Most significantly, black attorney James Dorsey publicly criticized the Milwaukee NAACP leadership for supporting the MUSIC boycott rather than pursuing the "dignified" path of legal redress and resigned from the organization of which he had been a past president and leading member for several decades. Dorsey also blasted integration leaders who used children "as guinea pigs" to achieve their "personal ambitions," a jab at Barbee, who was launching his own candidacy for the state legislature. But Dorsey's numerous critics questioned his own political motivations for opposing the boycott. Two weeks earlier, he had been the first black appointed to be a Milwaukee County court commissioner, one step below a judge. The young integrationists dismissed the sixty-seven-year-old black establishment figure as a sellout. This generational conflict overshadowed any public expression of historical memory about black Milwaukee activism. None of Barbee's supporters mentioned (or perhaps few knew of) Dorsey's role in leading Milwaukee's version of the March on Washington protest in 1941, nor did Dorsey publicly recognize the contradictions that his prior activism now raised in his criticism of Barbee's tactics.[16]

Despite all of these objections, MUSIC's first school boycott and Freedom Schools successfully brought masses of black Milwaukeeans under the school integration banner. Approximately 11,000 children—roughly 60 percent of the black inner-city school population—stayed out during the one-day action, although the number who attended Freedom Schools was somewhat lower, around 8,500. MUSIC had found a strategy to mobilize the largest, most united group of black supporters and white allies that the city had witnessed thus far. The school desegregation movement carved out participatory roles for thousands of citizens, in interracial settings, to speak their minds about changing public policy on race and education. Beyond Milwaukee, these widely publicized mass protests significantly raised the city's standing as a full-fledged member of the NAACP's Northern struggle for integrated education, something that the parent organization had been encouraging for several years.[17]

Yet Mildred Harpole did not participate in any MUSIC events after the 1964 Freedom Schools. Although her belief in quality education seemed compatible on the surface with MUSIC's integrationist stand, she soon discovered deep differences of opinion in her conversations with Barbee and Morheuser. "They believed that integration . . . was a goal in itself," Harpole realized, "and I believed that quality education can occur in a mixed group or a segregated group." In other words, MUSIC's leaders saw integration as both the means and the end of black school reform, while Harpole pursued a different goal—quality education for black students—which was not necessarily linked to integration. MUSIC's Freedom Schools attracted her because they provided the means to achieve quality education.[18]

Harpole's belief that educational quality was not dependent upon a school's racial composition emerged from her personal experience as a student in both all-black and all-white schools. During the segregated 1940s, her family sent her to an all-black Catholic boarding school in Baltimore, where she received an "excellent" education. Later, she became the first black student to enroll in an all-white Catholic high school in Cleveland. "But when I transferred to this all-white school," Harpole proudly noted, "I didn't miss a beat." The quality of instruction at the all-black Baltimore school matched the all-white Cleveland school. As Harpole reflected on this experience in Milwaukee, it led her to doubt MUSIC's claim that "integration in itself was going to bring about quality education." She parted company with Barbee and Morheuser, believing that they were moving along a parallel but different track. "I felt that the integrationists had their goals in mind, and I wished them well," she recalled. "However, while they were traveling along that line, something had to be done with the current situation. And all of the children were not going to be integrated, that was obvious, so I personally felt that my responsibility was to provide a quality educational program where I was." Harpole returned to focus on ways to achieve quality education, regardless of the racial composition, in her reading classroom at Wells Junior High, then Lincoln Junior-Senior High, and then outside the public school system.[19]

By the end of the 1960s, Harpole put her ideas about quality education into action on a broader scale. After serving on the steering committee for a new organization, the Concerned Parents for Quality Education, and receiving her master's degree in reading education, she became the head administrator of the Harambee Community School in 1970. Harambee was located at the former St. Elizabeth's parochial grade school, where the black student population had risen to nearly 20 percent by the mid-1960s, leading many whites to leave. As enrollments declined, the white pastors supported a proposal to convert St. Elizabeth's school into an independent community school with a more innovative curriculum and broader neighborhood participation in 1969. That same year, over 1,000 white families (nearly half the total) moved out of the parish. A remaining coalition of committed parents and pastors negotiated with the archdiocese to use the space and staffed it with hand-picked Catholic and secular teachers, eventually placing Harpole in charge.[20]

Harambee, translated from Swahili as "Let's pull together," strived to meet local demand for quality education with community control, a rarity in Milwaukee's inner-city schools. About 200 children and two dozen teachers learned together in an ungraded, multi-age environment that stressed individualized instruction and community awareness. An elected parent board oversaw school policies. After Harpole began, 82 percent of Harambee's students were black, yet a significant number of white families continued to enroll their children in the school. "We had a quality program and we had integration," Harpole explained. "We didn't have to talk about integration. It came about because we had a quality program. And some of the first registers were white parents, and some of them were from the suburbs. So it just brought out what I already knew, that if you have a quality program and it's in demand . . . they'll come from all corners." Six other Catholic schools in the central city also experienced similar reorganizations into secular institutions and affiliated themselves into the Federation of Independent Community Schools in 1970. Together, they educated over 2,000 students per year: some in predominantly black settings, some in racially mixed settings, and one, on the city's south side, which was largely Mexican American and Puerto Rican. Through the federation's black coordinator, Jesse Wray, the group collectively solicited donations from local philanthropists to sustain its educational alternative to the Milwaukee public schools.[21]

The federation almost succeeded in bringing federally funded tuition vouchers for private schools to Milwaukee in 1970. At that time, the Nixon administration's Office of Economic Opportunity announced that it would award a planning grant to one city in the United States to test whether free-market tools would increase low-income and minority parental choice and thereby improve the responsiveness and quality of both private and public schooling. Federal officials designated Robert Bothwell, the director of the Center for the Study of Public Policy in Cambridge, Massachusetts, to recruit applications from prospective cities, and he made several trips to Milwaukee to promote the concept. Vouchers had strong support from some white conservatives and Catholic leaders, such as Father Virgil Blum, a Marquette University political scientist who for many years had lobbied for federal aid for parochial schools in the form of grants to individual families. But Bothwell also found significant interest among several black Milwaukeeans. Although the national NAACP opposed vouchers, Bothwell received endorsements from several local black organizations, such as the Milwaukee Urban League and its executive director, Wesley Scott. "We've been interested in Milwaukee from the very beginning," Bothwell told an audience at the predominantly black Northside YMCA. "Milwaukee already has ten independent schools which are new and prime to implement new programs," he explained, referring to the federation schools and others like Urban Day (a nondenominational private school that opened in 1967 and served many inner-city black families, though it did not join the federation). But in order for Milwaukee's voucher planning grant application to be considered by the Office of Economic Opportunity, it required approval by the local school board. After many hours of deliberation and several close votes, Milwaukee's school board committees blocked the proposal from advancing, and Bothwell finally gave up and looked for pilot sites elsewhere. Nearly two decades would pass before another black and white coalition for vouchers would rise again.[22]

While Mildred Harpole moved through different black school reform groups during the 1960s, she did not "abandon" integration, because she had never embraced it as the primary means for achieving quality education for black children. She believed that quality education would produce integration as a by-product, "because from my experience, white families sought out what they considered the best." But integration itself was not her main reason for participating in MUSIC. Instead, the Freedom School attracted her as a means of demonstrating high-quality instruction and challenging the Milwaukee public schools to do the same for black children on a daily basis. Six years later, the same reasoning applied to Harambee and the Federation of Independent Community Schools. Therefore, the story of her personal struggle for black school reform emphasizes continuity more than contradiction.[23]

Other activists also joined—and eventually left—the integration movement without seeing any contradictions in the steps they had taken. When Flo Seefeldt moved to Milwaukee in 1953, she expected the schools to be far better than the legally segregated ones she had left behind in rural Mississippi. But she began to have doubts over the next few years. In 1962, when she and her four children lived near the predominantly black McKinley Elementary School, the two oldest ones were bused intact to the nearly all-white Garden Homes Elementary School. The experience awakened her to Northern-style racism. "Kids would tell us horror stories," she recalled, unable to believe that all of them were true. "They couldn't play at the same time the white kids was playing, they didn't have lunch at the same time, they couldn't go to the bathroom until after the white kids had gone. . . . I was just dumbfounded because I thought when you left the South and came to the North . . . everything was going to be different, and it wasn't." Seefeldt became so angry that she started a petition drive at the neighborhood grocery story to end intact busing and to integrate her children into the receiving school. "I wanted my children to go to an integrated school," she remembered, noting that "they shouldn't be bused to be segregated." In 1964, she participated in MUSIC's boycott to protest for better schooling for her children.[24]

Although Seefeldt joined the school integration movement, she was not driven by MUSIC's ideological vision of an integrated society as the ultimate goal. Seefeldt had no objection to integration. She fondly remembered participating in a controversial integrated Bible camp as a child in Mississippi, had several white friends in Milwaukee, and later married a white man. But when it came to schooling, Seefeldt's goal was simple: obtain better educational resources to improve black children's learning. At this point in her life, she was a single mother living on public assistance and highly conscious of every dollar spent on her four children. She supported integration only as an instrument to obtain better resources. If her children could sit alongside white children, Seefeldt reasoned, then "they would be getting the same education as other kids in that classroom."[25]

In Seefeldt's view, integration made sense in a world where "green follows white," a colloquial expression meaning that dollars flowed in the direction where whites went to school. Like many black Milwaukeeans, she supported the school integration movement as a means to secure the same resources for black children. Wesley Scott of the Urban League elaborated on this way of thinking. "In the minds of most black individuals in the community at that time, we just felt, rightly or wrongly, that over here were the white schools that were getting all the resources, and those that were predominantly black

were being deprived," he explained. Many blacks felt that "if it was integrated, then we could take advantage of some of these resources, just in
terms of equipment and space, to educate our kids." Scholars Robert Newby
and David Tyack described this logic as the "hostage thesis." According to
this view, white educators would provide high-quality instruction to black
children "only if there were white children as hostages in their classrooms.
. . . Only then would there be adequate facilities and supplies."[26]

But Seefeldt's subsequent experiences with uncaring white teachers led
her to question the value of integration as an instrument for reaching her
true goal. When she moved her children to a Milwaukee neighborhood with
a predominantly white school in the mid-1960s, it achieved her short-term
goal of placing them in the same classroom with whites but led her to realize how "one would get an education and the other one wouldn't." Teachers
told her children that reading and writing were too hard for them. Seefeldt
asked the teachers to offer extra help to catch them up, but their lack of response told her that they didn't believe her children were worth the effort. "I
didn't realize that the educators could sit in a classroom with a group of kids
and realize that one wasn't learning, and didn't take the time to help them."
As a reform strategy, school integration was not bringing Seefeldt any closer
to her real objective. Her participation in MUSIC activities ended.[27]

Seefeldt began meeting with other black and white women on welfare to
make dinners together and study the laws to learn more about their rights
in the system. After Milwaukee's brief but intense riot in 1967, an opportunity opened up for her to redirect her efforts on school reform. Wisconsin's Republican governor Warren P. Knowles offered over $4 million for
emergency funding to inner-city schools in an attempt to address ongoing
concerns about educational opportunity for black students. School administrators and several teachers recommended spending the funds on security
guards to protect themselves from attacks and on a special school for disrup-
tive students. But Seefeldt and others objected and organized an alternative.
"We started a group called the United Community Action Group [UCAG]
because we didn't want no prison schools," she recalled. "We wanted our
children to get a better education."[28]

Chaired by Seefeldt, UCAG was comprised of mostly black and white
women, including several who had been active in MUSIC. They quickly
learned that the governor's legislation prohibited funds from being spent
without community approval and drafted their own proposal. In late 1967,
UCAG called for the creation of Inter-related Language Skill Centers to
teach reading skills to small groups of elementary-level students who were
two years below their level. Teachers would be screened to eliminate those
with prejudicial views of black and Hispanic children, and inner-city residents would serve on an advisory committee to plan and implement the pro-

gram. Indeed, UCAG members advocated for a community-controlled version of compensatory education to address recognized reading deficiencies in inner-city children without the "cultural deprivation" racist pathology found in many earlier programs.[29]

Milwaukee's ensuing crisis over community control paralleled events that were also unfolding in New York City's Ocean Hill–Brownsville district. Wisconsin state officials approved funding for UCAG's proposal, to be administered by Milwaukee school officials. But conflicts arose when administrators insisted on hiring two teachers who had been rejected by UCAG representatives. The two sides clashed over different interpretations of governance over the program. In August 1968, UCAG members picketed against a center that administrators were opening without community approval. Police broke the picket line, knocked Seefeldt to the ground, then arrested her and twenty-eight others. Seefeldt later testified to visiting members of the federal Kerner Commission, who investigated the riots, that the Milwaukee schools "have failed our children and are still failing. . . . Unless we have more control, there is little hope for the children." The *Milwaukee Courier*, a black weekly newspaper, observed that "the reading centers are not the issue. The issue is POWER. By uniting and standing their ground, parents have shown that they do have power. And the administration is doing everything it can think of to crush this power before it grows."[30]

At the beginning of the 1960s, Seefeldt had joined MUSIC's protests for school integration, yet by the close of the decade, she advocated for language skills centers to provide a revised version of compensatory education within a greater degree of community control. These type of actions did not please Lloyd Barbee, who opposed creating additional schools for black children in the inner city. Did Seefeldt, in her frustration with white educators, abandon integration? Some said yes, including a faction of UCAG members who favored racially integrated centers; the organization subsequently broke apart. But in Seefeldt's mind, the answer was no. She had never embraced integration as the primary reason for joining MUSIC protests. Seefeldt had always been consistent about her true objective—better resources for black children—and used the most appropriate means to achieve it within her given context. Ideological differences between integration, compensatory education, and community control did not bother her, since what mattered most were results.[31]

MERGING INTEGRATION AND BLACK POWER: VADA HARRIS

Some activists embraced two ideologies commonly defined as polar opposites and seamlessly merged them during the decade. When Milwaukee's school integration movement was just beginning, Vada Harris was a teenage black student at St. Boniface parochial school, one of the few racially integrated Catholic schools still located in the inner city at that time. She came to identify herself as an integration activist through the work of her pastor, Father James Groppi, a white priest who became radicalized during his participation in Southern civil rights marches. When Harris completed eighth grade at St. Boniface, she insisted on attending an integrated high school rather than the all-black North Division High School located next door. "I didn't want to go to an all-black school," she recalled. "I begged my mom . . . to take me to the school board to get a transfer, and that's how I ended up in Riverside," a predominantly white high school on the east side of the Milwaukee River. With Groppi's encouragement, Harris became active in MUSIC and volunteered to teach black history to a Freedom School class in 1964. Harris acquired her own knowledge of black history at St. Boniface, along with a strong dose of racial pride. "Father Groppi always instilled in us to be 'black and proud,'" she remembered. "Ever since I heard that, I had an awakening, and from that moment on, I just pursued every issue there was to be recognized." As a young woman coming of age in the 1960s, Harris internalized a positive black identity that bolstered her political commitment to integration rather than conflicted with it.[32]

By 1967, Harris still defined herself as a pro-black integrationist, but MUSIC was no longer the vehicle for her activism. She began organizing her black classmates at Riverside High to promote black history and pride in the public schools. Harris led the first "textbook turn-in" protest. On her signal, thirty-five students joined her in walking out of their classrooms. "We went directly to the principal's office, laid all of our books on his counter, and then we proceeded to read the letter," she recounted. "We are sick and tired of receiving an inferior education, a biased one, and one that deprives a large group of our citizens of their rightful recognition as people who have contributed to the development of our democracy," the letter read. "We want books that picture the true history of America so that we have a better chance to become real Americans, and not just second-class citizens of a country which tries to ignore our presence." With Groppi's assistance, Harris and her fellow students timed their protest to coincide with Barbee's introduction of a bill in the state legislature to outlaw school segregation and require an accurate portrayal of black history in Milwaukee public schools. All three activists—Harris, Groppi, and Barbee—believed that racial integration and black pride were complementary objectives, not competing ones.[33]

Over the next few months, Harris continued to press for integration through the city's newest and most popular black-led protest movement, the open housing marches. As an officer in the Milwaukee NAACP Youth

Vada Harris, reading a letter at right, led black students in a "textbook turn-in" to protest the absence of black history at the predominantly white Riverside High School in 1967. From *Milwaukee Star*, 6 May 1967; courtesy of Milwaukee Courier/Star, Inc.

Council, she helped lead thousands of black youth and their white allies in marches to support open housing legislation, which the city council had voted down four times since Vel Phillips first introduced it in 1962. With Father Groppi as their adviser, the NAACP Youth Council intensified the level of confrontation with white racism by marching deep into white residential neighborhoods to demand their right to live anywhere. The marches attracted thousands of black supporters, particularly young men, many of whom longed to become one of "The Commandos," whose function was to protect and maintain order among the marchers. The Youth Council trained in nonviolent protest tactics but refused to rule out violent retaliation if attacked. In late August 1967, the open housing marchers crossed into the city's virtually all-white southside neighborhood, carrying signs reading "Fair Housing" and "Black Power." They were verbally and physically assaulted by mobs of angry whites who threw rocks and bottles, shouted "Nigger go home!," and brought their own signs proclaiming "White Power." Violent clashes sometimes broke out between both groups and the police, and the Youth Council headquarters was destroyed in a fire. Yet Vada Harris and the marchers persisted for 200 consecutive days and nights, drawing national attention and mounting pressure on city officials until the legislation finally passed.[34]

Milwaukee NAACP Youth Council marchers, with Father James Groppi, crossed into the city's southside white neighborhoods to demand open housing legislation. From NAACP Youth and College Division, *March on Milwaukee,* 1968; photo by Ken Bedford; courtesy of the NAACP and Milwaukee Public Library.

To Vada Harris and many young black open housing marchers in Milwaukee, the "Black Power" slogan did not convey the same separatist message as it did in other circles. To the contrary, the marchers carried signs for both "Fair Housing," an integrationist demand, and "Black Power," a struggle to end the "White Power" that maintained segregation and prevented blacks from escaping substandard inner-city housing and exercising their right to live wherever they chose. "We defined black power for ourselves some time ago," explained Frederick Bronson, president of the NAACP Youth Council. "To us, it means a struggle for political and economic unity and self-determination for the black man." Being pro-black was not synonymous with anti-white; in fact, whites were welcome to join the marches or work in other ways to eliminate racism. The continual presence of Father Groppi, the white priest, shaped this interpretation. At the end of a church service in 1967, when several youth began chanting "Black power's coming, black power," Groppi interrupted to ask, "What do we mean by black power? Does it mean black people over white people?" "No, equal! It means opportunity," they responded, describing the many types of political, economic, and social power needed to change the white-dominant system. "What do we mean by educational power?" Groppi inquired. "We want to get a good education," replied one, and "Negro history," said another. Groppi affirmed both answers, and the youth began chanting again, "Move over whitey, black power," then singing, "We love everybody in our hearts." For these students, the two ideological themes from different halves of the decade—integration and black power—were merged together into one whole in their struggle against white supremacy. In fact, Vada Harris continued to follow this path after leaving Milwaukee to attend Wisconsin State University at Oshkosh, where she and nearly all of the 111 black students on campus were arrested and expelled in 1968 for demanding a stronger black presence at the predominantly white campus in the northern part of the state. For Harris and many others, being an integration pioneer and demanding black history and power were entirely compatible.[35]

Abandoning Integration: Milton Coleman and the Clifford McKissick Community School

To be sure, some former MUSIC activists explicitly discarded integration and embraced black power, in accordance with the familiar abandonment narrative. For instance, a black teen named Milton Coleman taught in MUSIC's Freedom Schools in 1964 and later marched for open housing. Yet by 1969, while enrolled at the University of Wisconsin–Milwaukee where he was a founding member of the Alliance of Black Students, he decided to "forget about white folks and come on back to where we belong." Coleman joined a black Episcopalian priest, Father Kwasi Benefee, in launching the Clifford McKissick Community School, named in memory of the black youth shot by police during the 1967 Milwaukee riot. Unlike other independent community schools, McKissick did not focus on building a sizable regular enrollment. At its peak, only a dozen full-time students and perhaps forty part-timers attended after their regular school or in the evenings. But many of those who came found it to be one of the most important transformative experiences of their lives.[36]

Teenagers and adults both came to McKissick to immerse themselves in black poetry, history, African rituals, and community-building work projects that mainstream schools had failed to deliver. "The operating ideology of McKissick is Pan-Africanism," explained a black weekly news report. "This means that students at McKissick learn of their proud African heritage and the links that exist between people of African descent wherever they may be." Here, Coleman continued to teach black history as he had done in MUSIC's Freedom Schools. Yet while MUSIC's curriculum had been shaped by Morheuser and a large proportion of white teachers, Coleman and McKissick's all-black staff constructed their own history lessons. Teenage students like Fred Hopkins attended North Division High School by day and Clifford McKissick at night. "It opened up a whole new different awareness," he recalled. "It knocked 'Tarzan the King of the Jungle' out of my head and let me know about empires like Kush, algebra, astronomy, great ivory carvings, and our relationship as black folks in America to the continent of Africa." According to Hopkins, many of his conventional teachers at North Division believed that "we were the ones that supposedly didn't want to learn," but he and other black students dispelled that myth at McKissick, where learning became a lifelong journey into one's self and the world.[37]

In Milwaukee, black power embodied more of a cultural awakening than a concrete political agenda. According to local historian William Dahlk, the McKissick Community School was the city's most organized expression of black cultural nationalism since a local chapter of Marcus Garvey's Universal Negro Improvement Association briefly flourished in the early 1930s. Similar educational ventures in the late 1960s included black business training at the House of Truth, lessons in Swahili and African dance at the Soul Shack, the black history collection at the House of Peace, and black plays performed at the Panther's Den. Milwaukee's black Muslims renewed their activism in the early 1960s but did not open their first schools until 1972, when the University of Islam elementary school opened at Muhammad's Temple Number 3 (under the guidance of the Honorable Elijah Muhammad) and the Sister Clara Muhammad School welcomed its students (under the supervision of the World Community of Islam in the West). Out of all of these black cultural institutions, the McKissick Community School became influential by introducing black Milwaukeeans to leading figures in the broader black nationalist and Pan-African movements, such as Detroit's Rev. Albert Cleage and the founder of Malcolm X Liberation University, Owusu Sadaukai (more commonly known to Milwaukeeans as a hometown boy originally named Howard Fuller). Although the school closed its doors in 1974, due to staff turnover and limited funding, it had enlightened black Milwaukeeans from many walks of life for five years. By contrast, the politically oriented Milwaukee branch of the national Black Panther Party lasted for less than one year. After opening their doors in early 1969 and gaining about 100 members, the Milwaukee Panthers attempted to launch a political campaign against police brutality. But one month later, in November 1969, the Panther's Central Committee dissolved the Milwaukee branch for "counter-revolutionary leadership" and opportunism. In Milwaukee, cultural expressions of black power by grass-roots organizations seemed to last much longer than political expressions by national ones.[38]

Unifying the Street and the Courtroom: Lloyd Barbee

Under the direction of attorney-activist Lloyd Barbee, MUSIC served as the umbrella organization for two different types of supporting groups that did not easily coexist: those eager to confront segregation (like Milwaukee CORE and the Wisconsin NAACP) and those more comfortable with advocating change within the system (like the Milwaukee NAACP). In total, over a dozen political, religious, and labor groups (with black, white, and integrated memberships) became sponsoring organizations of MUSIC. Over 100 individuals also became dues-paying members, evenly divided between blacks and whites. Even the Milwaukee Urban League, while not an official MUSIC sponsor, aligned itself with Barbee's school integration movement. Roy Dingham, the white president of the Urban League chapter and vice president of personnel at the A. O. Smith Corporation, called upon the school board to take a stand against school segregation on the grounds that the city "cannot continue to waste its valuable manpower resources." Wesley Scott, the Urban League's executive director, also provided behind-the-scenes organizational support for MUSIC and helped build more diplomatic ties with Barbee on issues facing black teachers. Scott issued a report describing how intact busing impaired not only black student learning but also black teacher effectiveness. While Barbee had collided with black teachers' interests earlier in the decade, they now shared some common cause as the coalition expanded.[39]

MUSIC reached its pinnacle in 1965. Between May and June, over seventy MUSIC protesters (many of them women) were arrested for blocking intact buses, and NBC's *Huntley-Brinkley Report* broadcasted a four-minute segment about MUSIC activism on its national television evening news program. Attorney Barbee filed a federal school desegregation lawsuit on behalf of forty-one schoolchildren, representing both black and white families, the first integrated group of plaintiffs for a legal action of its kind in the nation. Barbee alleged that Milwaukee school officials maintained segregation through its school zone boundaries, construction decisions, transfer policies, intact busing, and teacher assignments. A *Milwaukee Journal* opinion poll stated than more than 80 percent of blacks sympathized with civil rights organizations, and almost 30 percent reported belonging to at least one such group.

When respondents were asked to name the individual who was doing the most for civil rights in Milwaukee, Lloyd Barbee polled the highest at 34 percent. Voters from the city's predominantly black Sixth District had elected him to the Wisconsin State Assembly during the previous fall.[40]

Yet for movement leaders like Barbee, the challenge of the 1960s was not only to build MUSIC but to hold this coalition together during the stresses and strains of the decade. Mass support for MUSIC began to falter in the latter part of 1965. A second boycott in October attracted about 7,000 people, fewer than the 11,500 who had participated in 1964. While it was intended to last a full week, Barbee called it off after three and a half days and publicly declared it a victory. A third MUSIC boycott was postponed twice due to continuing concerns about school officials' disciplinary reprisals against black students. When this final boycott eventually took place, targeted only at North Division High School for one day in March 1966, no more than 500 students participated. Freedom School attendance steadily declined across all three boycotts, and financial contributions to MUSIC's treasury decreased sharply from 1965 to 1967.[41]

One explanation for MUSIC's decline points to its changing mission and organizational structure in light of the political obstacles faced by the school desegregation movement in the mid-1960s. Two years of intensive mass protests may have raised public awareness and produced several favorable reports, but they did not force the conservative school board majority away from their firm stance against racial balancing. Milwaukee resembled other Northern cities in this respect. According to social scientists, the most influential factors regarding the outcome of school desegregation struggles were the ideological composition of the school board and the role played by civic elites and other elected city leaders. Protest tactics alone did not make a significant difference.[42]

Meanwhile, as MUSIC's demonstrations and boycotts dragged on, the 1965 desegregation lawsuit demanded greater attention from the two lead community organizers, Barbee and Morheuser, who also served as the legal team. Originally, Barbee had intended to file the lawsuit during the first school boycott in 1964, but Robert Carter from the national NAACP had sent it back for major revisions. After resolving those issues and filing the lawsuit, the massive research required to prove their court case drained their time and energy. Under Morheuser's leadership, MUSIC shifted its mission from organizing mass community protests to functioning as the headquarters for a small team of legal researchers. They investigated decades of school district files on enrollment patterns, school zoning and construction decisions, and transfer and busing policies. Participatory roles for ordinary black Milwaukeeans to join the freedom struggle through MUSIC declined; the work was now being done by a small number of well-educated and predominantly white individuals. "The movement is not over," Barbee declared to the daily press, "but it has lost its dramatic, eye-catching aspects, which is good because the leaders can concentrate on more serious things." After the 1965 boycott, one group of black families broke off from MUSIC to launch a new organization, the Parents Action Committee for Education (PACE). These parents sought to obtain immediate school integration by working within the existing system to obtain transfers and reassign their children from inner-city schools to those in predominantly white outlying neighborhoods. Most of their activities concentrated on informing parents about the bureaucratic transfer process and raising donations to coordinate bus transportation. While PACE remained affiliated with MUSIC, the group's shift in tactics made clear that the long-term protest strategy was losing mass appeal. In 1966, the remaining MUSIC board members officially restated their organizational purpose. "For too long we have engaged in expensive demonstrations which have provoked studies of the school system," Barbee declared. "With our demonstrations we have indeed educated many people in the city to facts they were unaware of. It is time now, however, to focus on action which will change the system." While MUSIC maintained some involvement in community organizing, such as voter education, its primary focus shifted from mass protests in the streets to courtroom battles between lawyers. At that time, no one knew that the legal battle would last well into the late 1970s.[43]

A second explanation for MUSIC's decline comes from looking more closely at different activists' particular reasons for joining the movement. In addition to the female participants described above, MUSIC also attracted a significant number of black male activists, including some who were drawn to Barbee's bold, confrontational image, perhaps even more than to his integrationist ideology. The school integration movement emerged during an era when Milwaukee's established black leaders negotiated diplomatically with white power brokers behind closed doors. By contrast, Barbee took a vocal stand for civil rights and confronted white racists in public. He established this reputation during his activist years in Madison, then began introducing it to black Milwaukee. In 1962, as president of the Wisconsin NAACP, he condemned the "Uncle Toms" who were frightened by the threat of white violence in the South and slowed down the movement's progress. "The Negro must become aggressive in his efforts for equal opportunities," Barbee wrote, "perhaps even over-aggressive." Looking back on this era, Cecil Brown vividly recalled one of the reasons why he joined MUSIC. "It was wonderful, because it was the first time that the African American community and its supporters set up a new organization that The Man did not control, could not influence, could not intimidate, could not coerce." During another interview, Reuben Harpole (Mildred's husband) pointed to old photographs of MUSIC's predominantly male leadership and praised them for being "tough, tough, tough," yet added that he didn't necessarily agree with their integrationist agenda. Even Barbee's 1964 campaign literature emphasized that he was a "Fighter on all Fronts" and urged voters to "Give yourself a fighter" for the state assembly. Barbee's politics of protest spoke directly to many black Milwaukeeans, especially men, who identified with confrontation rather than accommodation. Crowds of supporters marched with Barbee during MUSIC's peak years of protest, yet by 1967, their interests took them elsewhere. A newer and more exciting confrontation was brewing, as Father Groppi and the Youth Council began their open housing marches into the city's all-white neighborhoods. These young marchers did not abandon the integration movement, since both Barbee and Groppi led protests for that cause. Instead, they simply shifted from one part of the movement to another, searching for its strongest, most intense expression of black liberation.[44]

Rising popular support for calls for "black power" did place integrationists like Barbee on the defensive in the late 1960s, since he sought to maintain political momentum for the school desegregation lawsuit. At times he lashed out against parent groups that he described as willing to settle for "better ghetto schools" and criticized black nationalists for trying to improve schooling without integrating it. Yet Barbee did not dismiss black power. To the contrary, he argued in a 1966 essay that integration and black power, despite their differences, shared much more in common than most people realized. On one side, integrationists believed that dispersing black children throughout the entire school system would improve their access to educational opportunity. On the other side, black power advocates believed that self-determination over the nature of schooling would improve their access to educational opportunity. Yet both strategies faced the same obstacle: majority white domination over the school system. "The dilemma of black control is the dilemma of integration," Barbee wrote, "for it means the ability to have enough weight in the educational system to determine all of the goods and services which will be provided in black schools." Whites remain hostile to both strategies, he argued, "because both mean abdicating power to a dissident group constituting a minority in the school system." Whether blacks advocate for integration or black control, they will continue to be a minority seeking to take political power away from the white-dominated system. "The forces of integration and black control should join together," Barbee concluded. "While integration does not speak in terms of black control, [it] is implicit in the concept, in that black people of the community must band themselves together and determine at one level or another that black students should receive their fair share of the available goods and services." By the early 1970s, Barbee commended the national

Black Panther Party while participating in one of their national conferences in Oakland and regularly contributed a column to the Black Panther newspaper. Thus, in the eyes of Barbee, who brought black Milwaukeeans together in the coalition called MUSIC, even the seemingly polar ideologies of integration and black power could be united into one movement for improving black education.[45]

No one activist's story completely tells the saga of the 1960s. In Milwaukee, the decade is best understood by weaving together the perspectives of both movement spokespeople and ordinary participants. Together, they force us to consider the limitations of the familiar abandonment narrative. Although this literary device does apply to some black Milwaukee activists, like Milton Coleman at the McKissick Community School, it fails to explain the pathways followed by so many others. Juanita Adams and her white friend Arlene Johnson remained firmly dedicated to MUSIC's integrationist vision during the 1960s. From their perspective, they did not leave the movement; it had left them. Others who participated in MUSIC protests, like teacher Mildred Harpole and parent Flo Seefeldt, explained how they were drawn to the movement by their long-standing commitment to improving educational quality and resources, not by the integrationist ideology of its leadership. Still others, like student Vada Harris and attorney Lloyd Barbee, maintained a sense of continuity during the decade by merging integration and black power into their own coherent, unified worldviews.

Once we recognize how these various strands came together to form Milwaukee's school integration movement in the early 1960s, it becomes easier to understand how and why they later unraveled. Barbee and his early supporters focused the black community's attention on key symbols of white racism, such as intact busing and Harold Story, chairman of the Special Committee on Equality of Educational Opportunity. These symbols enabled disparate forces to unite into a broad yet temporary coalition under the umbrella of MUSIC. The organization provided a forum for activists with divergent visions of black education reform. In the Freedom Schools, for example, staunch integrationists could work alongside advocates for black history and proponents of quality black education. Yet political coalitions are never permanent, and new symbols of racism arise while old ones fade in the public's mind. When the school board refused to bend, and when MUSIC's courtroom duties overwhelmed its community-organizing capacity, the ties between different activists came undone, and the activists continued onward in various directions. Movement leaders, like Barbee and Morheuser, devoted their attention to a long legal battle that would last until the late 1970s, while many ordinary activists remained involved with classroom and school-based struggles that offered the possibility of more immediate results. From a traditional historical perspective, it appears on first glance that most black Milwaukeeans abandoned integration. Yet when we listen to activists' own accounts, their movements for black school reform simply evolved, as they had done many times before and would continue to do in decades to come.

6

NEGOTIATING THE POLITICS OF STABILITY

AND SCHOOL DESEGREGATION

I n Milwaukee, as in other cities, the politics of race and school reform have been largely shaped by geography. From the 1930s through the 1950s, the boundaries of the black community were widely recognized as the city's Near Northside neighborhood. The vast majority of Milwaukee's black residents lived there, and schools such as Fourth Street Elementary, Ninth Street Elementary, and eventually North Division High School became centrally identified with the plight of black education. Not all blacks attended these particular schools, but the trajectory of black education reform politics centered around these predominantly black institutions and their students' educational experiences.

By 1970, however, the racial geography had shifted, and it became harder to identify the "black community" and a specific cluster of schools that served it. First, Milwaukee's black population climbed another 68 percent during the 1960s, rising to over 105,000 (or 15 percent of the city total) in 1970. Second, black residents continued to move out of the crowded inner city to neighborhoods in the north and west, such as those feeding into the Washington High School cluster. In 1960, barely 100 black citizens (of all ages) lived in the Washington High district, but this figure rose to over 11,000 by 1970. In the early 1960s, Washington had been a virtually all-white

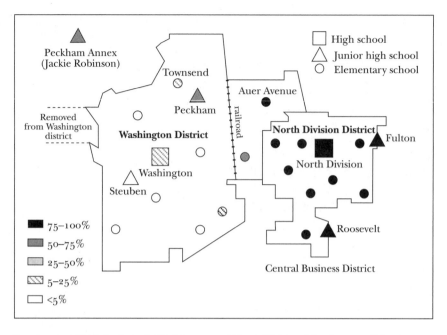

Percentage of Black Students in Washington and North Division Schools, 1970. School reform movements in the 1970s arose around the diverging experiences of blacks in two high school neighborhood areas: the racially transitional Washington High district and the predominantly black North Division district. Adapted from "Map of the City of Milwaukee: Schools," in McEvilly, "Teacher and Student Images," and box 226, folder 2, Barbee Papers.

high school with scarcely any students of color, yet the number of black students rapidly climbed to over 200 by the end of the decade. In these racially charged times, a second black community was forming in Milwaukee with its own vision of school reform tied to common experiences at Washington High.[1]

This chapter draws upon spatial analysis to interpret the stories of activists who were affiliated with two different communities: the inner-city black families committed to improving the all-black North Division High, and the black pioneers who boldly integrated the formerly all-white Washington High. At the beginning of the 1970s, their stories were geographically distinct yet thematically related. In the central city, North Division activists organized to secure a stronger voice in governing their downtrodden institution and to replace the ancient building with a brand-new facility that would serve as an anchor for the impoverished community. On the west side, where alarmist whites perceived a racial invasion at Washington High, black activists worked with white allies to restore calm and negotiate a smoother demographic transition for their neighborhood. In both areas, black activists struggled to reform schools in ways that would bring greater stability to their fragile communities. Yet both groups defined stability in their own way. At North Division, stability meant strengthening the all-black community's role in determining the future of the neighborhood school, while at Washington High, it meant negotiating a stable integration plan that would soothe white anxieties and end the turmoil for pioneering black students there. At the close of the 1970s, after Lloyd Barbee finally settled the fourteen-year school desegregation lawsuit, the stories of North Division and Washington activists came together—and collided due to their conflicting approaches to advancing blacks through schooling, reflecting each community's particular response to shifting patterns of racism.[2]

"Not Wanted" at Washington High School

During the 1960s, white families in the upper-middle-class west-side neighborhood around Washington High praised their school as one of the city's most prestigious academic institutions. It had long been identified as an all-white institution, yet by mid-decade, the student body began to experience a small yet noticeable change in its racial composition. One or two black students enrolled in 1964, followed by a dozen or so over the next two years. In the eyes of many white families on the city's west side, who watched uneasily as civil rights activists rose up in the inner city, these hints of demographic change provoked them to defend their neighborhood schools from perceived threats of a racial invasion.

Early white attempts to contain black students were most readily apparent at the elementary level. When Milwaukee's black population expanded outward from the inner city, many black families moved into the east side of the Washington High district. During the 1960s, the district was composed of eleven elementary schools and divided by a railroad track. Most schools were on the west side of the tracks and remained predominantly white, but those on the east side of the tracks underwent a dramatic transition and became predominantly black. Part of this demographic change can be explained by the individual choices of white families who moved west across the railroad tracks to attend predominantly white elementary schools within the Washington district, or farther out into the western suburbs. Part of the change can also be explained by the higher birth rates of younger black families versus those of older white families. But the racial transformation as a whole cannot be understood without reference to the official actions taken by Milwaukee school authorities to separate black and white students.

Contrasting the stories of two adjacent elementary schools—Townsend Street and Auer Avenue—located on opposite sides of the railroad tracks clarifies the crucial role played by school officials. In the early 1960s, both schools were predominantly white. Auer Avenue School, located on the east side of the tracks (close to the inner city), soon became overcrowded with larger numbers of black families moving into the neighborhood. One solution to relieve overcrowding would have been to redraw the attendance boundary between the Auer Avenue School and its western neighbor, the Townsend Street School, to redistribute a portion of the students. But Milwaukee school officials refused to take this step on the grounds that the railroad tracks served as a "natural or man-made boundary" and a potential hazard for children walking to school. Instead, school officials attempted to relieve overcrowding at Auer Avenue through intact busing. Beginning in 1966, as many as 600 Auer Avenue students were bused daily as intact classrooms to under-utilized schools, where they were taught in separate classrooms rather than mixed in with the general (typically white) population. When overcrowding increased and intact busing became more difficult, school officials took the controversial step of placing twenty portable classrooms on the Auer Avenue School playing field to contain the excess student population. Two years earlier, Chicago school superintendent Benjamin Willis had resigned under pressure for using "Willis Wagons" to contain the black population in his city, but the threat of controversy did not stop Milwaukee officials. Their policies successfully slowed the pace of racial change. By 1970, the black population at Townsend Street School remained only 12 percent, while at the neighboring Auer Avenue School it had risen to nearly 90 percent.[3]

Although racial containment strategies like these succeeded to some extent at the elementary level, they were more difficult to achieve at the secondary level since both white and black elementary schools in the area fed into Washington High. The number of black students attending the formerly all-white high school rose slowly but steadily to about 4 percent in 1968. White families who desperately sought to avoid all contact with black students had limited options. Either they could abandon their prized high school or do their best to make the pioneering black students feel unwelcome. Judging from the racial conflicts that followed in the late 1960s, many whites seem to have chosen the latter.

For the 100 black students at Washington High in 1968, stability meant searching for a positive sense of community and black identity somewhere inside the enormous building where the white majority did not welcome their presence. E'Allyne Perkins, one of the few black teachers at Washington during this period, heard numerous student concerns and printed at least one of them in her weekly advice column in the *Milwaukee Star*, the black weekly newspaper she edited as her second job. "Dear Perki," one letter began, "I go to an integrated school and we never have the chance to be in school plays and things like that. We have to work very, very hard to be in things like the drill team, cheerleaders, and almost anything else. . . . We feel left out of things, and never are made to feel that we are welcome in the school. Some of the kids are mad and want to start a fight with the white kids all the time. I am mad, too, but I don't like to fight. What can we do? Signed, Integrated, but Hated."[4]

In her reply, Perkins urged the black student not to give up her place at Washington. "That is YOUR school, paid for dearly by precious tax dollars from YOUR parents," she reminded her. Perkins then encouraged all black students to walk into the school "with your heads up, with your minds determined, and with the intention of learning everything you can." Whatever happens, Perkins warned, "don't get so disgusted that you transfer from the school. This is precisely what some of those teachers and administrators want!" In her accompanying newspaper editorial, Perkins asserted that, compared to the predominantly black inner-city schools, life was "far worse" for black students at the "so-called integrated schools" because "they are very obviously not wanted" by the many white teachers who make a "subconscious attempt to 'wish' them away."[5]

With Perkins as their faculty adviser, black students at Washington formed an organization named Soul Folk in 1968, which sponsored student plays and musical performances for blacks who rarely felt welcomed into the white-dominated extracurricular activities of the school. At first, Washington's principal gave his approval to the group but changed his mind after it became clear that Soul Folk members wanted to publicize the "unique culture of Black people" throughout the all-white school. Although Soul Folk insisted that their organization was open to all students, it was clearly a black-identified organization and therefore unacceptable to white school authorities. The principal insisted that it become an integrated student organization with a more acceptable name and mission statement. After adding a number of hand-picked white students to the organization, the principal successfully transformed Soul Folk into an interracial organization named Move Together, with the goal of improving race relations within the increasingly tense atmosphere at Washington High. Perkins sharply criticized the principal's actions in the pages of the *Star*, then left her position at Washington High on an extended medical leave.[6]

By the fall of 1969, racial controversies flared into violent confrontations. A fight between a black and a white student erupted into one week of disturbances, injuries, building damage, and police patrols in the hallways. The initial incident had been relatively minor: a white hall monitor reportedly followed school rules by refusing to allow a black student back into the building before the end of the lunch hour. But it had clearly intensified racial divisions. "Large numbers of black and white students use separate doors to enter the school," wrote one observer. "They segregate themselves by choice. . . . It is not uncommon to see halls clear of white students immediately after school is over, militant blacks standing in isolated sections of the building during class periods, or occasional confrontations between blacks and white students that could set off a new series of disturbances."[7]

Black students organized to demand more black history courses, black teachers, and the removal of the police "forces of aggression" from Washington High. Yet many whites dismissed these claims and questioned whether black students even belonged at the school. "The white kids aren't going to like it if there's an all-black faculty," one white student told a reporter. "After all, we're 85 percent of the population here." Another responded, "If they want black history, let them go to King," referring to Rufus King High School, a former academic rival, whose prestige dropped sharply in white eyes after black students enrolled in increasing numbers in the mid-1960s. Some leading white teachers publicly criticized black students' defiant behavior. Helen Goetsch, chair of the social studies department, wrote a letter to the *Milwaukee Journal* criticizing the "loud, crude, vulgar speech of many of the blacks—and their rough, unwarranted militant behavior in absolute defiance of all authority." She described how black students created chaos in the hallways, ignored class bells, and walked around all day wearing hats and coats to challenge teachers' authority. "Education is the fundamental ingredient in black progress for a decent job and for decent housing," Goetsch lectured her readers, and she warned black parents to "please stop this militant behavior or your young people won't get to first base." Anonymous antiblack leaflets distributed around the school predicted that the increasing number of black student "outlaws, muggers, hoodlums and social degenerates" would eventually lead to the "fall of Washington." If whites did not pressure school and city officials to expel and prosecute black students, the leaflets warned, "Washington will become another 'North Division,'" referring to the all-black high school located in the adjacent district.[8]

Washington High supporters rallied to save "their school" from turning into another North Division during redistricting hearings in 1970. In the previous decade, Milwaukee public school enrollments had risen nearly 30 percent to 130,000, the peak figure in the history of the district. Massive overcrowding had prompted school superintendent Richard Gousha to propose a major reorganization of the clusters of feeder schools in the area. His plan called for removing two all-white elementary schools on the west side of Washington High and adding ninth graders from an overcrowded junior high school that drew students from the predominantly black east side of the district. Overall, the redistricting proposal would increase black enrollments at Washington High from 12 percent to as much as 25 percent while maintaining a nearly all-white population at Marshall High School, located farther northwest. Rev. Paul Larsen, chairman of the Washington Parent-Teacher-Student Organization, warned a meeting of 150 members that the proposed boundary shift would "quickly extend Milwaukee's existing ghetto" and "hasten the deterioration of still another desirable part of our city." The PTSO membership responded with a unanimous vote to oppose the redistricting plan, gathered over 6,000 signatures in one weekend, and held a subsequent opposition meeting attended by more than 1,000 people. Over 95 percent of the faculty signed a petition against the redistricting, stating that they did "not want the social, the cultural, and the moral character of present and future Washington High School students to be jeopardized." Their words expressed the same concerns as those identified by researchers like Gerald Grant at other formerly all-white elite public high schools in the urban North.[9]

Despite these arguments, the school board faced overwhelming enrollment pressures and voted in favor of redistricting Washington High. By 1971, the proportion of black students rose higher than predicted to over 30 percent. Racial tensions peaked again as violence flared between students, teachers, principals, and police. White flight became more apparent across the city as a whole; the 1970 census reported a loss of over 70,000 whites (down 10 percent) over the previous decade. Some Washington High supporters sought increased school security forces as a solution to the problem. But a new group of black and white neighborhood activists took a different approach. Rather than fighting to maintain all-white schools, they began exploring how to integrate schools in ways that would maintain some degree of racial stability within their tense and fragile community.[10]

STRIVING FOR STABLE INTEGRATION

As times became more uncertain in Washington's transitional neighborhoods, some residents searched for a new approach to address underlying racial anxieties. In Sherman Park, a predominantly German-Jewish neighborhood located east of the high school, six liberal white couples came together in 1970 to create a new organization. The Sherman Park Community Association took the lead in promoting stable integration for both the neighborhood and local schools. Members lobbied against aggressive realtors' tactics such as blockbusting, where agents pressured whites to sell at low prices when the first black family moved onto the block, then profited by reselling those homes to more black families at higher prices. The association urged other white residents not to sell out but to stay and accept life in an increasingly diverse community. At the same time, members also spoke out against the construction of a new north-south freeway to the west of

Marian McEvilly (center, with dark-rimmed glasses) lobbied the school board for a desegregation plan to promote racial stability at Washington High. From *Milwaukee Courier*, 23 February 1974; courtesy of Milwaukee Courier/Star, Inc.

their neighborhood, which many believed would replace the racial boundary created by the railroad tracks and thus push their neighborhood deeper into the geography of the predominantly black inner city. Peter Mazurek, the association's president, acknowledged that his group walked a very fine line between accepting racial change and maintaining the status quo. "If we talk about stability, blacks think we are trying to keep them out. If we talk about integration, we make some whites nervous. They think we are trying to bring blacks in." So the Sherman Park activists blended the two ideas into one rhetorical strategy, emphasizing how a steady, gradual acceptance of racial change would preserve their neighborhood stability.[11]

When Marian McEvilly joined the Sherman Park Community Association in 1971, she was gladly welcomed into a group that had previously been all white. Raised in Gary, Indiana, McEvilly had attended segregated schools, until she moved to Milwaukee in 1963 and later that decade settled in the Sherman Park neighborhood. She soon became chairperson of the association's education committee and a leading spokesperson for its unique stance that carefully planned racial integration could bring stability to the group's transitional neighborhood. In many ways, McEvilly's family represented the new ideals of the association: she was black; her husband, John, was white; and both were well-educated, respectable, progressive citizens. McEvilly worked as the general manager of the *Milwaukee Star* black weekly newspaper, studied sociology as a graduate student at the University of

Wisconsin–Milwaukee, and parented a son who attended Washington High School.[12]

McEvilly spent many hours at Washington High, both as a parent volunteer and as a researcher for her master's thesis on racially transitional schools. She objected to school supporters who proposed simply hiring security guards to resolve racial tensions, because her observations confirmed that students' perceptions of safety inside the school were intimately linked to racially unstable social changes on the outside. White residents cautiously watched their neighbors in the Washington area, always fearful that if one white family moved out, it might spark panic selling that would leave them in an all-black neighborhood almost overnight. McEvilly spent a year working on human relations programs to ease tensions at Washington but soon became convinced that such piecemeal solutions were not sufficient. Instead, the best way to deal with fears of racial instability in the neighborhood was to address them head-on with a comprehensive integration plan. "The problem [that] we have got to face up to is race," McEvilly realized. "We should integrate these children before they get to Washington High School, then we [won't] have all of this turmoil between blacks and whites."[13]

McEvilly believed that racial conflict at Washington High might be averted by integrating students at an earlier age. By 1972, the two junior high schools that fed students into Washington were racially polarized. At Peckham Junior High, which drew students from the east side of the district, the black population had risen from 30 to over 90 percent in only four years. It quickly became a predominantly black school located in a predominantly white neighborhood. Meanwhile, at Steuben Junior High, which drew from the predominantly white west side, the black population had only grown to 9 percent during the same period of time. Sherman Park activists charged that the racial differences were not caused simply by residential patterns. Instead, they pointed to Milwaukee's open enrollment policy, which the school board had approved as a partial response to school desegregation protesters in 1964. Open enrollment broadened the potential for students to transfer from one school zone to another, if space was available and if they provided their own transportation. In theory, some desegregation activists had favored the policy in the mid-1960s as a way to promote racial balancing, but it had the opposite effect by the early 1970s as disproportionate numbers of whites requested transfers from Peckham to Steuben. "Every white kid in my neighborhood takes the [city] bus to get out of the neighborhood," complained McEvilly's husband, John, whose family lived near Peckham. School officials reported that if all of the white neighborhood children had remained at Peckham, the black student population would have risen only to 60 percent. But open enrollment facilitated white flight from the local school without requiring families to sell their homes. The Sherman Park Community Association criticized the policy for reducing white families' sense of commitment to their local junior high school and destabilizing the neighborhood as a whole.[14]

Marian McEvilly and the Sherman Park Community Association called upon the Milwaukee school board to address this racial instability, and the board responded by chartering the Washington Cluster Committee to propose a solution. The Cluster Committee was composed of delegates from all of the neighborhood schools feeding into the district, and McEvilly was elected chairperson. Meetings were dominated primarily by concerns about preventing schools from reaching the "tipping point" (around 40 percent black), when residents felt most white neighbors would panic and leave. One-third of the Cluster Committee delegates were black, though black families from predominantly white Sherman Park participated more regularly than those from the predominantly black Auer Avenue neighborhood. For many people, McEvilly's voice soon came to represent the leading black perspective in the Washington High district. According to white reporters, McEvilly did not seem to be offended by "the idea that the city and the schools must be 'saved' from becoming in parts all-black."[15]

McEvilly guided the Washington Cluster Committee through proposals for promoting neighborhood stability in the midst of a racially changing environment. In her mind, whether whites supported or opposed the concept of school integration was irrelevant. Regardless of these opinions, black students from Peckham and whites from Steuben were already being mixed together during tenth grade at Washington High. The common goal for the Cluster Committee, in McEvilly's opinion, was to prevent this sudden "culture shock" by creating a more peaceful transition to interracial education at the junior high school level. Therefore, McEvilly and a majority of the delegates drafted bold proposals for the school board in 1973. First, the Cluster Committee called for freezing all student transfers both in and out of schools in the Washington district in order to reduce destabilization caused by the open enrollment policy. Second, it proposed to pair Steuben and Peckham Junior High Schools for desegregation. Seventh graders from both schools would attend Steuben together, then advance as eighth graders to Peckham. Over time, increasing numbers of ninth graders from the paired schools would begin their studies at Washington High. But McEvilly did not have unanimous support within the Cluster Committee. A minority faction of white delegates quickly organized to oppose the proposals, and the ensuing controversy strongly resembled the fury over redistricting Washington High only a few years earlier. Russell Audi, president of the Parent-Teacher-Student Organization at Steuben, circulated a flyer calling on parents to challenge any proposal that would be "*forcing* your children to attend Peckham," the school from which many whites had fled. "Don't allow others to DICTATE where your children will be educated!" he warned.[16]

Opponents of school desegregation prevailed yet again. Although the Milwaukee school board had originally chartered the Washington Cluster Committee to propose its own resolution to the problem, the board voted against its recommendations for freezing transfers and pairing the junior high schools. White supporters of racial containment maintained control over "their" schools once again, but this time black parents lost control over theirs. To resolve overcrowding among black students at Peckham, the school board voted to bus seventh graders to another building rather than integrate them at Steuben. The new Peckham annex was located more than thirty blocks away, outside of the Washington district, in a former Catholic high school and adjoining garage that had been converted into classroom space. Later, the annex was renamed the Jackie Robinson Middle School in honor of the first black major league baseball player to break the color line. The choice of name was bitterly ironic, since the school board created the annex to avoid racial integration.[17]

After their proposals were defeated, McEvilly and her black and white supporters publicly resigned from the Washington Cluster Committee to call attention to the school board's disgraceful decision. In her resignation letter, McEvilly criticized the "forced busing" language of white opponents to the pairing plan to underscore the hypocrisy of applying it to only one segment of the population. "If Peckham is unfit for white children," she argued, "black children should not be forced to attend the school," nor forced out on buses to a distant, substandard annex. While the school board defended the right of white opponents of the Cluster Committee proposal to make choices for their own children, it gave little consideration to parents who were "unable to make choices" due to the expense of transportation for a transfer, moving to a new home, or tuition at a private school.[18]

The setback taught McEvilly a hard lesson that would shape her activism for years to come. White panic over "forced busing" sent an entire year's worth of biracial committee work down the drain. Although pairing the two junior high schools would have treated both races fairly, powerful whites successfully blocked any proposal that would jeopardize white rights to attend the predominantly white schools of their choice. McEvilly eagerly awaited September 1973, when Lloyd Barbee's desegregation trial was slated to begin; she would testify on behalf of the plaintiffs. But if Barbee were successful at persuading the court to mandate desegregation, the real challenge would shift to the negotiating table, where the details would need to be worked out for a plan that incorporated whites without causing them to disrupt—or abandon—the Milwaukee schools. McEvilly refused to give in to conservative white demands, but she now recognized the need to deal with their concerns to maintain the racial (and financial) stability of schools in the Washington district.

SEEKING VOICE AND STABILITY AT NORTH DIVISION

By contrast, maintaining racial stability was no longer a concern for black activists in the North Division High School. Nearly all whites had fled from the thirteen neighborhood schools in this district, whose boundaries lay within the official "Inner Core" perimeter. During the late 1950s, the neighborhood's flagship institution, North Division, had transitioned from a predominantly white to a predominantly black high school. Even though whites made up 37 percent of the population in census tracts around North Division in 1960, the percentage of black students rose to over 99 percent in 1963, due to white families obtaining school transfers and to black families with larger numbers of children moving in. By 1970, nearly all white families had abandoned the North Division neighborhood as well, and the black population in surrounding census tracts rose to 91 percent. The concerns of education reform activists in this neighborhood were therefore quite different from those of the Washington High district.[19]

North Division supporters demanded that white school officials grant them a stronger voice in determining how to improve the quality of education for black students from their community. Specifically, these activists called for incorporating black history into the curriculum, increasing community control over neighborhood schools, and seating black representatives on the citywide school board. During the late 1960s and early 1970s, black protesters occasionally forced school officials to respond to their demands, but real power still eluded them. Milwaukee administrators often subverted activists' original aims by granting them the appearance of authority while maintaining a strong degree of control over black children's schooling.

Struggles over teaching black history illustrated the power dynamics between activists and administrators at North Division. In February 1968, over a thousand black students at several city high schools, including North Division, staged walkouts to protest the absence of black history in the curriculum. Their complaints followed in the footsteps of prior efforts to include black history, led by William Kelley and the Milwaukee Urban League Community Center in the 1930s, Lloyd Barbee and MUSIC's Freedom Schools in the mid-1960s, Vada Harris and the textbook turn-in at Riverside High in 1967, and the innovative curricula of independent community schools such as Harambee and Clifford McKissick in the late 1960s. In response, the

Milwaukee central office curriculum planners quickly produced a mimeographed booklet, *The Negro in American Life*, designed to supplement the standard eleventh grade U.S. history textbook. Although black students had expressed a strong desire for an integrated text, meaning one volume that included the histories of all racial groups in America, administrators explained that this demand could not easily be accommodated. Even if major textbook publishers had such an item on the market, the school district's five-year cycle for textbook adoption, required by state law, constrained their efforts. Not all students were pleased with these answers. One unnamed black male student criticized the mimeograph as nothing more than a "comic book. And all that's in it are black achievements within the last ten to fifteen years. We know all about that stuff already." Yet for the most part, the booklet seemed to quiet the immediate crisis, and curriculum planners encouragingly noted that "pupils seem to have accepted the 'companion volume' as an interim measure."[20]

Although school officials allowed black history into the curriculum, they continued to maintain very tight control over how it was defined and who would teach it. At North Division, a black teacher named Jake Beason responded to student demands by introducing his own course for seniors titled "Africa in Perspective," which examined the relationships between African history and modern black America. Beason decided that the textbook assigned by central office planners was inadequate, so he supplemented the course with readings adapted from his graduate studies at Roosevelt University, a guest instructor in Swahili from Kenya, and a field trip to experience self-reliance among black Muslims in Chicago. The objective of the course, Beason explained, was to teach his students that "Afro-Americans are descendants of great civilizations." He also reminded school administrators and teachers of their "tremendous responsibility to dispel the distortions, the misunderstandings, and the misrepresentations that cause white people to feel superior and black people to feel inferior."[21]

Although many North Division students and parents praised Beason's work, both white and black school officials moved to stop him. Central office administrators claimed that Beason was "advocating anarchy and teaching hate." North Division's first black principal, Lloyd Howell, who had recently been hired from Mississippi's segregated system, gave Beason an unfavorable evaluation and requested that he be transferred. Rising to Beason's defense, many students questioned why their favorite instructor at North Division, "the only teacher there who knew he was black," was being punished. Rose Benning, chair of the North Division Parents Group for Quality Education, observed that "German, French, Spanish, and Latin are being taught in schools. But now that we want black history, they are accusing him of teaching hate." Despite these protests, Beason was involuntarily transferred to another predominantly black school, Lincoln High, where the principal issued him a second unsatisfactory evaluation. In 1970, the assistant superintendent of personnel ordered Beason to appear at a dismissal hearing to respond to charges that he had "ignored scope and sequence" in his teaching, engaged in "excessive lecturing," and "failed to exercise leadership and class control" in study halls. Beason's numerous supporters charged that school officials had singled him out for daring to teach an unauthorized interpretation of black history, which emphasized connections to Africa and racial solidarity rather than assimilation into white America. After a black school boycott and a prolonged series of hearings over two years, Beason finally won reinstatement as a teacher, but not to his former position at North Division. While school officials did respond to the general demand for black history, they retained considerable power over how it was taught.[22]

Black efforts to exert a stronger voice in local school governance over the North Division district were also thwarted. For several years, neighborhood parents and activists had complained about their limited role in shaping the school policies and practices. In response to this criticism, Milwaukee officials submitted an experimental school decentralization proposal to the federal government, which resulted in a three-year $900,000 grant in 1968. The plan created a model subsystem of school governance for the cluster of all-black neighborhood schools feeding into North Division. In some ways, it resembled the community control efforts also underway in the East Harlem and Ocean Hill–Brownsville neighborhoods of New York City. According to the Milwaukee proposal, residents of the North Division district would elect four community representatives to serve on an advisory council along with four principals, four teachers, another teacher representing students, and two administrators. Together, the advisory council would exercise "considerable latitude for local school decisions" under a framework established by Superintendent Gousha and the citywide school board. In theory, increased parental involvement and local autonomy would overcome centralized regulatory obstacles, presumably leading to improved educational programs and higher student achievement. The North Division subsystem model soon became a public relations cornerstone in Gousha's broader effort to decentralize school administration across the entire city.[23]

Yet black Milwaukeeans who supported the concept of community control criticized the subsystem plan as a fraud. First, it had been created entirely by the school administration without consultation from the community that was supposedly empowered by the plan. At one of the first public meetings, held nearly four months after the proposal had been submitted for funding, North Division parents sharply criticized subsystem planners for failing to include them in its development. Some charged that the proposal had been illegally funded, since federal regulations mandated parental involvement in its creation. "My name is in this proposal as a member of the superintendent's advisory committee," complained one mother. "It got there because I attended a meeting months ago on an entirely different matter. I didn't even know that this proposal existed." Second, critics charged that the subsystem failed to grant "real power" to parents, since their four seats on the advisory council were outnumbered by eleven other voting members, all of them school system employees. Moreover, any resolutions approved by the subsystem board were merely nonbinding advisory recommendations that might or might not be sent up a long chain of command to the superintendent and school board. Activist Flo Seefeldt and the United Community Action Group, whose own proposal for school-based community control had been blocked by school officials, called the plan "a trick to keep black students in bad schools while making black parents think they have some influence in running the schools." Another parent sarcastically complained that "we are supposed to jump at the chance to have anything that hints of black control, good or bad." The subsystem model would force black parents to wade through "unnecessary layers of administrators and advisors," they argued, rather than allow them to directly voice their complaints to the school board, which held the real power. National observers criticized the dependent subsystem model as "more of the same" without the accountability of genuine community control.[24]

Nevertheless, Milwaukee administrators launched the flawed subsystem decentralization experiment, and a number of North Division supporters eventually decided that it was in their best interest to participate. A storefront administrative office was established in the North Division neighborhood to act as a liaison between area residents and the distant central school office. Federal funds were primarily used to pay the expenses of involving parents and additional staff to develop new educational programs, such as a reading program. Three years later, Rev. Joseph McNeil, chairman of the North Division Advisory Council, looked back and acknowledged that "there were a lot of growing pains, but there were also a lot of frank expressions and exchanges. And as a result, we got some movement." But the Milwaukee school district's formal evaluation concluded that the decentralization experiment had done little to raise test scores or participants' perceptions of their own roles in the decision-making process. When federal funds ran out in 1972, the Milwaukee school board refused to carry the program in its own budget. The powers that had created school decentralization for black Milwaukee—without initial community input—now let it die.[25]

Amid these debates over school governance, new reports surfaced about the quality of education received at North Division. Similar concerns had been heard many years earlier, when whites had fled the high school in the late 1950s and when blacks had criticized the diminished curriculum and uncaring teachers at the Story Committee hearings in the early 1960s. But new evidence appeared in 1972, when the school board voted to release standardized test score data to the public. Compared to other city high schools, North Division students had the lowest combined test scores, approximately 75 percent below average norms in reading and mathematics. The school also had the second lowest attendance rate (80 percent) and the second lowest rate of teachers with six years or more experience (37 percent). Additional reports, using longitudinal data from the 1960s, noted that test scores of inner-city children steadily declined as they moved through elementary school. At North Division High, while black students' scores increased somewhat when they entered the tenth grade, the result was temporary at best. North Division still had the lowest standardized test scores among all high schools in the city.[26]

The question, of course, was, What should be done about North Division High? Integration activists, such as Lloyd Barbee, had called for black students to be dispersed into the white school population so that they would receive the same resources and benefits as white students. Although the school board had refused to accept his proposal, many blacks did leave the North Division district on their own. From 1960 to 1970, the population in the neighborhood census tracts declined by 2,000 black residents (5 percent). Some of them moved into housing that became available to the north and west, particularly in the adjacent Washington High district. But several of those who remained in the neighborhood, either by choice or circumstance, became North Division supporters in the 1970s. Dispersal into the white population was not part of their agenda. Instead, these activists wanted to strengthen and rebuild their impoverished community, and they turned their attention to the key centralizing institution in their neighborhood—the local high school.[27]

North Division High School, originally constructed in 1907, was one of the oldest facilities in the city, and supporters lobbied hard for a new building. History teacher Jake Beason and community members Rose Benning and Reverend McNeil began working together on the issue in the late 1960s. "We all must face the reality that even if a fair housing law or any other Utopia would come to pass," Beason declared, "there would still be a need for quality schools to serve the approximately 30,000 children in the Inner Core–North. Most of the residents would find it difficult to handle the cost of living in the suburbs and outer city." McNeil, who chaired the North Division Parent Teacher Organization and served on the subsystem advisory board, spoke out on his preference for a new type of facility. "It must not be just a new building," he cautioned. "It must be an integral part of the total community." McNeil envisioned a building that served as a school during daytime and as a community center during late afternoons, evenings, and weekends. McNeil's interest in designing a building to serve both purposes was motivated not simply by cost efficiency but by his goals of strengthening ties between school personnel and neighborhood families and of encouraging parental involvement to combat low-performing schools.[28]

North Division students played an active role in mobilizing support for a new school. During his freshman year in 1968–69, Fred Hopkins attended Washington High, but the white hostility he encountered led him to walk the extra distance and transfer to North Division. Between the two schools, he recalled years later, "you could easily see the inequities" in curriculum, staffing, and physical structure. "There were many times while we were in North Division that we would have to leave because the wiring in the walls would start smoking. . . . If that is not enough of an issue to get you involved, I don't know what is." Hopkins joined several adults on the North Division School-Community Committee, but deliberations over site selection dragged on for two years. Black advocates had divided opinions. Some argued for rebuilding North Division at its current location, which they believed would assist the neighborhood economy, where black unemployment rates eventually rose to 20 percent, the highest in the nation, reported the *New York Times*. Others insisted on relocating the school to a site near Carver Park, about halfway between the current site and the downtown business area, where there was more space and better highway access for buses, if North Division were to be desegregated at some point in the future. Anxious to end the prolonged debate, student council president Yolanda Love led 400 classmates in a walkout to protest the delay in 1973. "We want a high school that looks like someone cares," she insisted, adding that North Division lacked "even half the facilities or room that other Milwaukee public schools have." Political pressures mounted as the physical condition of the building deteriorated. Finally, after the intervention of white school board member Anthony Busalacchi, labeled a conservative by many, a deal was made to erect the new North Division on a site adjacent to the old school, within the heart of the black neighborhood.[29]

The long series of struggles over the future of North Division taught supporters an important lesson. White school officials could not be fully trusted to honor both the letter and the spirit of black demands for improving the quality of education at North Division. Time and time again, blacks perceived their reform agendas to be subverted by powerful interests bent on holding back the advancement of the race. After years of organizing for better schooling, North Division activists had one tangible achievement to show for their efforts: a new school. Groundbreaking ceremonies for the $15 million state-of-the-art facility began in December 1975. Although the new building would not be finished for another two years, North Division supporters kept a vigilant watch on their prized possession. If white school

Student Council president Yolanda Love (left) and concerned student Brent White objected to the deteriorating conditions at North Division, calling all sides to reach agreement on a site for constructing the new school. From *Milwaukee Courier*, 28 April 1973; courtesy of Milwaukee Courier/Star, Inc.

officials dared to make any attempt to take it away from them, they would not give it up without a fight.[30]

Taking Milwaukee Schools to Court

While black activists from Washington and North Division worked to improve schooling in their respective neighborhoods, attorney Lloyd Barbee continued pushing the long-awaited school desegregation lawsuit to a courtroom trial. The case, initially known as *Amos v. Board*, was named after Craig Amos, from the alphabetical listing of forty-one black and white schoolchildren whose families had signed on as plaintiffs in 1965. Since filing the suit, it had consumed about half of Barbee's time and diverted him from his regular law practice and elected duties as a state legislator. Marilyn Morheuser, the lead researcher, worked full-time on the case from 1966 to 1970, receiving only a token salary from MUSIC fund-raisers and private donations. Together, with the assistance of several volunteers, Morheuser and Barbee systematically researched the case against the Milwaukee public schools. During the early years of the movement, MUSIC activists documented that the number of predominantly black schools had increased in the city, from four in 1940, to seven in 1950, to twenty-three in 1964. Yet merely demonstrating the existence of predominantly black schools was insufficient. The plaintiffs had the burden of proving that school officials had intentionally maintained or fostered racial segregation through their policies and practices on intact busing, student transfers, boundary changes, new construction, and personnel decisions, and that required digging through decades of paperwork stored at the three-story central school office.[31]

Barbee and Morheuser faced tremendous obstacles while researching the *Amos* case. First, Milwaukee officials claimed that student and teacher racial demographics had not been collected until 1964, when MUSIC had insisted upon it, so the plaintiffs had to resort to class photographs and census materials to reconstruct racial data back to 1950. Second, Milwaukee school administrators slowed down the pace of the investigation by releasing only the exact documents requested rather than allowing researchers to browse through files. Third, defense lawyers attempted to block access to personnel records on transfers and promotions, arguing that these were confidential matters, and only relented after receiving a court order to cooperate. Finally, when Barbee and Morheuser had prepared several legal exhibits and were ready for a trial in 1970, defense attorneys stalled the proceedings for several months by arguing that they had no way of verifying the accuracy of items that had been compiled from their clients' own records.[32]

Even Barbee's allies sometimes ran up against him. The national NAACP had spent over $60,000 on the *Amos* case, mostly to support the work of attorney Joan Franklin Mosley from the NAACP Legal Defense Fund. But the two national organizations clashed over other matters in 1969, leading to the resignation of Robert Carter, who was Barbee's primary contact, from the Legal Defense Fund. As legal expenses continued to pile up in Milwaukee, national NAACP executive director Roy Wilkins complained to attorney Mosley that "the *Amos* case has become a Frankenstein monster. . . . There does not appear to have been any effort by the NAACP forces in Wisconsin to rally behind the *Amos* case. . . . The people have not been rallied to its support." Although the national NAACP had originally inspired Barbee to join its campaign against school segregation in the North and West during the early 1960s, Wilkins withdrew financial support from the Milwaukee case in 1969 and privately recommended that Barbee drop the entire lawsuit. Barbee refused and continued onward without the national NAACP.[33]

Yet the truth was that the decline of MUSIC's protest coalition had made it very difficult for Barbee to keep the plaintiffs united from the mid-1960s into the early 1970s. Even the family of Craig Amos, the black child for whom the original case was named, had grown doubtful. His father, Prince Amos, conceded during an interview in 1973 that if he had it to do again, he probably would not join the lawsuit. "Integrated schools are fine," at least in the abstract, Prince Amos told a reporter, but in practice, "integration has been rejected by whites." He told people to "look at all of the court suits that are still trying to implement the 1954 decision," which proved to him that whites "had never accepted [integration] in the first place." As Barbee recalled, Amos told him that "the white man . . . isn't going to do right by us" and then decided to have no further contact with the case.

While some plaintiffs distanced themselves because they no longer held out hope for integration, Barbee failed to keep contact with others. Rochelle Savage joined MUSIC's protests in 1964 and knew Barbee through her father, Aaron Toliver, a black Milwaukee labor activist since the 1940s. She and her husband, Roosevelt, agreed to sign their children on as plaintiffs to Barbee's complaint in 1965. But as the case dragged on into the 1970s, the gap widened between the legal proceedings and their everyday lives, hers as a paraprofessional aide at the predominantly black Palmer Street School and his as a minister of a black church. Over the years, the Savages recalled hearing from Barbee only on two or three occasions. "That was something that really disturbed me," she confided in an interview years later. "We never got together with Lloyd Barbee, we never knew the results, we never knew anything about it." In fact, after the Amos children left the Milwaukee public schools, the lawsuit was eventually renamed *Armstrong v. O'Connell*, with Rochelle Savage's sons, Kevin and Kraig Armstrong, as first plaintiffs. (Their surnames came from her previous marriage.) But during an interview years later, the boys' father, Roosevelt Savage, expressed surprise, since he had never heard of this fact, and their mother only vaguely remembered reading it in the newspaper at the time. In any case, the family clearly did not form a lasting identity as plaintiffs on the school desegregation lawsuit. While Barbee's attention was consumed by preparing for the trial, the evolving school integration movement had gone in one direction and Rochelle Savage's family in another.[34]

Barbee pursued the desegregation lawsuit amid a politically hostile climate in the early 1970s. In President Nixon's executive branch, the "Southern Strategy" to win Republican voters derailed much federal activity in school desegregation litigation and enforcement. Wisconsin's two Democratic U.S. senators split their votes on a racially charged bill against "forced busing" in 1972. Even closer to home, Wisconsin's first black state senator, Monroe Swan, a Democrat elected from the inner city, publicly opposed integration in 1973. "I think a lot of people realize now that integration is more myth than reality," Swan announced. "Not only can it not be achieved, but it is no longer desirable on the part of a lot of people," he contended.

A majority of black voters continued to return Barbee and his integration agenda to the state legislature through the mid-1970s. But over time, he became more vulnerable by taking political positions at the forefront of the most controversial issues of his day. He proposed that Wisconsin repeal laws on "victimless crimes" and thereby legalize abortion, gambling, homosexuality, prostitution, and marijuana use. He called for lowering the voting age and reducing all maximum prison terms to five years. Mainstream Democrats and Republicans called him "the outrageous Mr. Barbee" and often dismissed his proposals as "immoral," "weird," or "crazy," even though some were accepted by the state over time. Barbee ignored these critics and defined his legislation as a serious campaign to serve the rights of marginalized people. "I take the initiative, and the Assembly has to respond to it," Barbee declared. "I educate as I legislate."[35]

On the eve of Milwaukee's school desegregation trial in September 1973, Barbee's legal team abruptly resigned over a bitter dispute about courtroom strategy. Joan Franklin Mosley, the black former NAACP attorney who continued working on the case even after her employer stopped funding it, strongly disagreed with Barbee over who should question the expert witnesses. Her opinion was shared by Marilyn Morheuser, the longtime MUSIC activist and Barbee's closest white colleague, who had earned her law degree while researching the case. Both Mosley and Morheuser walked away from Barbee's legal team. Morheuser moved to New Jersey, where she continued her legal activism on urban education for the next two decades, though shifting from racial integration to school finance reform. Officially, MUSIC was still alive. But without Morheuser, whose work had carried the organization through the past several years, the mass organization diminished to a small handful of supporters whose primary function was to publicize the upcoming trial. Barbee's circle of activists was growing smaller and smaller.[36]

The long delay in starting Milwaukee's courtroom trial—over eight years since the lawsuit had originally been filed—brought two important legal changes in Barbee's favor. First, after several years of assertive decisions on Southern desegregation cases, the U.S. Supreme Court ruled on *Keyes v. Denver* in June 1973, only months before Barbee's trial began. It was the Court's first major school desegregation case involving Northern or Western states, where there had been no law (or de jure segregation) requiring the separation of race, as had been the case in most Southern and border states. When the *Keyes* plaintiffs charged that Denver schools were segregated, the school board blamed the problem on residential patterns, or de facto segregation. Yet when the Court examined the evidence, it ruled that the Denver school board had intentionally confined black residents by its policy actions on student transfers, school boundaries, new school construction, and the use of mobile classrooms. In addition, the Supreme Court ruled that if intentional segregation was proven to exist on one part of the Denver school system, then the Court could assume that segregation in other parts of the system was not simply caused by residential patterns. In other words, if Barbee could prove that Milwaukee officials had intentionally segregated one part of the city schools, then the burden of proof would fall on the defendants' lawyers to show that the whole system was not segregated in the same way. A second favorable legal development caused by the delay was the transfer of the trial to the courtroom of U.S. district judge John Reynolds, former Democratic governor and attorney general of Wisconsin, who had actively sought black Milwaukee votes while campaigning in 1962 and who was perceived as being liberal on racial issues. After years of facing political and legal obstacles, Milwaukee's school integration movement would receive a fair (and perhaps sympathetic) hearing.[37]

Barbee opened the trial with testimonies from several black parents, teachers, and former students who had personally experienced school segregation. Ivory Watkins, one of the original black plaintiffs who had stayed with the suit, began by testifying about the conditions her three children had encountered at segregated Milwaukee schools in the 1960s. Another witness, Washington High activist Marian McEvilly, described more recent efforts by the school board to maintain segregation in her racially transitional neighborhood. But the key expert witness was Robert Stuckert, who had been McEvilly's professor of sociology at the University of Wisconsin–Milwaukee. Under Barbee's questioning, Stuckert walked the court through mountains of statistical data and more than 500 exhibits documenting patterns of intentional segregation by school officials.

After the initial fanfare in September 1973, the trial slowly inched along over the next five months. Courtroom spectators dropped to no more than twenty-five regulars. Newspaper reporters, eager for good stories, seemed disappointed by the second week. "The testimony has generally been less than exciting," one wrote, "with spectators sometimes nodding off to sleep and even the judge occasionally yawning." Reynolds tried to speed the trial along, at times calling on everyone to take a brief stretch break or join him in a brisk walk around the courtroom rather than calling a longer recess. The trial continued through October, then recessed until January 1974; closing arguments were heard in February. Then the wait continued while the court pondered its ruling.[38]

Judge Reynolds waited two years before issuing his ruling, perhaps to give school board members an opportunity to change their ways voluntarily. Apparently, they had not done enough. The court issued its first ruling in favor of the plaintiffs in January 1976. "I have concluded that segregation exists in the Milwaukee public schools," Reynolds wrote, "and that this segregation was intentionally created and maintained by the defendants." Detailed research on the past twenty-five years of school board policy and practice had persuaded him to accept Barbee's charge of deliberate segregation. For example, Judge Reynolds found that the student transfer policy "facilitated the flight of white families from black schools" prior to the "comparable departure of white residents from black neighborhoods." School boundaries were most often drawn with the effect of increasing the concentration of black students rather than decreasing it. The board attempted to relieve overcrowding with intact busing rather than other practices that would have mixed children of different races together. The board also constructed large additions to inner-city schools that contained black student population growth rather than new schools in areas that would promote racial balance. For each of their actions, Milwaukee school authorities could supply a nondiscriminatory explanation. But in their totality, over a long period of time, the court ruled that they constituted "a consistent and deliberate policy of racial isolation and segregation."[39]

Judge Reynolds instituted a three-year school desegregation plan to be overseen by the court's special master, John Gronouski. Reynolds sought to strengthen white Milwaukee's acceptance of the ruling by appointing Gronouski, a former Wisconsin state politician, postmaster general, and U.S. ambassador to Poland. In a subsequent ruling, Reynolds also issued numerical goals. To be in compliance, black student enrollments in one-third of Milwaukee schools needed to fall between 25 to 45 percent in 1976–77 with the remaining two-thirds of the schools meeting that goal over the next two years. Continuing their legal defense of neighborhood schools, the Milwaukee school board voted to appeal Judge Reynolds's decision all the way to the U.S. Supreme Court. But on a pragmatic level, even prior to the court ruling, an increasing number of moderate school board members had moved closer toward the inevitable by beginning to negotiate the politics of a school desegregation plan.[40]

Negotiating the Politics of School Desegregation

Milwaukee's racial landscape changed considerably during the eleven years between the origin of the lawsuit and Judge Reynolds's first ruling. First, studies confirmed that the system had become one of the most segregated in the urban North. Out of 158 schools, over 100 were racially segregated, meaning that more than 90 percent of their students were of one race. Second, the percentage of black students in the system had risen from 21 to 34 percent by the 1975–76 school year, and future projections anticipated that it might rise to 50 percent by the end of the decade. Although whites still held a majority in the total city population, many feared the implications of being a minority in the public schools. The white-owned daily newspapers praised signs of white "stability" in the mid-1970s, when the rate of white flight out of city schools slowed down from 2.5 percent to only 1.5 percent.[41]

Despite a continued increase in the black population, the level of black representation on the Milwaukee school board did not keep pace. Although black Milwaukeeans comprised nearly one-fifth of the city population in 1975, the continued at-large election process made it extremely difficult for them to win a seat in the majority white city. After the first black board member, Cornelius Golightly, lost his reelection bid in 1966, not a single black candidate won sufficient votes to take his place for five years. Harold Jackson, the city's first black assistant district attorney, was appointed to fill a vacancy on the school board in 1970, then kept his seat in a 1971 election. Jackson became personally involved in calming racial tensions at Washington High, and his colleagues selected him to preside over the school board for a period of time until he resigned for personal reasons in 1972. Four years later, Clara New, a former black teacher and administrator at the University of Wisconsin–Milwaukee, was also appointed to fill a vacancy on the board. But overall, black representation did not increase in proportion to the population.

Black candidates from both the North Division and Washington High districts campaigned for school board elections in the mid-1970s, but Washington candidates were much more successful. In 1973, inner-city activists failed in their attempts to increase black representation by organizing the first Black Community Caucus for School Board Elections. None of their candidates succeeded in winning the citywide elections. One year later, at a similar community meeting titled "Blac-a-vention," inner-city activists unsuccessfully lobbied for a black neighborhood candidate to be appointed to fill a vacancy. In 1975, when three black candidates finally won election to the school board, they clearly represented the interests of blacks on the west side rather than the inner city. Marian McEvilly, the Washington district integration activist, won a seat on the board, as did Leon Todd, a black computer programmer and fellow Washington area resident, and black incumbent Clara New. None of the three had been nominated by the inner-city Black Community Caucus nor by Blac-a-vention in earlier years. While the three black board members were sympathetic to the plight of North Division area residents, they were more likely to identify with the struggle for stable integration in the Washington neighborhood. McEvilly, the most prominent member of the trio, was best positioned to negotiate the politics of desegregation. She had assisted Barbee in the research phase and had testified on behalf of the plaintiffs on the first day of the school desegregation trial. Now, as a member of the Milwaukee school board, she officially became one of the defendants and lobbied hard for her version of the best possible implementation.[42]

Even before Judge Reynolds issued his ruling in 1976, the school board had begun to shift its stance on school desegregation by taking some incremental steps. A growing number of white liberals had won election to the board by earning the votes of Milwaukee residents who wished to distance themselves from white segregationists of the past and to regain the city's progressive image. This minority faction of liberal school board members, plus some moderates, occasionally persuaded or outvoted the conservative majority. For example, when black attorney Harold Jackson served on the board in 1971, a strong majority voted to end the disgraceful intact busing policy and to merge students into regular classrooms at the receiving school, affecting about 800 black pupils. But other board actions, while appearing to be more liberal on school desegregation, were primarily intended to address concerns over white flight, not necessarily those of black students. In 1974, the board instructed central office staff to work with neighborhood residents at schools that recently had become 25 percent non-white in order to prevent their schools from becoming all-black. (Schools that were already past this limit did not receive this type of assistance.) The board also banned student transfers into seven schools undergoing racial transition (including Washington High), thus capping the number of blacks who could move in (but not preventing whites from moving out). Finally, the board converted the Jackie Robinson Middle School into Milwaukee's first citywide magnet school in 1975 with a specialized open education curriculum designed to attract both white and black families who volunteered to send their children. However, they limited black enrollment to 35 percent so that the former predominantly black school would be transformed into a white majority one. Overall, these decisions marked a dramatic shift away from the board's prior official position that maintained color-blind school policy (a position challenged in court by Barbee). Now, the board officially began to make some color-conscious policies on student enrollments and community relations, though often with the primary, unstated goal of protecting white interests.[43]

The genius behind Milwaukee's emerging magnet school plan was Lee McMurrin, the new superintendent hired by the board in 1975. After having watched racial violence erupt over busing in Boston and Louisville, and while still waiting for Judge Reynolds to make a decision, McMurrin's strategy appealed to most Milwaukeeans' desire for an alternative approach to school desegregation controversy. The superintendent crafted a rhetorical strategy to appeal to both sides. McMurrin vowed to anti-desegregation forces that he would not permit mandatory busing in the city, yet he promised desegregation supporters that he could integrate the schools through voluntary means. Milwaukee's emerging solution relied heavily on magnet schools. One of McMurrin's first proposals, prior to the court's ruling, was to reorganize the city's fifteen high schools into citywide magnet schools, each with its own specialized curricular offering, to encourage student enrollment from outside the traditional neighborhood boundaries. In theory, the stronger the attraction of special offerings at each magnet school, the greater the likelihood that black and white students would voluntarily cross neighborhood boundaries and obtain a high quality education at a racially integrated school. Furthermore, McMurrin knew how to obtain new federal funding to make it possible.[44]

But magnet schools also opened a new set of questions and controversies. First, as sociologist Mary Haywood Metz has argued, they openly contradicted the myth of equal educational opportunity in American public schooling. For magnet schools to attract students, they needed to offer something more than what students typically received in their traditional neighborhood schools. School desegregation supporters had long demanded equality for all students, but the magnet school remedy sought to resolve the issue by designating some schools as superior in resources or reputation. McMurrin's initial plan to transform *all* high schools into magnets theoretically addressed these concerns about inequality, but if all high schools were equally good, why would anyone move? Second, McMurrin's administration faced difficult pragmatic questions about the magnet school location and enrollment. Would white families send their children to a magnet school in the middle of an inner-city black neighborhood? Would they come if the percentage of black students was guaranteed not to rise above a certain level? And would sufficient numbers of whites participate in this voluntary integration plan? McMurrin and his assistants brushed aside these questions and pushed ahead on Milwaukee's magnet school plan, expressing confidence that it would eliminate "some of the negative imagery of desegregation" in the minds of many white Milwaukeeans, replacing the concept of "forced busing" into black neighborhoods with the rhetoric of voluntary "choice."[45]

After Judge Reynolds finally issued his ruling in 1976, political negotiations intensified over what kind of desegregation plan should be implemented in order to meet the requirement that all schools have 25 to 45 percent black students within three years. Special Master Gronouski toured Milwaukee schools and spoke with various community groups, expressing his deep concern that McMurrin's magnet school plan would fail to attract whites to the all-black North Division High School. Not only did North Division students have very low average achievement scores, but the school was viewed as the center of black protests and disruptions over the past decade and represented the heart of the black ghetto that whites had fled since the 1920s. Gronouski also candidly explained his concerns at a North Division community meeting in the spring of 1976. "I've read several hundred letters from Milwaukeeans," presumably meaning whites. "They are not negative toward integration. But they are negative toward busing their children into the center of black communities." He turned his attention toward new North Division High School, currently under construction at that time. "I'm persuaded that the building of [the new] North Division, combined with a voluntary integration plan, however admirable it may be, will result in an all-black North Division three years hence." Aware of his court-mandated duty to oversee the desegregation planning, Gronouski feared that the new North Division's neighborhood location might make it impossible to integrate, regardless of any special magnet program. His worries raised public concerns that construction might be halted.[46]

North Division staff, students, and community members spoke out in defense of their school amid these tense political negotiations over desegregation. "There's a great deal of pride here," claimed acting principal Donald Trythall, "and it's directed at the new building. The students seem to be finally getting it together. Once you integrate, you're not a Blue Devil [North Division team name] anymore. You can adjust to the other kids all right, but you lose your identity." Students like Joseph Smith recognized Gronouski's power to halt the construction of the new North Division but pleaded with him to let it continue. "The new school will have to be integrated anyway, no matter what, so why not put it where it is?" Rev. Joseph McNeil, who had lobbied for the new facility for seven years, warned against any delay. "Let them stop building that school and you'll see some trouble." His colleague, Pauline McKay, the president of the North Division Parent-Teacher-Student Organization, observed that years earlier, she had supported locating the new school at the Carver Park site to allow for better highway transportation for future desegregation. But since the white-dominated school board voted to place it on the current site, "why change it now?" McKay worried that any delay would rob the black neighborhood of its dire need for a quality high school. "We need the school in the community. It will help us socially, economically, you name it. If they want to bus white students in here, fine. But integration must work both ways."[47]

Marian McEvilly, the leading black school board member (though not a North Division resident), urged Gronouski to halt construction. It would be "a serious mistake" to build the new North Division deep inside the black neighborhood or to build its counterpart, the new South Division High School, deep within the white southside neighborhood due to the "clearly defined ethnic patterns" of both locations. McEvilly argued that strong racial identities for either high school would make desegregation more difficult, perhaps leading to a crisis similar to that in Boston, where South Boston whites attacked Roxbury blacks during mandatory busing in that city two years earlier. She publicly voiced the possibility of reversing the board's previous decision to build North Division in its current location.

"Just because we made a promise to a certain group is not reason enough to build a school," McEvilly warned. "We build schools for the future." Gronouski made clear that he was leaning toward McEvilly's position when he spoke to her core supporters, the Sherman Park Community Association from the Washington High area, who applauded his criticism of McMurrin's magnet school plan.[48]

In the wake of Reynolds's 1976 ruling, the school board also created a citizen advisory group, known as the Committee of 100, where representatives elected from each of the city's high school districts could participate in shaping the desegregation process. They reported directly to school board member McEvilly, who oversaw the board's relations with community organizations. One of the committee's co-chairs, Cecil Brown Jr., had worked with Lloyd Barbee as the vice president of MUSIC during the mid-1960s, and like McEvilly, he was deeply suspicious of Superintendent McMurrin's magnet school plan. With support from Brown and McEvilly, the Washington High delegates advocated for the mandatory participation of all whites and blacks in busing to desegregate all schools in the city. By pairing or clustering black and white schools into the same attendance zones, all children would be integrated. The Washington High delegates opposed any voluntary desegregation plan, like magnet schools, on the grounds that most whites would probably seek ways of avoiding being schooled with blacks. But the Committee of 100 was a large, unwieldy organization that played only an advisory role to the school board's desegregation negotiations, and white southside residents came out to defend their interests in far larger numbers than did inner-city blacks, who had little faith in the process.[49]

Negotiations between all parties dragged on through the summer of 1976, just months before the first school year of desegregation was scheduled to begin. But the power rested in the hands of the white conservative majority on the school board; they were convinced that their legal appeals might erase Judge Reynolds's ruling and objected to any plan mandating white participation. The board voted 8 to 7 against proposals by the Committee of 100 and subsequent modifications offered by McMurrin and Gronouski. Finally, in early July, an exasperated Judge Reynolds agreed to a compromise with the hard-line conservatives. The compromise yielded twenty-four magnet schools, which the school board publicized as a triumph for voluntary integration. But in reality, the compromise included mandatory busing, though primarily for black students. About 3,300 blacks were reassigned to white schools due to overcrowding or to the closure of inner-city schools, and another 1,300 blacks (but only 200 whites) were reassigned when their neighborhood schools were converted into magnets. One of these magnets was North Division. While construction continued on the new building, half of the enrollment in the old building (about 750 black students) was transferred out to make room for incoming white students. Attorney Barbee agreed to the compromise, since he expected that blacks were more likely to be reassigned than whites, given that white schools typically had better quality resources. Furthermore, he won guarantees from Reynolds that if the voluntary magnet school experiment was insufficient, more mandatory integration measures would be taken in the following year.[50]

At the opening of the 1976 school year, Superintendent McMurrin proudly announced that Milwaukee had surpassed Judge Reynolds's first-year goals. With tremendous effort from desegregation supporters, more than one-third of the public schools now had black enrollments between 25 and 45 percent, well on their way toward the three-year goal. Most important, in the eyes of white officials, was that the desegregation process seemed relatively peaceful. Since magnet schools were designed to be voluntary, whites had no reason to violently protest against "forced busing," as they had done in the streets of South Boston. In addition, under a new state law promoting voluntary metropolitan desegregation, commonly known as Chapter 220, about 270 black Milwaukee students transferred into participating white suburban schools, whose districts were lured by the incentive of increased state funding for accepting them.[51]

Yet further desegregation abruptly ground to a halt. The U.S. Supreme Court heard the Milwaukee school board appeal and ruled in its favor, vacating Judge Reynolds's decision and remanding the case back to the lower court for further consideration, in June 1977. Although the Supreme Court did not declare the school board to be innocent of all charges, it eliminated the power behind Judge Reynolds's remedy, such as the position held by Special Master Gronouski. The Supreme Court's intervention in Milwaukee was based on an earlier ruling in a related Northern school desegregation case, *Dayton v. Brinkman*. In this ruling, the Court narrowed the scope of school desegregation remedies, arguing that a systemwide solution would be appropriate only if evidence could be shown that the original violation had a systemwide impact. The Milwaukee case was remanded back to Judge Reynolds's courtroom to determine more precisely whether local school officials had deliberately intended to segregate all schools or if their actions had simply led to segregation in some areas. Attorney Barbee was forced to go back to trial in September 1977 to meet a stricter legal standard. Conservative school board members were elated.[52]

PROTESTING THE BURDEN OF ONE-WAY DESEGREGATION

The most disappointed Milwaukeeans were supporters of black neighborhood schools, who were deeply troubled by what they saw—and by what everyone else ignored—during the first year of desegregation. While Mc-Murrin's magnet schools created more choices for white students, they actually limited choices for most black students. Inner-city neighborhood schools were disproportionately converted into magnets, and since the majority of seats were reserved for whites, that bumped blacks out and gave them no opportunity other than to enroll outside of their neighborhood school. Magnet schools, the epitome of choice for whites who wished to participate, came to represent a "forced choice" for blacks whose neighborhood schools disappeared. "We were told to choose a new school," one black parent reported at the beginning of the 1976 school year. "They put kids out of the old school, then asked us to 'volunteer' for schools in white neighborhoods. What choice did we have?"[53]

Although several residents had previously voiced concerns about one-way desegregation, Larry Harwell was the first black community organizer to pinpoint the issue. In the early 1960s, Harwell became active in racial integration issues as a black Catholic in the Christian Family Movement and joined MUSIC to picket against intact busing. But in the late 1960s, he gradually abandoned the integration cause to focus on black community empowerment. In 1967, he became executive director of the Organization of Organizations (commonly known as Triple O), funded by the federal Office of Economic Opportunity to promote greater participation by low-income residents in governing anti-poverty programs. Through Triple O, Harwell rallied black parents to demand their right to participate in decision-making over programs funded by Title I of the Elementary and Secondary Education Act. He repeatedly organized attempts to win inner-city black representation on the school board, even running for a seat himself in 1975, though without success. During all of this time, Triple O was frequently investigated for allegedly violating federal guidelines by conducting political work for Harwell's longtime colleague, state senator Monroe Swan, who strongly advocated community control rather than Lloyd Barbee's integration agenda.[54]

After the first year of Reynolds's court order, Harwell organized a new group, Blacks for Two-Way Integration. Backed by Triple O community organizers, the initial group of twenty-eight parents called for the burden of desegregation to be equally distributed between both white and black communities. Harwell worked hard to compile evidence and publicize their case. "Blacks Forced to 'Volunteer,'" read the headlines on their handouts, with data sheets indicating how many more blacks than whites were displaced from their neighborhood schools due to mandatory reassignments, closures, and conversions into magnet schools. "The community is led to believe that integration is from the gods, so we don't question them," Harwell told listeners. "But this agency took ordinary black people and, with a little math, we put a plan together without a doctor or a computer." Blacks for Two-Way Integration issued its demands in 1977, calling for a halt on black school closings and magnet conversions, for vacancies in black schools to be filled by white students, and for the preservation of some 55 percent black majority schools in the inner city.[55]

Harwell's "black burden" argument initially fell on deaf ears among whites who supported efforts to stabilize Milwaukee through voluntary desegregation. In an interview with the *Milwaukee Community Journal* black weekly paper, Superintendent McMurrin responded that "I've been confused from the first by what people mean when they say 'burden.' Is it a burden to ride the bus to better facilities? Is it a burden to seek better opportunities?" Like many whites who recalled Milwaukee's recent history of MUSIC protests for school integration, McMurrin seemed puzzled at the thought that blacks were now complaining about the privileges they had won. "Years ago, people were jumping at the chance to ride the bus across town to a better school," he continued. "Now all of a sudden it's a 'burden.' Is it truly a burden to close down a few overcrowded, deteriorating schools and replace some of them with the most modern and better facilitated schools in the system?" Over a year's time, as Blacks for Two-Way Integration continued to press the issue, more whites came to understand the "black burden" argument, yet eventually dismissed it as an inevitable outcome. On the question of closing inner-city black schools to promote desegregation, the white-owned *Milwaukee Journal* editorial board wrote: "Perhaps the only argument is one of sociopolitical realism: If the city's once segregated school system is to be integrated in a peaceful and enduring way, the responsibility for pupil movement will tend to fall more heavily on blacks. This requires of blacks a higher degree of forbearance. Yet it can be hoped that the long range benefits of integration will justify any short range inequity." Political pressures to win peaceful white compliance through a voluntary desegregation plan simply meant, in the editorial board's view, that blacks had to pay the price. Two decades later, McMurrin's former deputy superintendent, David Bennett, publicly acknowledged that "white benefit" was the driving force behind Milwaukee's magnet school plan at that time. "I think it was an unspoken issue with the school board at that time," agreed Anthony Busalacchi, former school board president in 1978–79. "It was an issue of how do we least disrupt the white community."[56]

Some black desegregation supporters, like board member Marian McEvilly, were initially sympathetic to the "black burden" concerns. The arguments raised by Blacks for Two-Way Integration were similar to her own criticisms against the "forced busing" of black Peckham Junior High students in the early 1970s. At first, McEvilly agreed with the group's demand for a moratorium on magnet schools in black neighborhoods until comparable numbers were established in white areas. But Cecil Brown Jr., Committee of 100 co-chair and a fellow black desegregation supporter, warned McEvilly to think twice about the consequences of her decision. "If you think you're going to have voluntary integration and you don't create a lot of [magnet] schools in the central city," Brown cautioned, "how do you think you're going to get white parents to send white children to ordinary schools in the central city?" According to Brown, who played a vital role in negotiating the politics of desegregation with white community groups, the trade-offs were clear. "In order to have an integrated school system, sacrifices are going to have to be made," and Brown predicted that much of that burden "is going to fall on black children."

McEvilly faced a difficult dilemma. If she supported Blacks for Two-Way Integration and insisted that whites make their sacrifices by reassigning their children to black neighborhood schools, it might provide ammunition for integration opponents and scuttle the entire magnet school compromise. So she pulled back her initial support for Harwell's group and lent it instead to other organizations, like the Coalition for Peaceful Schools. Known as the city's "desegregation boosters," the Coalition for Peaceful Schools began as a volunteer organization, then later received federal funding, to conduct human relations workshops and ensure that the desegregation plan would succeed without violence in local schools. For McEvilly and other longtime Washington area activists, the goal was not simply racial integration but a plan that would also maintain the city's sense of racial stability.[57]

Blacks for Two-Way Integration continued to focus on its North Division area constituents. At the organization's height, over 600 blacks convened at the inner-city Bethel Baptist Church for "Decision Day." According to Harwell's data for the upcoming 1977 school year, the number of blacks forced to "volunteer" increased to almost 8,000 to be dispersed to nearly 100 formerly white schools across the city. One-third of those participating in the "Decision Day" vote supported a one-day school boycott to protest the magnet plan. But nearly two-thirds of the participants decided to simply ignore their official school reassignment notices and reportedly attempted to enroll their children in a black neighborhood school. One of these parents was Annette "Polly" Williams, a rising figure in local Democratic politics, whose four children attended Urban Day Academy, the predominantly black private school whose program ended after eighth grade. Although Williams filled out the public high school assignment forms for one of her teenage daughters, she was not granted any of her choices because her presence would not enhance racial desegregation at a predominantly black school. But Williams vowed to defy school authorities and take her daughter to her preferred school anyway. "Next week they won't have to worry about sending her anywhere," she announced. "We will take a chair . . . and they are going to enroll my daughter in the school of my choice."[58]

Despite drawing large numbers, Blacks for Two-Way Integration did not succeed in building an enduring broad-based coalition to influence school desegregation policy. According to Scott Anderson, a journalist for the *Milwaukee Courier* black weekly paper, Harwell played up the rhetoric of blacks "having a choice" but spoke candidly in private conversations about Triple O's black separatist ideology. Internal disputes arose within Blacks for Two-Way Integration about whether the group sincerely supported an equitable approach to integration or simply sought to stir up black opposition to being "tricked" into desegregation. Some members, distrustful of Harwell's motives, openly criticized his relationships with desegregation opponents on Milwaukee's white south side. Other organizations, such as the Committee of 100 and the Coalition for Peaceful Schools, avoided Harwell's group and worked to support desegregation in the face of white conservative opposition. After "Decision Day" and its one-day school boycott, the organization did not sponsor another major event nor meaningfully participate in the politics of desegregation. Blacks for Two-Way Integration disappeared, but its underlying concern about the black burden did not, and the language of "choice" by Polly Williams and Larry Harwell would propel another black school reform movement in the decades to come.[59]

SETTLING THE DESEGREGATION LAWSUIT

After the remanded case forced Judge Reynolds to hold a second desegregation trial, he ruled in favor of the plaintiffs again in 1978, with stronger language against the defendants. Barbee had presented more witnesses who spoke directly to the question of intent. Former white school administrators and liberal board members testified that the majority of board members had openly expressed support for segregation in private conversations. "Anything that would increase the mix of black and white students would be detrimental," reported one. Furthermore, Barbee presented a number of black teachers, and a white teacher union representative, who testified about school officials' intent to segregate teachers. These testimonies about motive, in addition to years of documentation on policies and outcomes, led Judge Reynolds to conclude that school officials "acted with a discriminatory intent in their decisions and actions" regarding boundary changes, site selection, school construction, student transfers, and teacher placement. "They deliberately separated most of the whites from most of the blacks, and this the Constitution forbids."[60]

Reynolds did not issue a remedy but ordered the plaintiffs to submit one, a move that prompted the school board to begin discussions for a settlement. Lloyd Barbee clearly hoped for a metropolitan desegregation plan. "Bigots are going to Washington County or to Waukesha," he declared, and the only way to force them to integrate was through a remedy that reached into the outer suburbs. But Barbee's dream for metropolitan desegregation was unlikely to become reality. The U.S. Supreme Court had ruled against a mandatory metropolitan remedy in its recent *Milliken v. Bradley* decision regarding Detroit and its suburbs. And in Milwaukee, reaching a political agreement on a plan requiring suburban participation seemed very unlikely. Four years earlier, state representative Dennis Conta, a white Milwaukee Democrat, proposed to merge two predominantly black city high school districts with two white, wealthy suburban districts. Despite the support of several cosponsors for the bill and the promise of financial incentives, suburban town governments soon derailed all discussion of a metropolitan merger.[61]

Barbee's inclination to seek a solution by looking outward, toward the suburbs, underscored the widening gap between him and many of his inner-city constituents. Two years earlier, Barbee had realized that he had been spreading himself too thin. His service as a state representative in Madison, his private law practice in Milwaukee, and the desegregation litigation (for which he had still not received a dime in legal fees) fragmented his time and drained his energy. In 1976, he decided not to run for the State Assembly seat he had held for the past twelve years and endorsed his longtime supporter, Marcia Coggs, the widow of the black politician Isaac Coggs. Yet it was still impossible for Barbee both to litigate the case and to hold the leading role in negotiations with black and white community groups about the details of desegregation implementation. Barbee's metropolitan strategies took him farther away from inner-city realities. Immediately after Reynolds's decision in 1978, he spoke to the *Milwaukee Community Journal* black weekly, stating that "the best is not too good for blacks. We should enjoy the same things as the white community. I don't care how we accomplish that. If students must crowd into a Volkswagen or take a helicopter . . . [these are] extremes that we must live through as long as we receive the same type of education the whites receive." By giving scant attention to real concerns about the black burden of desegregation, he distanced himself even further from his North Division constituents. For Barbee, the end goal of integration had become even more important than the means for achieving it.[62]

While settlement talks continued, the 1978 school year began with Superintendent McMurrin's announcement that the Milwaukee public schools had met the goal for two-thirds of its schools to enroll 25 to 50 percent black students. The brand-new North Division opened up as a traditional neighborhood high school, with specialized academic resources for medical-dental health careers and outstanding athletic facilities. Next door, the wrecking ball knocked down the seventy-year-old former North Division building. Yet the brand-new high school did not meet the court's desegregation goals. On opening day, only 36 white students voluntarily enrolled at North Division, with more than 1,400 black students. The multimillion dollar educational facility and its specialized curricular offerings had failed to attract significant numbers of whites into the black neighborhood, as several observers had previously warned.[63]

As the school board moved closer to meeting the third year's goals of the desegregation plan, black neighborhood schools became even more vulnerable to closings. Citywide public school enrollment had fallen by 29,000 students (23 percent) from its peak year, as the baby boom trailed off and white suburbanization grew in the late 1970s. Economic pressures on the city school system intensified while the most crucial period of desegregation negotiations neared. As the school board looked for ways to hold down costs, meet their numerical racial goals, and not alienate whites, closing black neighborhood schools was the most obvious solution. Black board member Leon Todd recognized that their decision would be opposed by those who had supported Blacks for Two-Way Integration. "I'm biting my lip at times about it because there should be equity between black and white, but there is no other way to bring about integration peacefully," he commented. In later months, when board colleague Marian McEvilly voted to close several black neighborhood schools, she argued that her decision was forced by the fact that, for decades, school officials had spent more money on white schools, building better libraries, science labs, and physical education facilities. Segregative practices in the past now tied her hands in the present. Confronted by jeers from angry black neighborhood school supporters, McEvilly replied, "I didn't run for the school board to be popular . . . [but] to take care of all the interests of the children of the City of Milwaukee."[64]

Yet to North Division area residents, these words from Washington area black board members sounded like they had forgotten the inner city. Evidence of the black burden of desegregation grew larger. Since 1970, nearly half of the thirteen neighborhood schools in the North Division area had been closed or converted into magnets. During the spring magnet school lottery, nearly all of the losers had been black; being white sharply increased one's chances of gaining entry to one of the "better" schools, even if it was located in your neighborhood. Over 90 percent of the students bused for desegregation were black. Adding insult to injury, the school board initially refused to award contracts to either of the two black-owned school bus firms in the city.[65]

In the spring of 1979, attorney Barbee and the school board defendants finally negotiated a settlement that was approved by Judge Reynolds. It was not the metropolitan solution that Barbee had hoped for but was perhaps the best citywide desegregation plan he could secure under less than ideal conditions, since time was not on his side. The terms guaranteed that at least 75 percent of the city's students would attend a desegregated school (rather than the 100 percent in the initial ruling). These racially balanced schools would be defined as 20 to 60 percent black (an increase in the upper level). Although the settlement would permit the existence of about twenty all-black schools, it disallowed all-white schools and guaranteed every individual student the right to attend a desegregated school, if she or he chose to do so. Milwaukee's model for attracting volunteer whites to desegregated magnet schools would continue to prevail. The school board would drop all appeals, and the federal court would appoint a monitoring board to resolve disputes over the next five years. Outraged by these terms, Marian McEvilly and other black board members voted against the settlement, since it would not desegregate a substantial number of all-black schools, but the majority of board members prevailed and voted to accept the deal.[66]

"Let this truly be the last word," wrote the *Milwaukee Journal* editors, speaking on behalf of white Milwaukeeans who hoped to put years of racial controversy behind them. Even most Barbee supporters welcomed what they believed to be the end of the prolonged struggle for black school reform, which in their minds had begun with MUSIC over fifteen years earlier. State representative Marcia Coggs, who now held Barbee's seat, noted that the court's approval of the settlement coincided with the twenty-fifth anniversary of the *Brown v. Board* decision and praised everyone who had fought hard to win both victories for the race. "Now we can close this chapter in our history books," she proclaimed. But at North Division High School, a new struggle that would transform future reform movements had only just begun.[67]

7

TRANSFORMING STRATEGIES FOR BLACK

SCHOOL REFORM

"Enough is enough," chanted hundreds of marchers, waving banners in protest against the black burden of desegregation. "Save North Division," they shouted, seeking to reverse the school board's proposal to close the all-black neighborhood high school. At first glance, it appeared to many that the actors in Milwaukee's epic school desegregation saga had simply switched roles. Black activists were now fighting for the right to retain their "neighborhood school," the same phrase that white segregationists had used to defend their all-white institutions for the past two decades. The school board's conservative white attorney, Laurence Hammond, who had defended the district against Lloyd Barbee's lawsuit, now became the legal enforcer of a school desegregation policy against black citizens who refused to participate. But there was much more to this story than a simple reversal of roles.

This chapter explores the rise of the Coalition to Save North Division in 1979, a broad-based movement that was much more than one struggle over the fate of a single black neighborhood high school. The Coalition became a popular and sustained challenge to Milwaukee's magnet school policy, which fulfilled the legal requirements of school desegregation while favoring white political interests over those of many blacks. The Coalition

Coalition to Save North Division protesters opposed the closure of their brand-new school and its conversion into a citywide magnet school, which would displace black students in order to attract whites. From *Milwaukee Journal*, 11 January 1980; copyright Milwaukee Journal Sentinel, Inc.; reproduced with permission.

represented the breaking point between two black communities that had steadily grown apart since the 1960s: inner-city residents who clung to their dream of quality schooling in all-black settings, and those moving outward who pinned their hopes on integration as the means to guarantee equal standards and resources for the entire city. Black activists from North Division and Washington High struggled against one another, not only over politics of the day but also over historical memories of black schooling during the age of segregation.

Participants in this local struggle joined forces with a growing national movement of black activists and academics who questioned whether the methods of school desegregation were consistent with the stated goal of equal education for all. This broader movement began in the South during the 1950s and 1960s, when white-dominated school officials typically implemented one-way school desegregation plans. Under pressure to act by federal authorities, many Southern districts reassigned black students to formerly all-white schools (though not vice versa) and commonly displaced or fired black teachers, coaches, and principals by downgrading or closing formerly all-black schools. As legal and political pressures for integrated education spread to the North and West in the 1960s and 1970s, school districts like Milwaukee followed a similar pattern by implementing a magnet school desegregation plan that privileged white interests. To respond to these new forms of racism embedded within school desegregation, some black activists redefined the popular meaning of *Brown v. Board* to address the context of their particular struggles. They came to the same conclusion reached in 1978 by Robert Carter, a leading attorney with Thurgood Marshall in the *Brown* trial. Looking back on over twenty-five years of litigation, Carter recalled that the NAACP's major challenge in 1954 was to destroy the "separate but equal" doctrine of the 1896 *Plessy v. Ferguson* decision. To do so, Carter and his colleagues "fashioned *Brown* on the theory that equal education and integrated education were one and the same," thereby equating the two concepts. But after their initial legal victory, the real target of their attack—racism—had changed over time, adapting itself to privilege white interests in school desegregation arrangements in several locations. While Carter personally continued to support integration, he eventually came to understand "the goal was not integration but equal educational opportunity," thereby distinguishing between the two concepts he had fused together during the 1950s. Once Carter and other black education reformers had clarified these terms, they opened their minds to consider alternative strategies for reaching their goal.[1]

In Milwaukee, the aftermath of the Coalition to Save North Division's actions transformed the city's agenda on race and school reform for the next two decades. During the 1980s, competing groups of black education reforms sought to advance the race by gaining the ability to influence—and to exit from—the Milwaukee public schools, but their strategies for doing so sharply diverged. On one hand, black activists affiliated with the Washington High area continued to exercise political power on the school board and insisted on expanding the right for blacks to be integrated into white suburban schools, where they perceived expectations and resources to be greatest. If the city schools could not be saved, their preferred exit strategy was to attend the public schools of the suburbs. On the other hand, some blacks affiliated with the North Division movement initially sought greater administrative authority within the Milwaukee public schools, while others allied with white conservatives to demand state-funded vouchers to attend private schools, where they perceived expectations and resources to be superior. In their eyes, if Milwaukee's public education system could not be saved, their preferred exit strategy was to attend the private schools of the city. By tracing the divergence of these two black-led movements in recent years, we can better understand the dynamics of race and school reform today.

North Division had long been the scene of racial struggle in Milwaukee, ever since the majority of the student population had shifted from white to black in the late 1950s. During the early 1960s integration movement, black activists questioned whether school officials had watered down its curriculum. Later in the decade, North Division became the rallying point for black youth participating in the open housing marches and an important battleground over who would define the teaching of black history. In the early 1970s, the North Division governance subsystem served as a white-run phony experiment in black community control, which largely failed. In the late 1970s, after years of institutional neglect and declining student achievement, the all-black multimillion-dollar school became a target in the heated politics of school desegregation.

In May 1979, Marian McEvilly and her black school board colleagues had been furious with Judge John Reynolds's approval of the settlement in the school desegregation case, since it allowed nearly twenty schools to remain nearly all-black, racially isolated from the rest of the desegregated city school system. McEvilly had decided upon a political solution for this legal problem and proposed a resolution to close the new North Division High School as a traditional neighborhood school, then reopen it as an integrated citywide magnet school with a health and science focus. The board's vote— 12 to 1 in favor of her resolution—would soon become the most controversial decision in the politics of desegregation at that time. In order for the citywide magnet school to attract white students to North Division successfully, the board required black junior high students who anticipated enrolling at the all-black school in September 1979 to be transferred to other schools. At the end of the 1979–80 school year, sophomores and juniors from the all-black school would also be reassigned elsewhere. When North Division reopened as a magnet the following fall, it would have an entirely new student body, one that would be virtually "cleansed" of the past. The number of black students allowed to enroll would be limited to the equivalent number of whites, to ensure racial balance. Therefore, this brand-new facility, with a potential capacity of over 2,000 students, would soon displace many black students who resided in the neighborhood and anticipated enrolling there, except those few who were lucky enough to secure one of the limited seats available via the magnet school lottery.[2]

News of the impending closure brought school life to a halt at North Division. At a meeting with angry students, Superintendent Lee McMurrin, the leader of Milwaukee's magnet desegregation policy, tried to convey a hopeful message. "Integration is going to be painful, I know, but it's for the good of all parents, students, and the community." Yet North Division students quickly grew frustrated by his unwillingness to act on their concerns, and about 500 walked out, marching to the central administration office with parents and civil rights activists. Their primary objection was that black students were being forced to leave North Division solely in order to attract whites. "I want to stress, we are not opposed to integration, as long as the students at North get to remain there," explained student spokesperson Willie Washington. "How can the board make room for 1,000 white students when they don't have them?" Others pointed out that North Division currently had space to hold 700 white students without displacing a single black student.[3]

Faced with growing student protest, Milwaukee's school board agreed to hold a special hearing on the matter. Several students and community members spoke out on various concerns, scattering the agenda in all different directions. But the audience became more unified—some would say electrified—when a tall, bearded black man named Howard Fuller, a 1958 North Division graduate, stepped up to the podium and delivered a powerful speech about "our" school. "We say that it is ours because it does indeed belong to us," he began, laying the groundwork for a more personalized struggle over a bureaucratized issue. Fuller continued by raising the familiar "black burden" argument. "The black community is once again being forced to bear the brunt of the so-called integration process," he observed. "What sacrifice is the white community being asked to make?" Then Fuller focused attention on the board resolution that "cleansed" the brand-new North Division of its current black students before reopening as an integrated magnet. "If this school is going to be such a great thing, then why can't we stay there?" Fuller chastised the board for its recent conversion of two older, predominantly black high school buildings, Rufus King and Lincoln, into citywide magnets. "And now you want North. We say no! And ENOUGH IS ENOUGH!" School board members sat silent and stone-faced, while the audience roared its approval.[4]

Liberal board members were convinced that dispersing the current North Division student population was the key to saving the school. Lois Riley, the white board president, supported integration in both her political and personal lives; her daughter was one of the few whites to voluntarily enroll in North's special health sciences program. "The only way North Division is going to be a successful educational institution," she told reporters, "is to move some of those kids out of there. . . . A high school cannot function when 70 percent of the kids can't even read at an eighth grade level." Riley seemed most troubled by what she perceived as a black protest to maintain an underachieving, segregated school. "What those [North Division] kids are protesting is the exact thing hundreds of people have spent millions of hours and millions of dollars on over the last fourteen years to change," she confided. "It just shows how everything has gone full circle." Liberal white board members, together with McEvilly and the two other black board members, held their ground on closing the school and converting it into a citywide magnet.[5]

North Division advocates did not give up. Over the next few months, they banded together into the Coalition to Save North Division, a black-led organization with a broad base of supporters representing at least three distinct strands of reform. At the center of the Coalition stood longtime community advocates of North Division, like Rev. Joseph McNeil and Pauline McKay, who had lobbied for a new building for several years and now defended it from being taken away. They were joined by current North Division students as well as a younger generation of black neighborhood activists, like Eyelyn and Ralph Williams, who lived one block away from the school (Ralph's alma mater) and were active in local housing issues. For years the Williams family had watched other black families being forced to give up their homes when the city built an expressway through the Northside neighborhood and black workers being forced to give up their jobs when industries moved out of this rust belt city in the 1960s and 1970s. Evelyn and Ralph Williams joined the Coalition to Save North Division for access to better resources—the same reason that some black Milwaukeeans had joined the integration movement fifteen years earlier. "We wanted access to stuff. We wanted libraries, we wanted updated maps . . . we wanted a real gym for our kids," recalled Evelyn Williams. "Here we finally get, in North Division, some stuff that we had fought for . . . [and] they take your struggle and turn it around on you. Just because we wanted integration, they figured that they can do anything to us for the sake of integration."[6]

A second group of supporters came from the Coalition's failed predecessor, Blacks for Two-Way Integration, echoing its strong emphasis on black self-determination. One supporter, Hubert Canfield, had participated in the Clifford McKissick Community School during the 1960s and together with his wife, Anita Spencer, joined Blacks for Two-Way Integration and boycotted Milwaukee public schools after a dismal experience with the first year of desegregation in 1976. The couple also played an influential role in the United Black Community Council, a local organization dedicated to strengthening black people's ability to control every aspect of their own lives in a white-dominated society, and Anita became active in the Sisters group for black women. But in contrast to local North Division activists, whose immediate neighborhood stood to benefit directly from the new school, members of this second strand were motivated by an ideological desire to maintain black institutions within the community. "None of my kids went to North Division," explained Spencer, who lived on the eastern side of the Washington district. "It was the point of the thing that North Division was a school in my community. Whether my kids went to North Division or not, I wanted North Division to stay there."[7]

A third strand of Coalition to Save North Division supporters was a multiracial group whose members identified themselves as sincere advocates of fair integration. One was Brian Verdin, a multiracial community activist, who at age nineteen ran an unsuccessful campaign as a pro-integration school board candidate in 1972. Five years later, he had grown increasingly skeptical of McMurrin's magnet school strategy and the inequitable burden it placed on blacks by protecting whites from mandatory busing. For a brief period, Verdin worked as a community organizer for Blacks for Two-Way Integration but resigned after feeling betrayed by what he described as Larry Harwell's questionable allegiance to integration. He later became a staff member with the Coalition for Peaceful Schools, Milwaukee's federally funded "desegregation boosters," until he and fellow staffers Dwaine Washington and Sarah Spence took over the organization and refocused its mission to promote fair integration. "It was ridiculous to promote peaceful desegregation without talking about fair and equitable desegregation," Verdin recalled. "How the heck can you have peaceful schools if it's not fair?" When the decision to convert North Division into a magnet was announced in May 1979, Verdin and his colleagues rushed to the school to address students' concerns and help them to organize what later became the Coalition to Save North Division.[8]

Binding together these three diverse strands—neighborhood supporters, black self-determinists, and fair integrationists—was Howard Fuller, who possessed the unique credentials and organizing experience to unify and propel the movement forward. Fuller had personal ties to several local community institutions. He and his mother were Southern black migrants who had moved from Louisiana to Milwaukee in 1948, when he was seven years old, and they had lived in the Hillside public housing project in the Near Northside neighborhood. But Fuller did not follow the life of a typical child there. His mother enrolled him in the St. Boniface Catholic parochial school, where he was the only black student in his third-grade classroom. Fuller later attended North Division, adjacent to his former parochial school, when it transitioned from a predominantly white to a predominantly black high school in the late 1950s. At North Division, he was an extraordinary student leader, serving as president of the senior class and the student council and as the star center on the Blue Devils basketball team. Fuller's leadership abilities were nurtured by Wesley Scott of the Milwaukee Urban League; Scott mentored him through youth programs and was part of the supportive black community around him.[9]

After graduating from North Division in 1958, Fuller began a long ideological journey that spanned integrationism, Pan-Africanism, and Marxism.

Community organizer Howard Fuller crafted language to unite supporters of black self-determination, fair integration, and neighborhood groups into the Coalition to Save North Division. From *Milwaukee Sentinel*, 17 August 1981; copyright Milwaukee Journal Sentinel, Inc.; reproduced with permission.

He became one of the pioneering black students to attend the all-white Carroll College in Waukesha, Wisconsin, where his more affluent classmates later elected him to be president of the student senate. But Fuller's efforts to minimize the distance between himself and his white classmates worked too well, he later recalled. When his white college friends reassuringly stated that they considered him "not really black," he began to question deeply his racial identity and larger purpose in life. Fuller later moved to Cleveland, Ohio, to obtain a master's degree in social administration at Western Reserve University and then became involved in the city's school integration movement in 1964. At one demonstration, Fuller and other nonviolent activists were kicked and clubbed by police and hauled off to jail. On another occasion, they blocked the construction of a new school in a black neighborhood to protest its location, which would promote segregation, as MUSIC activists also did. But the Cleveland protest went horribly wrong: one of the bulldozers crushed a white minister who lay in its path.[10]

Fuller changed course and moved to North Carolina in 1965, where he directed anti-poverty programs and worked to enable low-income blacks to become more involved in making decisions affecting their own lives (as Larry Harwell also did in Milwaukee). The North Carolina struggles taught Fuller profound lessons about power and both the racial and class divisions that kept much of it out of ordinary people's hands. "Take the word 'power' and put 'black' in front of it," he explained to reporters in 1969. "All it means is that black people got to have power to make decisions about their own lives." Fuller's charismatic leadership and success in the state soon brought him national recognition. He broadened his role in the black freedom movement by adopting an African name, Owusu Sadaukai, and by directing the Malcolm X Liberation University in Durham in the early 1970s. Speaking tours occasionally brought him back to Milwaukee, where he visited fellow Pan-Africanists at the Clifford McKissick Community School. Then he traveled abroad, spending a month on the trail with guerrilla fighters in Mozambique. But after Malcolm X Liberation University closed due to financial pressures in 1973, Fuller began to question seriously whether a class struggle or a racial struggle was more appropriate for black America. He delved into black Marxist politics and attempted to organize black hospital workers at Duke University, but he found himself drained physically and intellectually by the unsuccessful union drive and the internal conflicts among fellow Marxists. On the edge of a total breakdown in 1976, Fuller left North Carolina and headed back home to Milwaukee to clear up both his political and personal life. He began selling insurance to pay the bills and within a year became the associate director of the Equal Opportunity Program at Marquette University, where he assisted black low-income students in bridging the gap between them and the predominantly white Catholic institution. When the North Division controversy arose in 1979, Fuller was ready to step back into the black freedom movement but with a renewed focus on local issues.[11]

Fuller shaped the thinking of the Coalition to Save North Division by redefining the meaning of *Brown v. Board* to fit Milwaukee's current situation (as Urban League director William Kelley and MUSIC spokesperson Lloyd Barbee had both done during their time). His genius was to craft a new language that appealed to supporters of both black self-determination and fair integration. Fuller forcefully challenged the prevailing interpretation of *Brown*, arguing that the Supreme Court's decision that all-black schooling was "inherently unequal" set the stage for racist remedies. "The *Brown* decisions were not in themselves based on racist tenets," he later wrote, "... [but] the manner in which desegregation has been carried out in many cities through America is racist." The prevailing methods of desegregating black students, Fuller argued, presumed that black schools had no value whatsoever and that black students were best served by being assimilated into white schools, where they "must give up their humanity and deny their self-image in order to reap the benefits of the system." Fuller supported advocates of a strong black identity, but he did not abandon integration in the traditional sense. Instead, he reclaimed *Brown* and reinterpreted its meaning for black Milwaukeeans, thereby transforming the local politics of school desegregation. Fuller held that *Brown* stood for the elimination of barriers against black progress, not the elimination of black schools. He questioned whether the school board's methods for attaining desegregation—the removal of black students from a new school and their dispersal across the city—were consistent with the true meaning of *Brown*. "I struggled for the integration of facilities in the South and have struggled for the integrated schools in Cleveland, Ohio, to eliminate any racial barriers that would exist," Fuller explained. "But when you take 600 to 700 black kids and put them out, in a sense 'cleanse' the school, so that you can bring in white students who won't come when you're there . . . when you use that as a basis for desegregation, it's inane, because you're going to create the type of hostilities that would make meaningful integration impossible." By reclaiming *Brown* rather than rejecting it outright, and by charging that its implementation was racist, Fuller kept the Coalition united around their primary goal: the preservation of a predominantly black, though integrated, North Division High School to stabilize the neighborhood.[12]

Fuller and the Coalition strategically merged community organizing and courtroom tactics to attain their objective, as Barbee and MUSIC had done years earlier. Through its lawyer, the Coalition filed complaints with the U.S. Office of Civil Rights and the monitoring board appointed by the federal judge to oversee desegregation disputes and also sought a court injunction to halt the proposed magnet conversion. Rather than fighting its battle over complex sets of racial percentages (as many community groups had done in the wake of Judge Reynolds's 1976 ruling), the Coalition emphasized its compelling story—about the fate of a once-proud black high school—to convey its broader message about the biased implementation of magnet school desegregation. The North Division story spread across the city through flyers, newspapers, radio, television, and even a short documentary film. Even the school's symbolic sporting victories took on new meaning, such as when North Division's boys' basketball team came from behind to win the state high school basketball championship in 1980, proving to sports fans that an all-black team could play a well-disciplined ball game and defeat a higher-ranked white team. Throughout this time, the Coalition maintained a consistent, uncompromising position: keep North Division as a neighborhood high school with a health and science specialized curriculum and integrate the school to be 60 percent black and 40 percent white, a goal that could be met without moving out any of the current black students. Realistically, most Coalition activists knew that large numbers of white students would most likely never voluntarily come to North Division, but their broader point was to shift the desegregation burden off of black shoulders alone. If Milwaukee was serious about integration, it was time to insist that whites ride the bus.[13]

The Coalition gained public support from the city's two oldest (and sometimes rival) black organizations, the Milwaukee Urban League and the Milwaukee NAACP. Wesley Scott, the Urban League's executive director and Fuller's mentor, spoke out on his organization's long-standing commitment to strengthening black communities as a means of increasing wider economic opportunity. He argued that dispersing North Division underachievers to other schools across the city would put them at a further disadvantage, since long bus rides into sometimes hostile white neighborhoods would exacerbate these students' truancy and dropout rates. Scott, who also held an influential position on the five-member desegregation monitoring board appointed by the federal judge, welcomed members of the emerging Coalition to meet in the Urban League's office on Center Street, just down the block from North Division. Meanwhile, Chris Belnavis, president of the Milwaukee NAACP, found a way for her organization to support the Coalition, despite the fact that it was simultaneously seeking support from its parent body to appeal the settlement approved by Judge Reynolds on the grounds that it did not go far enough to guarantee sufficient desegregation. Some local NAACP officials, like education chair Joyce Mallory, publicly stated, "We just cannot accept all-black schools." So NAACP chapter president Belnavis supported the cause by focusing on fairness. "Equity is the thing we are after," she announced to a North Division rally. "I feel that just as whites are being attracted, they never think of attracting blacks." The two veteran black organizations found common ground in the fight to save North Division, a struggle that merged the Urban League's commitment to black communities and opportunity with the NAACP's traditional focus on equity and integration.[14]

Fuller brought national attention to the North Division struggle by connecting with prominent black activists who had previous ties to Milwaukee. During the early 1960s, Rev. Lucius Walker had been one of the first black ministers to publicly support Barbee's integration movement, and he had become well known among CORE and MUSIC activists for organizing training sessions at the Northcott Neighborhood Center. In the late 1970s, he had directed the Interreligious Foundation for Community Organizations in New York City, where Howard Fuller had served on the board. Reverend Walker announced that a national conference would be held on the North Division issue as a "classical illustration of the problem that is emerging nationally" of displacing black students for the sake of desegregation. The conference, titled "Desegregation: A New Form of Discrimination?," was held at Rev. Joseph McNeil's inner-city Milwaukee church in early 1980. Delivering the keynote address was Derrick Bell, a black legal scholar-activist from Harvard Law School. This was not Bell's first trip to Milwaukee. He had previously visited the city in 1963, as an NAACP attorney with organizer June Shagaloff to rally community support for Barbee's fledgling school integration movement. At the 1980 conference, Bell spoke out on broader themes that also appeared in his controversial book of edited essays, *Shades of Brown: New Perspectives on School Desegregation*. He criticized civil rights activists who, like he had once done, rigidly held to the goal of racial balance and supported desegregation policies that resulted in the closing of black schools, whether or not these policies actually improved the quality of education for black students. "This is precisely what has happened in the long crusade for school desegregation," he told conference participants, declaring that the continuing persistence of racism required civil rights activists to reflect upon and revise their tactics.[15]

COLLIDING VISIONS AND COMPETING MEMORIES

But Marian McEvilly and other longtime Milwaukee school integration supporters saw no reason to change their tactics since, in their minds, settling for anything less than full integration was a betrayal to the cause of civil rights. McEvilly and her two black school board colleagues firmly held their ground against the Coalition to Save North Division's proposal to maintain North Division as a neighborhood school. The two sides sharply disagreed over the best strategy for improving the quality of black education. McEvilly presented her case for integration at a community meeting at the Urban League center in August 1979. She argued that it was fundamentally wrong to accept the continued existence of the current North Division school, where more than 80 percent of the all-black student body scored two years or more below reading level. Low achievement like this would never be tolerated at a white school, she charged, adding that "having different standards for black and white children is racist." During her four years on the board, she recounted dozens of previous efforts to provide extra staff and resources for North Division (as Coalition members presently proposed), but it had made no difference in student outcomes. Continuing to operate North as a racially isolated school was unwise because "the probability of significant, on-going board-funded resource allocations to all-black schools is remote, given competing demands." Instead, McEvilly argued on behalf of systemwide school integration as the best means of providing black students with the best educational resources that the city had to offer.[16]

On a deeper level, the disagreement between the black board members and the Coalition to Save North Division represented a growing split between the interests of two black communities: those living in the predominantly white Washington area and those living in the predominantly black North Division area. When McEvilly had come to Milwaukee in 1963, she recalled that it was difficult for black parents in the inner city to even conceive of their children attending white schools. But now this was possible, due to MUSIC's struggle and the desegregation court order. Although McEvilly was initially sympathetic to the black burden argument, she now felt confident that the thousands of black parents and educators who had left segregated inner-city schools over the past two decades proved her right. Many black families had moved outward in search of better housing and schools, as she had done. In fact, McEvilly felt even more compelled to act now in closing underachieving black schools like North Division because the exodus of middle-class blacks had left inner-city blacks even more economically and racially isolated than before.[17]

Harsh words widened the gulf between the two black communities. Mc-Evilly, who had spent hundreds of hours as a parent activist seeking to improve and stabilize Washington High in the early 1970s, did not see the same commitment from North Division parents. She reported being called to North Division in 1978 by a concerned staff member who worried that the school would soon "blow up." After personally observing truancy, tardiness, fights, and feuds at the school, McEvilly believed that the neighborhood community shared the blame with the school board for the abysmal situation at North Division. McEvilly told her Urban League audience that, except for debates over the location of the new school, "the community itself has been largely apathetic about the lack of quality in either the 'old' or the 'new' North Division." Leon Todd, another black board member from the Washington area, publicly declared that "North Division is an academic cesspool. It is a cancer that manifests itself in severe below-average test scores." Peg Kenner, a newly elected third black member of the school board, lived in the same vicinity as her colleagues and had also been employed as a paraprofessional at Washington High. Kenner pointed to the high percentage of low-achieving students at North Division and the stigma they placed on that school. "If you start moving those kids out," she urged, "then other communities start to have to share this gross deficit." Together, the black board members embraced the very "cultural deficit" language that Fuller and his colleagues strenuously opposed.

On the other side of the fence, Fuller blamed North Division's shortcomings on Milwaukee's black middle class, who he believed had abandoned the inner-city neighborhood. "The civil rights movement fizzled," he charged, "because those blacks who benefited from its gains sat out the rest of the struggle." His comments failed to recognize McEvilly's stated motivation: she felt compelled to act on North Division now because the black middle-class exodus had left them more isolated and vulnerable than before. As a school board member, McEvilly was now responsible for the system, while Fuller critiqued it from his position as an outsider, much like she had done as a community activist earlier in the decade.[18]

McEvilly's and Fuller's colliding visions of civil rights in the late 1970s paralleled a similar tension in the early 1960s. Back then, Lloyd Barbee had clashed with established black Milwaukeeans over competing civil rights agendas, where victories in hiring black teachers for increasingly segregated schools collided with the student integration movement. At that time, each side also brought along its own interpretations of all-black schooling. Newcomers like Barbee had emphasized how the substandard resources of segregated schools promoted ignorance and racial inferiority, while established blacks were more likely to recall the positive educational qualities and community ties found within black schools. In the 1970s, these same debates were being played out with renewed vigor, but this time the split came between black activists who identified with Washington High versus those who were affiliated with North Division. The two groups saw the world through such different lenses that they constructed strikingly different historical memories of black schooling in Milwaukee. For example, when Barbee was preparing for the desegregation trial in 1972, he had needed more detailed evidence about the pace of student segregation in inner-city schools during the 1950s, a time when school administrators had not officially collected racial statistics. McEvilly and other Washington-area desegregation supporters had come to his aid by leading a campaign to collect old elementary

Marian McEvilly and other Washington area activists supported Lloyd Barbee's lawsuit in 1972 by constructing a visual history of inner-city Milwaukee classrooms, stressing the increase of racial segregation and the decline of educational quality. From *Milwaukee Courier*, 18 November 1972; courtesy of Milwaukee Courier/Star, Inc.

school class photos, which also served as a way to publicize the upcoming trial. In the context of Barbee's court case, their photo essays told a familiar story: as Milwaukee's schools became increasingly segregated over the decades, the quality of education for black children had sharply deteriorated.[19]

Five years later, a different group of black Milwaukee school alumni used similar images to convey a much more positive historical memory of black education. Organizers of the "Fabulous Fifties Night" published classroom photos in the black weekly press to attract publicity for their upcoming class reunion, designed to bring together black Milwaukeeans who had graduated from inner-city elementary, junior high, and senior high schools during the 1950s. More than 400 alumni turned out for the reunion, and in their eyes, the photographs sparked nostalgic memories of a positive time when black education occurred in an increasingly segregated but tight-knit, caring community. One of the reunion organizers, Polly Williams, was also involved in the Blacks for Two-Way Integration movement in the mid-1970s and later joined Fuller to support the Coalition to Save North Division.[20]

Mixing historical memories with political activism did blur several important distinctions. A closer look at the 1950s classroom photographs used by both groups reveal several white children's faces in inner-city schools at that time, meaning that they were not entirely segregated inferior schools (as integrationists tended to portrayed them) nor entirely all-black proud institutions (as the reunion organizers portrayed them). Furthermore, any given individual's alumnus status and current geographical location in the city did not necessarily predict that person's movement activism. Cecil Brown Jr., a black North Division graduate from the 1940s, affiliated himself with the school integration movement in the 1970s. By contrast, even though Polly Williams graduated from North Division and supported Coalition efforts to save it, she no longer lived in the inner-city neighborhood, nor did she exert her limited power of choice (in the magnet school lottery) to attempt to send her children there. But historical memories are valuable for illustrating how activists on both sides of the 1970s struggles collectively reconstructed the past in order to shape interpretations of black schooling during the 1950s in ways that would advance their respective movements.[21]

Washington and North Division advocates even drew different conclusions from the same statistics, making nuanced interpretations about what these numbers might possibly tell about black student coercion and choice. Both sides agreed that in 1979, about 2,000 black students who had previously attended schools in the North Division district were now enrolled outside of that attendance area. But disagreements arose over how this transformation had occurred. McEvilly described these students as having "chosen" to attend either magnet schools or desegregated schools in white neigh-

In 1977, North Division advocates featured class photos during their "Fabulous Fifties Night" reunion that emphasized positive historical memories of a supportive black community and its schools. From *Milwaukee Courier*, 19 November 1977; courtesy of Milwaukee Courier/Star, Inc.

borhoods, since both of those moves seemed natural to her and her Washington area constituents. But Fuller referred to the same students as being "sent out" of the North Division district against their will. His criticism of Superintendent McMurrin's "forced choice" policy for black students, combined with his own personal identification with North Division, led him to label these students as involuntary transfers. Yet neither McEvilly's nor Fuller's interpretation of the data was entirely accurate. Judging from the existing studies of school application forms and black parent surveys, it appears that some inner-city residents clearly welcomed the opportunity to leave their neighborhood schools, while some others fought very hard to stay. Opposing views on black school reform led both McEvilly and Fuller to generalize about the data in ways that fit their particular visions for black education reform.[22]

To be sure, the differences between the black communities in the Washington and North Division neighborhoods did not appear by chance. Mc-Evilly and other Washington-area black activists were more likely to be middle-class professionals who had the economic means to afford the housing in this area. They also were more likely to share the integrationist views that originally would have led them to consider living in a predominantly white neighborhood. Milwaukee's two black communities and their leading spokespeople can be distinguished by these variables. But the variables of income and ideology alone do not fully explain how these two black education reform movements diverged during the 1970s. Black Milwaukeeans did not automatically take up different positions. Instead, black reformers created two distinctive activist communities, identified primarily around the challenges that jeopardized the two leading neighborhood public high schools that had become central to each of their collective identities. McEvilly and other Washington black activists fought for a desegregation plan that would reduce white flight and stabilize their racially transitional outlying neighborhood. Meanwhile, Fuller and North Division activists fought for a desegregation plan that would retain their brand-new facility to serve as an educational, cultural, and economic center for restabilizing their impoverished inner-city neighborhood. Given that the protection of white interests dominated all negotiations over school desegregation, the goals of the two black activist communities were pitted against one another. When the North Division controversy forced the two groups to address their irreconcilable differences, the split transformed the politics of black school reform in Milwaukee.

Transforming Struggles in the 1980s and 1990s

For a very long and bitter year, the Coalition to Save North Division continued to press the school board to reconsider its position, and by the spring of 1980 there were hopeful signs of progress. The Coalition gained significant support from the federally appointed monitoring board and eventually won the right to a hearing before the magistrate. The group's success can be traced to the broad base of supporters that Fuller organized, growing beyond the core black constituency to include a significant number of whites, as Barbee and MUSIC had done years earlier. The Coalition's emphasis on racial justice, not just racial solidarity, encouraged the participation of several liberal white academics from the University of Wisconsin–Milwaukee, whose research confirmed the Coalition's general claims and thus extended its credibility with other white audiences. The city's two white-owned daily newspapers, the *Milwaukee Sentinel* and the *Milwaukee Journal*, eventually shifted their editorial stances to recognize the black burden of desegregation as a major problem and to urge the school board to compromise. After mounting a final campaign and publishing a full-page petition with more than a thousand signatures in both white and black newspapers, the Coalition achieved its immediate goal in April 1980: the school board voted to keep North Division open to neighborhood students. The high school would enroll no more than 2,000 students; 60 percent of those seats would be allocated to black students, with the remaining 40 percent reserved for whites, if they chose to come.[23]

Although Marian McEvilly and her black school board colleagues opposed the Coalition, two different groups of white board members eventually voted in favor of the North Division compromise. On one hand, liberal white board members decided to change course, after a year of massive publicity for voluntary enrollment at the North Division magnet school had yielded only 41 white students and evidence of the black burden had grown larger. Doris Stacey, a leading white desegregation supporter on the board, explained that she now understood the "clear reality of the non-voluntarism of many black students in their choice of schools," adding that McMurrin's efforts in "counseling" current North Division students to transfer elsewhere was more appropriately labeled as "cajoling." On the other hand, conservative white board members, like Margaret Dinges, eagerly agreed to maintain North Division as a black neighborhood school in order to protect predominantly white neighborhood schools. One month prior to the North Division agreement, conservatives successfully overturned Superintendent McMurrin's plan to bus about 500 white students away from their southside neighborhood high schools. To avoid charges of hypocrisy, since black students were still being forced out of North Division, Dinges and other conservatives joined white liberals in resolving the matter. Coalition supporters savored the outcome, but it was a sober reminder of the harsh realities of race and school reform politics. The Coalition could not have maintained North Division without the votes of white conservatives, whose real interests did not necessarily coincide with their own.[24]

The victory won by Howard Fuller and the Coalition to Save North Division fundamentally transformed Milwaukee's history of black school reform by pushing Lloyd Barbee and MUSIC's accomplishments to the sidelines. A decade later, Barbee looked back on Milwaukee's school integration movement and counted the years when it had prevailed in the minds of the city's black residents. "I would say that from 1963 to 1980, the bulk of blacks in Milwaukee supported me, in general," he recalled. In the beginning, Barbee had launched the integration struggle with only a handful of supporters, then built a mass movement and was continuously reelected to the state legislature. But at the end, when he finally brought the desegregation lawsuit to a close, Barbee was backed by a relatively small number of supporters. The North Division struggle marked the endpoint of vibrant black popular support for his integration agenda because the demographic realities of white suburbanization led him to advocate for dispersing black students to better-resourced white schools, regardless of the consequences. During an oral history interview conducted with Barbee in 1990, when asked to comment on the Coalition's complaints against blacks carrying the burden of desegregation, he still interpreted the issue through 1960s lenses. "The process of desegregation is undoing what has been done by the segregators," he explained. "Sometimes that is hard on the people who have been segregated, like the Little Rock Nine [the first blacks to enter Central High in 1957] or James Meredith [the first black to enter the University of Mississippi in 1962]. The burden many times is uneven. But when you get integration, that burden disappears." While members of the 1979 Coalition to Save North Division perceived the black burden as their defining issue, it was, from Barbee's standpoint, merely a temporary inconvenience.[25]

After the North Division controversy, both white and black media sought to create a forum where Barbee and Fuller would debate one another. But this event never took place. "My enemy is not Dr. Fuller," Barbee insisted. "My enemy is the segregationists and the people who want to keep minorities ignorant." Fuller, who earned his doctorate by writing a critical study on the Milwaukee school system's implementation of desegregation, was careful to praise Barbee as a courageous civil rights activist of his time. During a 1990 public history conference on Milwaukee's integration movement, Barbee and Fuller sat onstage with other panelists and told their own stories of the struggle, each emphasizing the main points they had covered as activists building their respective movements. At the close, Fuller approached Barbee and privately discussed how they might possibly collaborate on a future project. It was a cordial conversation, but the two men, molded by vastly different experiences of race and reform, never talked about the idea again. A new age of black politics had clearly risen. Polly Williams, a rising black Democrat who supported Fuller's Coalition, was elected to represent Milwaukee's Seventeenth District in the Wisconsin state assembly in 1980. "We have a new movement of black people emerging," she declared. "This is not the 1960s."[26]

Fuller's inner-city activism reached beyond educational politics to raise public awareness about other historical burdens of the black community, such as police brutality. In late 1979, Fuller and other activists spoke out against the controversial death of Ernest Lacy, a young black man who died while in police custody. The case stirred memories of the fatal police shooting of Daniel Bell in 1958, which, during the "migrant crisis" of that era, had been the focus of intense black community meetings and debate over how best to respond. The Lacy incident coincided with an amazing revelation of a police cover-up. In 1979, a white policeman involved in the 1958 Bell shooting confessed that fellow officers had planted a knife in the dead victim's hand in order to falsely justify their actions and were encouraged by superiors not to tell anyone. Rev. R. L. Lathan, the black minister who had first tried to organize a "Prayer of Protest" against police brutality in 1958 (but who had faced black and white political pressure to call it off), now led his protest march, twenty-one years after the incident, with Fuller at his side. Their public demonstration contributed to the subsequent departure of Milwaukee's controversial police chief, Harold Breier.[27]

But after the Coalition's 1980 victory in saving North Division, Fuller soon learned a humbling lesson that many other black education activists had learned before him: winning one high-profile political battle for school reform did not necessarily improve the actual quality of education for black students. After the initial victory, the Coalition attempted to follow up on making North Division the best school possible by organizing a school-community committee to draft a "School Effectiveness Program." The program called for a new academic focus, revised curriculum, additional tutoring, higher expectations, and code of student respect. But the challenge was implementation. Fuller complained about the absence of authentic community control at North Division. School officials assigned a new black principal to the school a mere two weeks before it reopened, and teachers mistakenly expected community members "to come in and instantly motivate students." After the first year, while North Division had crawled up from the bottom of the academic rankings for city high schools, its schoolwide student grade point average remained a 1.07, equivalent to a D. Whites did not come in significant numbers to the school, which remained 96 percent black. The stark predictions of black board member Marian McEvilly, who warned that the Coalition's strategy would not transform the educational quality of North Division, could not be ignored.[28]

Meanwhile, Superintendent McMurrin proudly reported in 1982 that the Milwaukee school system had surpassed the racial balance goals established by the final court settlement. Over 85 percent of students attended a school that fell within the official desegregation range, ten percentage points higher than the minimum required by law. In addition, certain high-profile schools (like Washington High) were now comprised of balanced percentages of blacks and whites. But McMurrin's numbers did not reveal the entire story. Numerical integration had become easier to achieve in the Milwaukee public schools during the early 1980s because the overall student enrollment had become approximately 50 percent black and 50 percent white. But this change was caused, in part, by the falling numbers of white students, as the overall student enrollment declined from its 1970 peak of 130,000 to a 1982 low point of 87,000 (a 33 percent drop). Also, North Division and twenty-four other inner-city schools were not desegregated and remained predominantly black, as permitted by the terms of the controversial desegregation settlement. In addition to its citywide residential disparities, Milwaukee earned the dubious distinction of being named the most segregated major metropolitan area in the United States in 1981. Out of 150,000

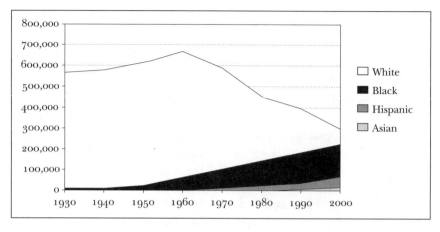

Milwaukee Population, by Race, 1930–2000. *Source*: U.S. Census Bureau, *Census of Population and Housing*, 1930–2000.

blacks in the four-county area, only 2.5 percent lived outside of Milwaukee city limits. From 1980 to 2000, the white share of the Milwaukee city population dropped from 71 to 50 percent. As in most Northern "rust belt" cities during this period, white suburbanites pulled farther away from the increasingly black and Hispanic central-city population, largely abandoning the city's pressing educational issues.[29]

During the 1980s, black Milwaukee education activists continued to move in two different directions, each group pursuing its own vision of how to harness real power to uplift the race through school reform. Integration supporters tried to pick up the *Armstrong v. Board of School Directors* school desegregation case where Barbee had ended it in 1979, but the federal courts denied an appeal filed jointly by the Milwaukee NAACP and its national parent organization to reopen the terms of the controversial settlement. The setback led integrationists to regroup and redefine their goal, from citywide desegregation to metropolitan integration, thereby earning greater rights for blacks to access white suburban schools and the resources they held. In 1980, black board member Leon Todd proposed that the Milwaukee school district file a lawsuit against suburban municipalities that refused to participate in Wisconsin's Chapter 220 voluntary city-suburb transfer program. Integration advocates supported this tactic and went a step further in 1984 with a bold proposal to dissolve political boundaries between Milwaukee and twenty-four suburban districts and to create six racially balanced subdistricts (shaped like slices of a pie) that would divide the black inner-city and integrate it with outlying white areas. Although this metropolitan proposal failed, increased political and legal pressure successfully persuaded all suburban districts in Milwaukee County to accept Chapter 220 students

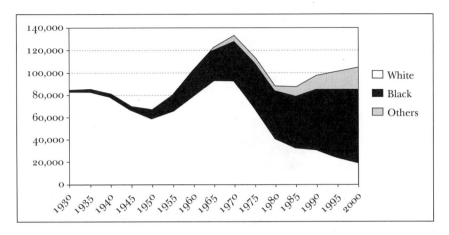

Milwaukee Public School Enrollment, by Race, 1930–2000. *Sources*: Milwaukee Board of School Directors, *Annual Report*, 1930–75; Washington and Oliver, "Identification of Strengths in the Black Community"; Barndt and McNally, *Return to Separate and Unequal*; and U.S. Census Bureau, *Census of Population and Housing*, 1930–2000.

(and the state funding that came with them). By 1987, the Milwaukee public schools sent over 3,000 student volunteers (mostly black) to enroll in suburban schools and received less than 800 white suburban students. But the overall impact on racial balance in city schools was minimal. The expensive Chapter 220 program gave new opportunities to individual students but effectively reduced Milwaukee's proportion of minority students only from 67 to 65 percent.[30]

At the same time, Howard Fuller and several activists from the former Coalition to Save North Division also reorganized their efforts to gain more political influence over public schooling in the 1980s. Fuller joined the administration of Democratic governor Tony Earl and began to fight more battles for Milwaukee schools at the state level. He and his allies sharply criticized the Chapter 220 program for diverting millions of dollars from education to transportation and furthering racist assumptions that quality schooling could not occur in predominantly black settings. After city officials voted to close additional inner-city schools, Fuller proposed state legislation to create the New North Division School District in 1987, which would be legally independent from the Milwaukee public schools. Integrationists charged that Fuller's plan would further segregation, but he responded that this was a moot point, since blacks already composed 97 percent of the school population in that area. Publicity for the newly proposed district prominently quoted from W. E. B. Du Bois's famous 1935 essay, "Does the Negro Need Separate Schools?," to make its case: "Theoretically, the Negro needs neither segregated schools nor mixed schools. What he needs is Edu-

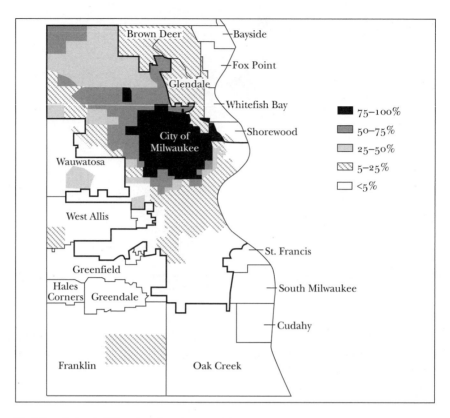

Black Population in Milwaukee County, 2000. The metropolitan Milwaukee area has become one of the most "hyper-segregated" regions in the United States. Adapted from U.S. Census Bureau, *Census of Population and Housing*, 2000.

cation." Fuller's proposal, with backing from state representative Polly Williams, made surprising advances in the state legislature but eventually was defeated. Yet the attempt sparked new ideas about potential strategies and unconventional political coalitions in the years to come.[31]

In 1988, Polly Williams and her administrative aide, Larry Harwell, rallied legislative support for a state-funded tuition voucher program by allying themselves with white conservatives such as Republican governor Tommy Thompson, business leaders, and the Bradley Foundation. Their political success shifted the discourse of black school reform at both local and national levels. When first implemented in 1990, the Milwaukee Parental Choice Program restricted eligibility to low-income city students, whose $2,446 voucher had to be accepted as full tuition by approved nonsectarian private schools. During the first year, only 341 students, about 90 percent black or Latino, participated in the program. In 1995, the Republican-dominated state legislature raised the voucher to $4,600 dollars and expanded the Milwaukee program to include religious schools, an action that was delayed but eventually approved by Wisconsin courts. By 2003, the number of students participating in the voucher program had risen to over 11,000, the vast majority of them still black or Latino. Milwaukee's voucher movement has drawn national attention as policy advocates and social scientists on both sides of the issue have hotly debated whether or not vouchers are a panacea for the ills of urban public education or a "false choice" that will undermine democratic schooling. Privately funded and publicly funded voucher programs have since arisen in other cities with large black and Latino populations, such as Cleveland, Indianapolis, and San Antonio.[32]

Most contemporary accounts of Milwaukee's voucher movement focus on the "strange bedfellows" coalition that suddenly arose between black Democrats and white conservatives in the late 1980s. But some writers have noted that the Milwaukee choice movement has deeper roots in the city's history of black education reform. Indeed, an earlier generation of black Milwaukee activists discussed vouchers as early as 1970, when the Office of Economic Opportunity solicited proposals for a federally funded pilot program. Some of the surviving independent schools from that era, such as Harambee and Urban Day, lobbied for vouchers then as well as in the late 1980s and today enjoy some of the largest enrollments of subsidized students in the city. Yet neither Williams nor Harwell played a significant role in the 1970 voucher debate. Instead, their activism for vouchers stemmed from the black protest against the white-dominated politics of school desegregation of the mid- to late 1970s. The prevailing magnet school strategy gave most whites a voluntary choice about moving to a newly desegregated school but presented many blacks with a "forced choice" since inner-city schools were disproportionately closed and converted into magnets, resulting in fewer options for enrolling in neighborhood schools. In 1977, when a younger Polly Williams announced that she was going to defy authorities who rejected her daughter's application and take a chair with her to enroll her "in the school of my choice," she was referring to options solely within the public school system. But since that time, Williams came to believe that the Milwaukee public schools had failed to serve her and her constituents, and she demanded a choice outside of the system, the same choice that most middle-class whites enjoyed.[33]

Throughout the 1980s, Howard Fuller initially believed that private school choice would be the "death knell for public education." But as local journalist Mikel Holt observed, Fuller surprised many Milwaukeeans by supporting Williams's voucher bill two weeks before a crucial legislative committee meeting in 1990. Fuller argued that "choice can be the savior of public education. The key to reforming the bureaucracy is progressive leadership at the top and empowering parents at the bottom." One year later, after working his way up through a series of governmental positions, Fuller was selected to fill the leadership role as superintendent of the Milwaukee public schools. He was the city's third black superintendent, stepping into the position after the relatively brief administrations of two black predecessors, Hawthorn Faison and Robert Peterkin. As superintendent, Fuller continued to focus his attention on transforming institutions to better serve the interests of inner-city black schoolchildren. He oversaw the opening of two African American immersion schools in the public system in the early 1990s, an effort that had been proposed by a coalition of black school principals and proponents of black cultural studies. But Fuller soon became frustrated with what he could not change. He resigned as superintendent in 1995, citing as his major obstacle the new school board majority who supported the Milwaukee Teachers' Education Association, the union that had begun amid the inner-city school crises of 1963 and had grown in power over time. Fuller left to take up a position as director of the Institute for the Transformation of Learning at Marquette University, where he has become more deeply involved in the national private school choice movement and has alienated some of his past supporters by accepting funding from right-wing voucher proponents. But Fuller has managed to hold together considerable black support for the voucher coalition in recent years by wrapping its agenda in the rhetoric of black self-determination. "Choice is not the issue in America," he declared to black Milwaukee parents at a late 1990s pro-voucher rally. "The issue is who has choice." In doing so, Fuller has translated the 1990s buzzword of "choice" into racial terms, just as he had done with the 1960s "black power" slogan as a North Carolina community organizer three decades earlier.[34]

At the close of the 1990s, black Milwaukee school reformers were largely split into two groups, each pursuing what it viewed as the real source of power to uplift the race. Metropolitan integration supporters fought for black rights to attend white suburban public schools, while voucher advocates campaigned for black rights to exit the public system and take public funding with them to the private sector. Both groups struggled to define "choice" in their own way. But the integrationists have clearly lost ground in Milwaukee over the past two decades. Enrollment in the state-subsidized Chapter 220 city-suburb school transfer program peaked at nearly 6,000 students in 1993; ten years later, it has declined to just under 5,000. The entire program was threatened with extinction in 1994 and faces pressure from state budget cuts again. Inside city limits during the late 1990s, school board and state officials campaigned to reduce the scale of Milwaukee's school desegregation busing to return to a vision of "neighborhood schooling," though this effort is currently more of a rhetorical agenda than a reality. Still, several contemporary black Milwaukee activists, operating independently or in conjunction with white conservatives, have recent argued for dismantling the desegregation court order that an earlier generation worked so hard to build. But that particular school reform movement is now history. After a long illness, Lloyd Barbee, Milwaukee's most prominent advocate of school integration, died in December 2002. More struggles over race, class, and education reform, based on people and ideas most appropriate to the region's unfolding context, are still to come.[35]

CONCLUSION

RETHINKING HISTORY AND POLICY IN THE

POST-*BROWN* ERA

As the nation prepares to commemorate the fiftieth anniversary of the 1954 *Brown v. Board* decision, the current status of black school reform appears to be very confusing. School desegregation policies that took more than a generation to achieve now are being partly rolled back in cities like Milwaukee, and several leading black activists are advocating for neighborhood schools, African American immersion education, or private school vouchers. Similar trends in desegregation politics have also appeared in other Northern and Western cities (such as Buffalo, Cleveland, and Denver) and across the South (including Charlotte, Jacksonville, Mobile, and Nashville). National observers point to three major U.S. Supreme Court rulings during the 1990s that curtailed the scope and duration of desegregation orders, enabling the return of segregated neighborhood schools and the evaporation of two decades of progress toward integrated education. For historians of educational policy, this apparent dissonance between past and present raises a troubling question. How do our historical interpretations of *Brown* explain—or fail to explain—how the nation arrived at these current policy dilemmas on race and education? This concluding chapter identifies three general types of scholarly writing on *Brown* and its aftermath — the unfinished struggle, the misguided struggle, and the continuing local struggles—and evaluates how each of them have shaped our understanding of the evolution of black education reform in recent years.[1]

The first, and most prevalent, historical interpretation portrays black educational history over the past several decades as a heroic yet unfinished struggle for integration. One of the best illustrations of this tradition is James T. Patterson's *Brown v. Board of Education*, an outstanding synthesis of the shifting strategies within the school desegregation struggle during most of the twentieth century. His story begins with the young cadre of NAACP Legal Defense Fund lawyers, such as Thurgood Marshall, and their courageous black plaintiffs who began challenging the "separate but equal" *Plessy v. Ferguson* ruling in the 1930s. At first, Marshall attacked the "equal" part of "separate but equal," forcing Southern states to live up to their promise of providing equal resources for black schools. He successfully persuaded the Court to force Missouri to accept the expensive remedy of opening a black law school in the 1938 *Gaines* decision. Over time, these precedent-building victories allowed Marshall to shift his legal strategy from the tangible benefits of equal resources to the intangible benefits of integrated education, thereby attacking the "separate" clause head-on. In the 1950 *Sweatt* and *McLaurin* decisions, Marshall convinced the Court that physically separating the small handful of black law and graduate school students from white professors and classmates deprived them of the free exchange of ideas, the fundamental basis of higher education. These favorable new rulings linked integration with equality, a concept that Marshall pressed the Court to expand for the elementary school cases in *Brown*.[2]

Despite the victorious *Brown* ruling in 1954, Patterson explains that the NAACP's battle continued to evolve after Southern whites erected new barriers to stall the pace of racial integration during the late 1950s and early 1960s. These ranged from crude intimidation against blacks seeking entry into white schools, to complex bureaucratic and legal obstacles to deter or delay black transfers, to the systematic approach of closing down an entire school district and diverting public funds into vouchers for whites to attend private schools. Confronted with these obstacles, NAACP lawyers went back to court and fought hard to win new rulings in the late 1960s that demanded results in racial integration, most often through affirmative steps such as busing and redistricting. But once again, white conservatives found new ways to protect their interests through the political process. President Nixon's "Southern Strategy" to win conservative white votes for the Republican Party slowed down the pace of federal desegregation enforcement in the early 1970s. Later, President Reagan's reconfiguration of the U.S. Supreme Court signaled a retreat on civil rights in the 1980s. Although the black-led school integration movement ended the travesty of legalized segregation and reminded America of its constitutional promises of equal protection under law, the campaign to fully integrate public schools remained unfinished at the close of the twentieth century.[3]

Although Patterson offers a broad survey, his account does not adequately explain the recent evolution of black educational activism since the late 1970s. Although the bulk of the book provides a careful historical analysis of changing reform strategies from the 1930s through the early 1970s, the final two chapters abruptly shift to a static characterization of two groups of activists in the last two decades. On one hand, Patterson writes, the "optimists" in the civil rights movement "kept the faith" in the promise of *Brown* and continued to "fight their good fight." On the other hand, "pessimists," like former NAACP attorneys Robert Carter and Derrick Bell and social psychologist Kenneth Clark, became "gloomy" and "bitter" about the prospects of integration in a racist society and turned their backs on the cause. By simplistically dividing historical actors into two fixed categories—optimists and pessimists—Patterson loses track of his previous analysis on how the black education struggle had changed over time. Furthermore, he sharply criticizes "pessimists" who advanced a "separatist nostalgia" about the positive aspects of all-black schooling during the Jim Crow era, dismissing it as a "poor reading of history and the product of disillusion" with the recent stalemates of racial progress.

Patterson issues a valuable warning against romanticizing the past, but his own narrative is not immune from this tendency. Consider an alternative interpretation of Patterson's story using the same categories and evidence. From the perspective of black voucher supporters in the 1990s, the integrationists could be renamed the "nostalgic optimists" for believing that the reform strategies devised in the 1950s and 1960s are still appropriate for today. Black voucher supporters might also label themselves "pragmatic realists" for creating a new strategy to achieve what the past decades of the school integration struggle had not fully attained. Like many historians of the civil rights era, Patterson centers his narrative squarely on *Brown*, and he creates a compelling account of this important story. Yet in doing so, he elevates the school integration movement as the only struggle in black educational history during the twentieth century, thereby casting aside all the other struggles observed in cities like Milwaukee: hiring black teachers, acculturating new migrants, exercising community control, teaching black history, and securing vouchers to leave the system. Viewing all of black educational history through the lens of *Brown* distorts our vision of the past because it obscures how reform movements have evolved with the changing historical context and limits our understanding of the scope of these movements' goals.[4]

A second trend in historical interpretation depicts the past half-century of black education reform as an originally noble yet eventually misguided struggle. The most influential work along this line has been Diane Ravitch's *Troubled Crusade*, a sweeping synthesis of changes in American education during the postwar era. She argues that when NAACP lawyers originally demanded the elimination of legalized segregation in the 1950s, they justified their case on the egalitarian principles of the Constitution and envisioned a color-blind society. Specifically, when Justice Felix Frankfurter asked attorney Thurgood Marshall what remedy he envisioned if the Court ruled in his favor, he replied that education officials should be prohibited "from segregating on the basis of race or color" when drawing school attendance boundary lines. "If the lines are drawn on a natural basis, without regard to race or color, then I think that nobody would have any complaint," Marshall added. After the Supreme Court's initial *Brown* decision led to confusion over implementation, this view came to be adopted by a lower court as the "*Briggs* dictum" in 1955, stating that segregation was illegal if forced by governmental power but still legal if voluntarily agreed upon.[5]

Over the next two decades, Ravitch contends, the integration movement veered away from this noble vision of color-blindness and pursued a misguided crusade for color-consciousness. Pressure from federal authorities, liberal social scientists, and militant black power activists led the federal courts to change course, she argues. The 1968 *Green* decision ruled that "freedom of choice" plans were insufficient because they did not desegregate students fast enough, and the 1971 *Swann* decision required schools to take affirmative steps to create racially balanced schools. Former tools of segregation—such as using race to draw school boundaries, as well as busing and quotas—were now considered to be fair tools for integration, states Ravitch. During the 1970s, as color-conscious advocates imposed bureaucratic mandates for multicultural curricula and affirmative action policies on schools, they distracted educators from their core teaching mission and undermined their moral authority to socialize youth. What began as a noble struggle resulted in a collapse of academic standards, she asserts, shortchanging the black students whom the integration movement was intended to serve.[6]

Like Patterson, Ravitch's interpretation is problematic because it fails to recognize the dynamic nature of black reform movements as they respond to the shifting historical context. Whereas Patterson faults selected black activists who changed their views on integration, Ravitch criticizes the entire integration movement for evolving over time. To be sure, Ravitch's account provides a valuable historical reminder that Thurgood Marshall initially envisioned *Brown* as the removal of segregative barriers in the early 1950s. But her account does not adequately address the transformation of white power in controlling the terms of desegregation in the 1960s and 1970s and the need for integration supporters to shift their strategies accordingly and press for race-based reforms. The white-dominated world of the 1950s and 1960s was certainly not color-blind in practice, even though the NAACP crafted a color-blind rhetoric as their best strategy for promoting black rights at the time. When the judicial system forced whites to accept color-blind principles in educational policy, many adapted new ways of protecting white privilege in schools, prompting new responses in turn from integration activists. In sum, both Patterson's and Ravitch's interpretations favor a static view of history and do not fully consider how black reform activists and movements may evolve over time, continually adapting to the prevailing context, seeking new ways to secure the broader goals that have not yet been fully achieved.

A third trend of historical interpretation examines continuing local struggles for black education, and this growing body of literature offers some insightful alternatives to both of the national-level narratives cited above. As political theorist Jennifer Hochschild has observed, local movements can sometimes be quite difficult to characterize since some definitions of "quality black education" may simultaneously attract both conservative and radical supporters. Yet local histories of black educational struggles, when carefully researched and written, offer several advantages: the ability to trace subtle developments in one location over several decades, to contrast viewpoints from multiple participants' perspectives, and to assess the varying influence of national-level factors. Furthermore, these rich local histories are most valuable when read in comparison to one another. By contrasting how local groups of black education activists defined goals on their own terms and how they exercised the limited power available to achieve their aims, we learn a great deal about the importance of historical context. Struggles over race and school reform vary from place to place, and even in the same location, they evolve from decade to decade.[7]

For example, compare how black activists in two different rural Southern communities responded to "freedom of choice" desegregation plans in the latter half of the 1960s. First, in Constance Curry's *Silver Rights*, Mae Bertha and Matthew Carter of Sunflower County, Mississippi, longed for their children to have a better life than sharecropping cotton on white plantations. Dilapidated black schools had far fewer resources than white schools did; in the 1950s, only a third of the black teachers in the county had even completed high school. Ten years after *Brown*, federal authorities eventually pressured local white officials to comply with the minimalist *Briggs* dictum. Sunflower County's all-white school board fulfilled the letter of the law by instituting a freedom of choice desegregation plan, whereby each family would choose a public school for its children. In truth, the plan continued to protect white interests, since blacks were intimidated from choosing white schools. In 1965, the Carter family was the only black family in the entire county who dared to cross the racial line. They courageously defied physical violence and economic retaliation to choose white schools in search of the best education available in the county. Two years later, "freedom of choice" had produced scarcely any movement away from the preexisting system of segregation. So the Carters and their allies filed a federal lawsuit to prohibit this so-called voluntary desegregation method and to replace it with the mandatory integration of all blacks into white schools. In the end, the Carters finally won their court battle against the cruel hoax of "freedom of choice," though their broader struggle for equal educational opportunity still continued.[8]

Yet in David Cecelski's *Along Freedom Road*, hundreds of black families rose up to protest the elimination of freedom of choice desegregation in the late 1960s in Hyde County, North Carolina. Black residents of this coastal fishing community had built their own one-room schoolhouses in the late nineteenth century and, despite limited resources, created a secondary school in the 1930s with high academic standards and respected roles for black teachers as community leaders. State aid for segregated schools increased in the 1950s, when North Carolina narrowed the resource gap with white schools in an attempt to avert desegregation litigation. A decade after *Brown*, Hyde County whites introduced freedom of choice plans (similar to Curry's account), and while twenty-one black children initially transferred to white schools, that number soon declined as blacks developed concerns over student mistreatment, the fate of black educators' jobs, and barriers against their full participation in the desegregation planning process. Eventually, after federal officials declared freedom of choice plans to be a failure for achieving significant racial balancing in Hyde County in 1968, the white-dominated school board closed the black community schools and mandated one-way integration to white institutions. Local black leaders responded that they were "tired of having to bear the burdens of integration" and, with the help of civil rights allies, held protest marches to the state capitol and a year-long boycott to demand the reopening of their schools. In contrast to Sunflower County, many Hyde County blacks demanded that freedom of choice be reinstated to protect black schools, one of the most essential cultural and political institutions in their community. After clashes with white police and Klansmen, Hyde County's black protesters negotiated a bilateral desegregation agreement, which reopened the black high school (though only as an elementary school) and guaranteed black educators' jobs and new positions of authority in school administration. Although several important concessions had been won, the Hyde County struggle was far from over.[9]

Contrasting Curry's and Cecelski's local narratives of black education struggles tells us how an identical reform policy can have different meanings and provoke very different reactions, depending upon the historical context surrounding its implementation. Understanding why blacks opposed freedom of choice in one Southern county yet supported it in another requires looking beyond the policy label and examining the fabric of each community. In Sunflower County, it appears that both white state officials and local blacks had invested fewer financial and cultural resources in their black schools over time, in contrast to the better-resourced schools in Hyde County that seem to have played a more central role in the life of the black community. As a result, "freedom of choice" had no fixed meaning across the South, so it did not provoke a uniform response from these two different communities. Simply put, there was more than one struggle.[10]

Whether in Mississippi, North Carolina, or even Milwaukee, black education reformers have pursued the same broad objective: to assert greater power over school policies and practices to uplift the race. Only the means of achieving that end have changed, over time and place. But the reasons why black reformers have engaged in so many different types of struggles become much clearer when viewed through historical lenses, particularly at the local level. As racism, the key factor underlying these struggles, has adapted to new situations and continues to privilege white interests, the definition of real, lasting power has sometimes eluded reformers since it, too, varies from place to place; even in one location, it continues to change over time. At first glance, many contemporary black school reform movements — for neighborhood schools, Afrocentric curriculum, and private vouchers — seem anomalous with the spirit of the fiftieth anniversary of *Brown*. But given the evidence that some school desegregation policies were fundamentally designed to protect white interests, as many describe Milwaukee's plans of the late 1970s, then it makes sense that some black activists would challenge these policies in the 1980s and 1990s. Therefore, from a historical perspective, the past and present struggles of black education reform are not so far apart. In fact, if black education movements had remained frozen in time, so that the struggles and strategies of 1954 were identical to those observed fifty years later, we would be facing an even greater state of historical confusion. This is the important, subtle lesson that local histories of race, power, and school reform can teach us.

Yet for policy-hungry audiences, the weakness of this third category of historical interpretation — continuing local struggles for black education — is its inability (or its refusal) to pin down a specific list of useful prescriptions for "what works" regarding race and education. Other interpretations that claim to deliver a definitive summary of the national legacy of *Brown* (whether the unfinished or the misguided versions) seem to satisfy this appetite, but only temporarily. Perhaps the fundamental problem here can be resolved only by rethinking the relationship between history and policy. Contrary to George Santayana's famous curse that those who fail to learn from history will be condemned to repeat it, most historians would never claim that the past will ever be repeated. Indeed, while some similarities may arise between past and future events, they will always be accompanied by differences in historical context, which is continually changing. Consider then what policy historians Richard Neustadt and Ernest May pose in their book, *Thinking in Time*, as an alternative reason for studying the past: its ability to simulate historical imagination. "Seeing the past can help one envision alternative futures," they write. While history cannot tell policy-makers what to do, studying the past can teach us how to ask probing questions, especially about our presumptions about contemporary policies. "The point is to get forward, as soon as possible, the questions that ought to be asked," they argue, "before anyone says, 'This is what we should do' or 'Here's how to do it.'"[11]

Following Neustadt and May's advice, what have we learned from Milwaukee's history of race and schooling, and how does it shape the questions we should be asking about contemporary educational policy, for both the city and the nation at large? This book has shown that education reform movements have evolved in Milwaukee from the 1930s to the present as different generations of black activists have responded to changing expressions of racism and their shifting perceptions of the needs of black communities. As each generation fought and won a bit of power over the system, its victories (and compromises) entailed serious consequences for the generations that followed. Beginning in the Depression era, when William Kelley and the Urban League organized to break Milwaukee's barriers against hiring black teachers, their eventual victory in the 1950s came at the cost of accepting an increasingly segregated school system. When Lloyd Barbee, Marian McEvilly, and MUSIC confronted school segregation in the 1960s, their subsequent legal victory in the late 1970s came at the cost of accepting a magnet school desegregation plan that privileged whites and disproportionately burdened inner-city blacks. More recently, when Howard Fuller and the Coalition to Save North Division fought to maintain North Division as a inner-city neighborhood high school, their victory in the early 1980s came at the cost of embracing a system that did very little to improve the standard indicators of academic quality for black students. During each of these decades, black activists brought vibrant coalitions of people together with slogans such as "Jobs," "Integration," and "Save North Division," but these slogans have been mere representations of the real, lasting power needed to continually improve education and uplift the race over the long haul.

Learning these difficult lessons from Milwaukee's past leads us to pose hard questions to the black education reformers of today. For example, if twenty-first century proponents of returning to neighborhood schooling, or expanding metropolitan integration efforts, should happen to gain victories in their respective efforts, what would be the long-term consequences for future generations? As for the private school voucher movement, which made the most visible political gains in the 1990s, how might white privilege be reasserting itself through the broader implications of this market-based reform? If we have learned anything from Milwaukee's past, it is to maintain equal amounts of hope and healthy skepticism for every reform effort. Each of them can point us in positive directions, yet none of them should be mistaken for a panacea. For example, cracks have already appeared in Polly Williams's fifteen-year-old coalition for private school vouchers. If the past teaches us that coalition memberships are often more fluid than the ideological positions voiced by official leaders, then perhaps we might witness an entirely new reform movement arise out of the voucher coalition in the not-too-distant future.[12]

Contrary to the popular impressions conveyed by national-level narratives of *Brown*, there is no steady historical march of progress for jobs, integration, black power, or choice. Rather, Milwaukee's experience in the twentieth century tells us that black education reform is best understood as an overlapping series of evolving struggles to gain power to uplift the race through improved schooling. If we fail to look at contemporary debates over race and education through historical lenses with a rich appreciation of both change and continuity across different contexts, then we will never fully understand them. Yet there is a hopeful message in all of this. From a historical perspective, the evolution of reform movements does not imply a mechanical process; instead, it is a process of creative adaptation. While activists in Milwaukee and elsewhere clearly have responded to political, cultural, and demographic changes in their local environments, they still make human decisions, point out new possibilities, build innovative coalitions, and cause historical change to happen. If we learn more about race and reform movements in the past—especially their subtle lessons about the dynamic nature of privilege and power—perhaps we can strengthen our collective capacity to make a difference in the future.

NOTES

ABBREVIATIONS

BARBEE PAPERS   Lloyd A. Barbee Papers, Golda Meir Library, University of Wisconsin–Milwaukee, Milwaukee, Wis.

BARNDT PAPERS   Michael Barndt Papers, in possession of author

DORSEY PAPERS   James Dorsey Papers, Milwaukee County Historical Society, Milwaukee, Wis.

MILWAUKEE CORE PAPERS   Congress of Racial Equality, Milwaukee Chapter, Papers, Golda Meir Library, University of Wisconsin–Milwaukee, Milwaukee, Wis.

MILWAUKEE NAACP PAPERS   National Association for the Advancement of Colored People, Milwaukee Branch, Papers, Golda Meir Library, University of Wisconsin–Milwaukee, Milwaukee, Wis.

MILWAUKEE URBAN LEAGUE PAPERS   Milwaukee Urban League Papers, Golda Meir Library, University of Wisconsin–Milwaukee, Milwaukee, Wis.

MORHEUSER PAPERS   Marilyn Morheuser Papers, in possession of author

NATIONAL NAACP PAPERS   National Association for the Advancement of Colored People Papers, Library of Congress, Washington, D.C.

NATIONAL URBAN LEAGUE PAPERS   National Urban League Papers, Library of Congress, Washington, D.C.

PETERSON PAPERS   Bob Peterson Papers, in possession of author

REUSS PAPERS   Henry S. Reuss Papers, Golda Meir Library, University of Wisconsin–Milwaukee, Milwaukee, Wis.

WILLIAMS PAPERS   Evelyn Williams Papers, in possession of author

ZABLOCKI PAPERS   Clement J. Zablocki Papers, Marquette University, Milwaukee, Wis.

ZEIDLER PAPERS   Frank P. Zeidler Mayoral Administration Papers, Milwaukee Public Library, Milwaukee, Wis.

INTRODUCTION

1. *Brown v. Board of Education* (17 May 1954); Wilson, "Exhibition Review"; *Eyes on the Prize*, video; Jacobs, *Getting around Brown*, xi–xii. On civil rights narratives in textbooks, documentaries, and popular culture, see Epstein, "Tales from Two Textbooks"; Link, "Film Review"; and Gardner, "Coming of Age in the Movement."

2. Harding, *Hope and History*, chapters 1 and 3.

3. Sullivan and Martin, "Introduction," xi–xii.

4. Goings and Mohl, "Toward a New African American Urban History," 288; Cecelski, *Along Freedom Road*; Walker, *Their Highest Potential*. For related works on Southern black community ambivalence over *Brown*, see Arnez, "Implementation of Desegregation"; Dempsey and Noblit, "Cultural Ignorance and School Desegregation"; Foster, "Politics of Race" and "Constancy"; Jones, *Traditional Model of Educational Excellence*; Philipsen, *Values Spoken and Values Lived*; and Pride and Woodard, *Burden of Busing*. See also recent histories of Mexican American educational struggles that decenter the conventional *Brown* narrative, such as Donato, *The Other Struggle*, and San Miguel, *Brown, Not White*.

5. On continuity in twentieth-century civil rights and black educational historiography, see Carson, "Civil Rights Reform"; Chafe, *Civilities and Civil Rights*; Dalfiume, "'Forgotten Years'"; Korstad and Lichtenstein, "Opportunities Found and Lost"; Lowe and Kantor, "Considerations"; Marable, *Race, Reform, and Rebellion*; Nasstrom, "Beginnings and Endings"; Newby and Tyack, "Victims without 'Crimes'"; Norrell, "One Thing We Did Right"; Payne, *I've Got the Light of Freedom*; and Tyson, *Radio Free Dixie*. For a caution against overemphasizing continuity, see Fairclough, "Historians and the Civil Rights Movement."

6. On multiple perspectives and gender analysis within the movement, see Blumberg, *Civil Rights*; Collier-Thomas and Franklin, *Sisters in the Struggle*; Crawford, Rouse, and Woods, *Women in the Civil Rights Movement*; Giddings, *When and Where I Enter*; Morris, *Origins of the Civil Rights Movement*; Payne, "'Men Led, But Women Organized'"; and Robnett, *How Long?*

7. On historical memory in civil rights and black educational history, see Shircliffe, "'We Got the Best of That World'"; Grim, "History Shared through Memory"; and Dougherty, "From Anecdote to Analysis."

8. On interactivity between community studies and national history, see Lawson, "Freedom Then, Freedom Now"; Payne, *I've Got the Light of Freedom*; and Lawson and Payne, *Debating the Civil Rights Movement*.

9. Some noteworthy book-length histories on race, reform, and twentieth-century Milwaukee include Trotter, *Black Milwaukee*; W. Thompson, *History of Wisconsin*; Orum, *City-Building in America*; Rury and Cassell, *Seeds of Crisis*; Aukofer, *City with a Chance*; Coleman, *Long Way to Go*; Gurda, *Making of Milwaukee*; Holt, *Not Yet "Free at Last"*; Byndloss, "Resistance, Confrontation, and Accommodation"; Carl, "Politics of Education in a New Key"; Dahlk, "Black Education Reform Movement"; P. Jones, "'The Selma of the North'"; and Nelsen, "Racial Integration."

10. Some noteworthy book-length histories on twentieth-century Northern black education include Danns, *Something Better for Our Children* (on Chicago); Douglas, *Law and Culture*; Franklin, *Education of Black Philadelphia*; Mohraz, *Separate Problem* (on Chicago, Indianapolis, and Philadelphia); Homel, *Down from Equality* (on Chicago); Jacobs, *Getting around Brown* (on Columbus); Lukas, *Common Ground* (on Boston); Mabee, *Black Education*; Mirel, *Rise and Fall of an Urban School System* (on Detroit); Perl-

stein, *Justice, Justice* (on New York City); Podair, *Strike That Changed New York*; C. Taylor, *Knocking at Our Own Door* (on New York City); and Tyack, *One Best System*. Some recent book-length studies of black freedom struggles in the North and West include Biondi, *To Stand and Fight* (on New York); Countryman, "Civil Rights and Black Power"; L. Moore, *Carl B. Stokes* (on Cleveland); Self, *American Babylon* (on Oakland); Stulberg, "Teach a New Day" (on New York City, Chicago, and Oakland); Theoharis and Woodard, *Freedom North*; H. Thompson, *Whose Detroit?*; and Woodard, *Nation within a Nation*.

11. See reflections on this theme in Dougherty, "'That's When We Were Marching for Jobs.'"

Chapter One

1. *Wisconsin Enterprise-Blade*, 4 August 1928; *Milwaukee Journal*, 2 June 1934, cited in Grover, "'All Things to Black Folks,'" 51.

2. J. Moore, *Search for Equality*, 43–49; Weiss, *National Urban League*, chapters 7–8. For biographies of Kelley, see *Milwaukee Star*, 11 September 1965; and *Milwaukee Sentinel*, 17 April 1960.

3. Still, *Milwaukee*, 479–85; Orum, *City-Building in America*, 96–97; Grover, "'All Things to Black Folks,'" 56. Quote from black steel worker John Williams appears in Trotter, *Black Milwaukee*, 47.

4. *Milwaukee Sentinel*, 16, 21 September 1924; W. Thompson, *History of Wisconsin*, 311; Trotter, *Black Milwaukee*, 67–71; Still, *Milwaukee*, 454; Vaeth, "Milwaukee Negro Residential Segregation." For sample restrictive covenants in Milwaukee County, see box 203, folder 11, Barbee Papers. In 1928, no blacks lived north of Galena Street, according to Kelley biography in *Milwaukee Sentinel*, 16 April 1960. By 1940, the northern line had shifted to North Avenue, according to a block-level analysis of census data in the Citizens' Governmental Research Bureau, "Milwaukee's Negro Community," chapter 1.

5. *Milwaukee Journal*, 1 August 1923; *Milwaukee Times*, 15 July 1926; H. Williams, "Educational Status of Colored Children."

6. Fultz, "African American Teachers," 406; Foster, "Constancy," 237; Walker, *Their Highest Potential*, chapter 5.

7. Virginia Daniels, "Attitudes Affecting the Occupational Affiliation of Negroes" (Ed.D. diss., University of Pittsburgh, 1938), 57, cited in Tyack, *One Best System*, 223–24; Imse, "Negro Community," 28–29; *Milwaukee Journal*, 23 May 1960, cited in W. Thompson, *History of Wisconsin*, 362. See similar story in *Milwaukee Journal*, 27 August 1959.

8. Table compiled from Porter, "Problem of Negro Education," chapter 3; Grace, "Effect of Negro Migration," 64–66; Herrick, "Negro Employees"; Mohraz, *Separate Problem*, 121; and Homel, *Down from Equality*, 28.

9. Ment, "Patterns of Public School Segregation," 81; Mabee, *Black Education*, 268.

10. Mabee, *Black Education*, 217–20; Tyack, *One Best System*, 117; E. Tatum, *Changed Political Thought*, 64–70.

11. Bunche, *Political Status of the Negro*, 580–81; Grace, "Effect of Negro Migration," 64–66; E. Tatum, *Changed Political Thought*, 71; Wye, "Midwest Ghetto," 59.

12. Gosnell, *Negro Politicians*, 37, 55, 285; Homel, *Down from Equality*, 6, 28; Herrick, "Negro Employees," 21, 87; Mohraz, *Separate Problem*, 23; J. Reid, "Race, Class, Gender," 144.

13. Pierce, "Beneath the Surface," 27–29; Thornbrough, *Negro in Indiana*, 395; Franklin, *Education of Black Philadelphia*, 85–86.

14. Thornbrough, *Negro in Indiana*, 338–39; Thornbrough, *Indiana Blacks in the*

Twentieth Century, 8–9, 51–62, 74, 140–41; Tyack, *One Best System*, 116–17; Douglas, "Limits of Law," 698, note 81.

15. Mabee, *Black Education*, 189–210, 268; Chase, "African American Teachers in Buffalo," 73–74; Watkins, "Black Buffalo," 62–69; L. Williams, *Strangers in the Land of Paradise*, 83, 87; S. Taylor, *Desegregation in Boston and Buffalo*, chapter 2.

16. Proctor, "Racial Discrimination," 14, 41; I. Reid, *Social Conditions*, 88.

17. Pechstein, "Problem of Negro Education," 198; Porter, "Problem of Negro Education," 22.

18. Du Bois, "Postscript," 313; Du Bois, "Does the Negro Need Separate Schools?"

19. Ettenheim, *How Milwaukee Voted*, 3, 10; Schmitz, "Milwaukee and Its Black Community," 72–75; Susan Bazzelle Ellis, transcript of testimony at *Armstrong v. O'Connell* school desegregation trial, 5 January 1978, p. 5622, box 148, folder 1, Barbee Papers. Compare with Kritek and Clear, "Teachers and Principals," 148.

20. *Wisconsin Enterprise-Blade*, 16 January, 13 February, 3 March, 2 April 1932; Trotter, *Black Milwaukee*, 118–19, 133; Milwaukee Board of Election Commissioners, *Biennial Report*, 1932.

21. Milwaukee Board of School Directors, Committee on Appointments, 26 October 1932, 1, 3, 7. For supporting evidence that black children performed at levels comparable to whites in their school, see H. Williams, "Educational Status of Colored Children," 90–92.

22. Milwaukee Board of School Directors, Committee on Appointments, 26 October 1932, 5–8.

23. Milwaukee Board of School Directors, *Proceedings*, 1 November 1932, 253; Vorlop, "Equal Opportunity," 79–85; Trotter, *Black Milwaukee*, 133; *Wisconsin Enterprise-Blade*, 3 May 1932; *Milwaukee Journal*, 18 March 1936.

24. John J. Williams, transcript of testimony at *Armstrong v. O'Connell* school desegregation trial, 3 January 1978, pp. 5159–71, box 147, folder 5, Barbee Papers.

25. W. Thompson, *History of Wisconsin*, 315; Milwaukee Board of School Directors, *Annual Report*, 1933–47. Compare Thompson's 1940 unemployment data with Trotter, *Black Milwaukee*, 155–64. Orum, *City-Building in America*, 102–3. On Depression-era teacher employment in general, see Tyack, Lowe, and Hansot, *Public Schools in Hard Times*, chapter 2.

26. Trotter, *Black Milwaukee*, 154; Grover, "'All Things to Black Folks,'" 71; J. Moore, *Search for Equality*, 82. On the CIO in Chicago, see Cohen, *Making a New Deal*; and Korstad and Lichtenstein, "Opportunities Found and Lost," 786. For a short-lived CIO effort to support black Milwaukee workers in the 1940s, see Meyer, "*Stalin over Wisconsin*," 142–43.

27. Schmitz, "Milwaukee and Its Black Community," 90–92.

28. Milwaukee Board of School Directors, Committee on Appointments, 31 May 1939, 4–9; Vorlop, "Equal Opportunity," 80–82; *Milwaukee Journal*, 1 June, 26 November 1939.

29. Milwaukee Board of School Directors, Committee on Appointments, 31 May 1939, 9–11.

30. Ibid., 13.

31. Ibid., 1–2; *Milwaukee Journal*, 26 November 1939; Wilkerson, "Negro in American Education," part 3, p. 54, table 8.

32. Grant and Lucinda Gordon, interview with author, 1995; V. Williams, "Wisconsin Negro History Makers [Grant Gordon]"; *Milwaukee Journal*, 17 January 1960.

33. Ruby Young, interview with author, 1996. On married female teachers, see Kritek and Clear, "Teachers and Principals," 151–62.

34. John H. Jackson, interview with Michael Gordon, 1989. Reference to Dean Lazenby's role in discouraging blacks from secondary school teaching also appears

in "Report on Negro Teachers in the Milwaukee Public School System [1956]," box 17, folder 14, Milwaukee Urban League Papers. Jackson also was hired as a substitute high school history teacher in the nearby suburb of Shorewood, but the principal was forced by school officials to resign after his attempt to offer Jackson a permanent position. See Washington and Oliver, *Identification of Strengths*, 59–60.

35. Jake Beason, interview with author, 1995; *Milwaukee Journal*, 31 October 1947.

36. Dr. John H. Jackson, transcript of testimony at *Armstrong v. O'Connell* school desegregation trial, 5 January 1978, pp. 5601–21, box 148, folder 1, Barbee Papers. In 1955, Jackson was reassigned to North Division High School, which had just become more than 50 percent black, rather than to either of the two high schools that he had requested, both less than 10 percent black.

37. Geraldine Gilmer Goens, interview with author, 1996; *Milwaukee Community Journal*, 17 November 1976.

38. Bob Harris Jr., interview with author, 1995.

39. Miller to Vincent, 12 January 1955, in possession of Thomas Cheeks and the author; Thomas Cheeks, interview with author, 1995; "Paul H. Jacks to Get Award" (undated; c. January 1951), *Milwaukee Journal*, in the "Negroes" newspaper clippings microfiche, Milwaukee Legislative Reference Bureau; Geraldine Gilmer Goens, interview with author, 1996.

40. "Distribution of White and Non-White Teachers," box 97, folder 35, Barbee Papers.

41. Milwaukee Board of School Directors, *Annual Report*, 1930–53; "Congratulations to Philadelphia" editorial, *Crisis*, August 1937, 241.

42. Parris and Brooks, *Blacks in the City*, 291; J. Moore, *Search for Equality*, 93–95.

43. For Kelley's participation in planning the march, see *Bulletin: Negro March on Washington Committee*, 22 May 1941, in part 2, section A, box 416, "March on Washington Committee. General 1940–41" folder, National NAACP Papers; *Milwaukee Journal*, 23, 29 June 1941; and *Chicago Defender* (national edition), 28 June 1941. Decades later, Dorsey gave a higher march attendance of 700, in Virginia Williams, "Negro History Makers in Milwaukee [Dorsey]," *Milwaukee Star*, 7 August 1965. Compare this event with an 1877 black protest march in Trotter, *Black Milwaukee*, 18.

44. Kersten, *Race, Jobs, and the War*, 71, 141; *Milwaukee Journal*, 21 January, 16 April 1942; Trotter, *Black Milwaukee*, 166–69; Schmitz, "Milwaukee and Its Black Community," 49–54. Although the 1940 census officially calculated blacks as 1.5 percent of the city population, estimates of the black population in 1943 were significantly higher. See *Milwaukee Sentinel*, 6 September 1942; and W. Thompson, *History of Wisconsin*, 309–10.

45. Kelley also attempted to strengthen his ties to the federal government by supplying information to J. Edgar Hoover's FBI during World War II. But his reports emphasize the pro-American quality of the Milwaukee Urban League's activities with CIO and American Federation of Labor unions in defense industries, in contrast to "agitators" such as the small number of black Communists (only thirty-six) and an even smaller number of black Muslim draft resisters in the city. See Hill, *FBI's RACON*, 160–66.

CHAPTER TWO

1. *Milwaukee Sentinel*, 12 October 1953.

2. Ibid.; *Milwaukee Journal*, 12 October 1953.

3. *Milwaukee Sentinel*, 12 October 1953; *Milwaukee Journal*, 12 October 1953; Williams, "Negro History Makers [Vel Phillips]."

4. *Milwaukee Sentinel,* 12 October 1953; "Non-White Enrollment Percentages, 1954–1955," box 127, folder 9, Barbee Papers.

5. Myrdal, *American Dilemma,* 879. Compare with unpublished material from his research assistant, Doxey Wilkerson, "Negro in American Education," part 3, 53–70.

6. For historical overviews, see Douglas, "Limits of Law"; and Bond, *Education of the Negro,* 372–90. On New Jersey, see Wilkerson, "Negro in American Education," part 3, 58–60; Granger, "Race Relations and the School System"; New Jersey State Temporary Commission, *Report to the Legislature,* 41–42; and Jensen, "Survey of Segregation Practices." On Pennsylvania, see Wilkerson, "Negro in American Education," part 3, 60–62; Smythe and Smith, "Race Policies and Practices"; and "The Nona Bragg vs. Swarthmore Case: The Facts [c. 1939]," part 2, box L15, "Education-General 1933–39" folder, National NAACP Papers.

7. Douglas, "Limits of Law," 738.

8. Back, "Up South in New York"; Goldaber, "Treatment by the New York City Board"; C. Taylor, *Knocking at Our Own Door;* Anderson and Pickering, *Confronting the Color Line,* 64, 76–77; Mirel, *Rise and Fall of an Urban School System,* 193–94; *Crisis,* February 1955, 110, and June/July 1955, 369. On the Chicago report, see early stages in *Crisis,* August/September 1955, 442, and final publication in November 1957, 563.

9. *Milwaukee Sentinel,* 15 December 1952.

10. *Milwaukee Journal,* 18, 21 May 1954; *Milwaukee Sentinel,* 21 May 1954. To ensure that the Milwaukee NAACP would never be branded as a Communist front, Dorsey sharply criticized the Wisconsin Civil Rights Congress. See *Milwaukee Journal,* 15 August 1952; *Wisconsin State Journal,* 30 August 1952; and Wisconsin Civil Rights Congress to Dorsey, 19 August 1952, folder 1, Dorsey Papers. The Milwaukee NAACP also purged suspected Communists from its membership lists and investigated charges of Communist dominance in the Madison NAACP branch, a concern initially raised by Lloyd Barbee. See Phillips to Black, 16 June 1955, part 2, section C, box 218, "Milwaukee 1954–55" folder; and Lucinda Gordon, "Report of Investigation of Madison Branch—Interracial Friendship Club Controversy," 22 October 1957, part 3, section C, box 166, "Milwaukee 1958" folder, National NAACP Papers.

11. Cecil Brown Jr., interview with author, 1995. On blacks elected to the State Assembly, see W. Thompson, *History of Wisconsin,* 322.

12. *Milwaukee Journal,* 29 May 1960; *Amos v. Board* (19 January 1976), 792.

13. Granger, "Does the Negro Want Integration?"

14. *Milwaukee Star,* 11 September 1965; *Milwaukee Journal,* 31 January 1932, 29 January 1948; *Wisconsin Enterprise-Blade,* 5 March 1932; Cecil Brown Jr., interview with author, 1995; Schmitz, "Milwaukee and Its Black Community," 105; Grover, "'All Things to Black Folks,'" 60–62.

15. *Milwaukee Sentinel,* 17 April 1960; *Milwaukee Star,* 18 September 1965; Williams, "Negro History Makers [Kelley]"; Kelley to Granger, 27 August 1954, marked "Not for public consumption," box 1, folder 84, Milwaukee Urban League Papers.

16. *Milwaukee Defender,* 14 February 1957, 15 March 1958, clippings located in part 3, section C, box 166, "Milwaukee 1958" folder, National NAACP Papers; *Milwaukee Journal,* 2 June 1960; *Milwaukee Sentinel,* 11 December 1962, 18 August 1965; Trotter, *Black Milwaukee,* 87–92; Halyard, interview with Greenlee, 1978, 23; "Milwaukee Branch NAACP" speaking notes by Ardie Halyard, no date, box 8, folder 2, Milwaukee NAACP Papers; "President's Annual Report of Activities of Milwaukee Branch NAACP," 14 December 1952, part 2, section C, box 218, "Milwaukee 1950–53" folder, National NAACP Papers. See Halyard on housing discrimination, absence of blacks in city governance, and job discrimination in *Milwaukee Journal,* 5 June, 19 November, and 15 December 1951.

17. *Milwaukee Journal,* 2 April 1951, 15 April 1952; Halyard to Zarem, 10 March

1951, and Halyard to Vincent, 29 March 1951, both in box 5, folder 9, Milwaukee NAACP Papers; "Milwaukee Alumni of Member Institutions," 27 March 1954, box 7, folder 18, Milwaukee NAACP Papers; Halyard, interview with Greenlee, 1978, 15.

18. Kluger, *Simple Justice*, 221; Current to Phillips, 10 June 1954, and *Milwaukee NAACP Newsletter*, November 1955, both in part 2, section C, box 218, "Milwaukee 1954–55" folder, National NAACP Papers; *Milwaukee Defender*, 31 August 1957; President's Annual Report, 8 December 1957, part 3, section C, box 166, "Milwaukee 1956–57" folder, National NAACP Papers.

19. On tensions between Granger and Wilkins, see Weiss, *National Urban League*, 57; and J. Moore, *Search for Equality*, 54, 164–82. Kelley to Marshall, 2 July 1954, with additional copy containing quote to Granger, part 1, box 108, "Milwaukee Urban League 1953–54" folder, National Urban League Papers. To compare the Milwaukee Urban League and the Milwaukee NAACP during an earlier period, see Weems, "From the Great Migration to the Great Depression."

20. Kelley to Vincent, 8 June 1954, and Vincent to Kelley, 16 June 1954, box 1, folder 84, Milwaukee Urban League Papers. For an observer's account of Kelley's five-year lobbying effort, see Banner, *Study of Urban League Services*, 13–15, 68.

21. Kelley to Vincent, 8 June 1954, Kelley to Granger, 27 October 1954 (marked "Very, Very Confidential"), and Kelley to Granger (with previous copy to Vincent), 3 November 1954, all in box 1, folder 84, Milwaukee Urban League Papers. See Granger's version of the correspondence in part 1, box 50, "Supreme Court 1954" folder, National Urban League Papers. See also Grover, "'All Things to Black Folks,'" 120–21; and J. Moore, *Search for Equality*, 95.

22. Kelley to Banner, 11 July 1956, enclosing survey results of "Sample Questionnaire: Pertinent Information with Reference to Negro Teachers in Public School System," part 1, box 108, "Milwaukee Urban League 1957" folder, National Urban League Papers.

23. Granger to Vincent, 19 January 1955, Kelley to Granger, 27 August 1954, both in box 1, folder 84, Milwaukee Urban League Papers; Kelley to Banner, 11 July 1956, part 1, box 108, "Milwaukee Urban League 1957" folder, National Urban League Papers.

24. Corneff Taylor, notes on Milwaukee Commission on Human Rights meeting with Vincent, 21 January 1955, Kelley to Granger, 22 March 1955, both in box 1, folder 84, Milwaukee Urban League Papers; Milwaukee Urban League, *Monthly Report*, December 1955; "Report on Negro Teachers in Milwaukee Public School System," first draft, Milwaukee Urban League, *Monthly Report*, November 1955. A more detailed second draft, dated 1956, appears in box 17, folder 14, Milwaukee Urban League Papers. "Report on conference with Vincent," 5 January 1956, box 17, folder 14, Milwaukee Urban League Papers; Milwaukee Urban League, *Monthly Report*, January 1956, September 1956, January 1957; Kelley to Granger, 13 June 1957, part 1, box 108, "Milwaukee Urban League 1957" folder, National Urban League Papers.

25. See detailed correspondence in box 1, folder 84, Milwaukee Urban League Papers; "Distribution of White and Non-White Teachers," box 97, folder 35, and Milwaukee Public Schools, "Report on Visual Count of Teachers," 1965, box 103, folder 16, Barbee Papers; and *Armstrong v. O'Connell* (1 June 1978), 830. See also *Milwaukee Journal*, 29 May 1960, which mistakenly exaggerated the degree of racial progress and reported the hiring rate as double the black population, perhaps because 1960 census data had not yet been released.

26. Wesley Scott, interview with author, 1995; W. Thompson, *History of Wisconsin*, 362–65. On civil service, see *Milwaukee Journal*, 30 May 1960. On Dorsey's struggle on behalf of black tradesmen, see *Milwaukee Journal*, 25 November, 11 December

1953; *Milwaukee Sentinel*, 18 October 1954, 1 December 1956, 20 November 1959; and *Milwaukee Defender*, 11 April, 6 June 1957. "Negro Teachers in the Milwaukee School System," 1965, box 8, folder 21, Milwaukee Urban League Papers. By comparison, black Milwaukee women in nursing occupations rose from 11 in 1950 to 129 in 1960, according to the U.S. Census Bureau, *General Characteristics of the Population*, Wisconsin, Milwaukee SMSA, table 77 (1950) and table 122 (1960).

27. Milwaukee Board of School Directors, *Annual Report*, 1950–60; Kritek and Clear, "Teachers and Principals," 157; Lamers, *Our Roots Grow Deep*, 20–24; W. Thompson, *History of Wisconsin*, 233–34; Cutler, *Greater Milwaukee's Growing Pains*.

28. O'Reilly, Pflanczer, and Downing, *People of the Inner Core-North*, 176.

29. "I Spent Four Years in an Integrated High School," *U.S. News and World Report*, 7 November 1958, 40–45. Although the anonymous student author used the pseudonym "Lakeside," it was identified as North Division High School by Maxine Jeter, interview with author, 1995, and Cecil Brown Jr., interview with author, 1995. *Milwaukee Journal*, 7 November 1958 editorial, reprinted in *U.S. News and World Report*, 21 November 1958, 10.

30. Kelley to Granger, 19 January 1955, part 1, box 108, "Milwaukee Urban League 1955" folder, National Urban League Papers.

CHAPTER THREE

1. *Milwaukee Journal*, 14 November 1952.

2. See Katz, *Improving Poor People*.

3. For reinterpretations of the "Golden Age" and racial uplift, see Kelley, *Race Rebels*, 39–40; and Gaines, *Uplifting the Race*, 76, 89.

4. *Milwaukee Journal*, 8 November 1967; *Milwaukee Sentinel*, 13 July 1965; Hamilton, "Expectations and Realities of a Migrant Group"; Geib, "Late Great Migration"; O'Reilly, Pflanczer, and Downing, *People of the Inner Core-North*, 172–75.

5. *Milwaukee Journal*, 6 January 1957; *Milwaukee Defender*, 10 January 1957; *Milwaukee Sentinel*, 8, 10 January 1957. For black conflicts with white police brutality in similar contexts, see H. Thompson, *Whose Detroit?*

6. *Milwaukee Defender*, 10 January 1957; *Milwaukee Sentinel*, 10 January 1957; *Milwaukee Journal*, 15 January, 2 February 1957. On "scare headlines" in 1959, see Banner, *Study of Urban League Services*, 101.

7. *Milwaukee Journal*, 3 December 1952.

8. Ibid., 19 November 1952.

9. *Milwaukee Sentinel*, 14 November 1952; *Milwaukee Journal*, 3 December 1952.

10. Trotter, *Black Milwaukee*, 215–18; Du Bois, *Philadelphia Negro*, 310–11; Frazier, *Negro in the United States*, 298. See also Grossman, *Land of Hope*, 123–60; and Phillips, *AlabamaNorth*, 165.

11. *Milwaukee Journal*, 5 August 1951, and "Better Programs Will Be Available," undated, "Negroes" newspaper clippings microfiche, Milwaukee Legislative Reference Bureau.

12. *Milwaukee Journal*, 7 March 1952.

13. French to Current, 23 May 1957, part 3, section C, box 166, "Milwaukee 1956–57" folder, National NAACP Papers.

14. *Milwaukee Journal*, 24 September 1959, 30 May 1960. Black crime statistics appeared in different (and conflicting) forms in the 1950s, ranging from 25 to 80 percent.

15. Frazier, *Black Bourgeoisie*; *Milwaukee Sentinel*, 11 August 1956; Trotter, *Black Milwaukee*, 218.

16. Zeidler, "Milwaukee's Racial Tension: The Problems of the New Negro Migra-

tion," *Socialist Call* 22 (March 1954): 8–10. For Zeidler's earlier criticisms of realtors, see *Milwaukee Journal*, 14, 19 November 1952. See also Fure-Slocum, "Challenge of the Working-Class City."

17. On Southern billboard rumors, see "Races: The Shame of Milwaukee," *Time*, 2 April 1956; Zeidler's handwritten notes, 5 February 1954, box 101, folder 5, and Zeidler, "A Liberal in City Government," unpublished manuscript, boxes 342–43, both in Zeidler Papers. On the street disturbance and its aftermath, see *Milwaukee Sentinel*, 26 August 1959; and *Milwaukee Journal*, 27 August 1959.

18. Mayor's Study Committee, *Final Report*, 3–9; W. Thompson, *History of Wisconsin*, 350.

19. W. Thompson, *History of Wisconsin*, 371.

20. Mayor's Study Committee, *Final Report*, 3, Appendix G: Housing, 14–16, Appendix H: Education, 5. See similar interpretations by Orum, *City-Building in America*, 132, and W. Thompson, *History of Wisconsin*, 371–75. The latter argues against the Study Committee's findings by noting that in general, Southern blacks made rural to urban transitions while migrating within the South before heading North. Conant, *Slums and Suburbs*, 2.

21. The 1933 *Annual Report of the Superintendent of Milwaukee Schools* refers to the problem of "the foreign family," cited in Vorlop, "Equal Opportunity," 83. On Milwaukee social centers, see Reese, *Power and the Promise of School Reform*, 203–6, although he emphasizes that they were contested institutions where immigrants sometimes affirmed their ethnic identities. Handlin, *Newcomers*.

22. *Milwaukee Journal*, 2 September 1959. The two other representatives from the Interdenominational Ministerial Alliance included Rev. John Bradford of St. Mark's African Methodist Episcopal Church and Rev. E. M. Kelly of Metropolitan Baptist Church.

23. *Milwaukee Sentinel*, 30 January 1955, 3 November 1956. See also a section titled "Incidents of Crowd Resistance to Arrests, 1952–55," in "Report on a Survey of Social Characteristics of the Lower Northside Community" by social work professor John Teter and students in the appendix of the Milwaukee Commission on Human Rights, *Annual Report*, 1956.

24. *Milwaukee Journal*, 21 February, 11, 18, 21 March 1958; *Milwaukee Sentinel*, 21 February 1958; *Milwaukee Defender*, 1 March 1958.

25. *Milwaukee Sentinel*, 11 February 1959; *Milwaukee Journal*, 4 December 1955, 10 February 1960.

26. *Milwaukee Defender*, 23 May 1957 editorial; *Milwaukee Sentinel*, 1 October 1959.

27. *Milwaukee Journal*, 3 September 1950, 3 December 1952, 8 December 1960; Grant and Lucinda Gordon, interview with author, 1995.

28. *Milwaukee Journal*, 27 August 1959. For Kelley's awareness of the broader role of teachers, see Wesley Scott, interview with author, 1995. On the role of black teachers upholding cultural standards, see Foster, "Constancy," and Walker, *Their Highest Potential*, 82–91.

29. *Milwaukee Sentinel*, 1 September 1959; *Milwaukee Journal*, 1 September 1959; *Milwaukee Community Journal*, 31 January 1979, Sarah Scott obituary; Fred Hopkins, interview with author, 1996. On Dunbar High School, see Jones, *Traditional Model of Educational Excellence*. On Taylor, see *Milwaukee Journal*, 15 January 1957.

30. *Milwaukee Journal*, 1 September 1959. Reverend Phillips's message was consistent with a speech he had delivered three years earlier to the Milwaukee NAACP, calling upon the group to "teach our own people about the operation of our city," in *Milwaukee Journal*, 1 October 1956.

31. Jeffrey, *Education for Children of the Poor*, chapter 1.

32. Callaway and Baruch, "Milwaukee Curriculum," 116. For Special B and Special

C classes, see the 1929 and earlier editions of Milwaukee Board of School Directors, *Manual and Roster.*

33. *Milwaukee Journal,* 6 October 1953.

34. Indirect quotation of Principal Paul Jacks, *Milwaukee Journal,* 28 November 1948. *Milwaukee Journal,* 12 October 1953. See also the recommendation in 1947 to create a "training center for young people of the colored community" at Ninth Street School, in Callaway and Baruch, "Milwaukee Curriculum," 123.

35. Bolz, "A Descriptive Analysis," 2, 3, 20, 26, 34, quotation from 39–40; "Nonwhite enrollment percentages, 1955–56," box 127, folder 9, Barbee Papers.

36. *Milwaukee Journal,* 29 May, 2 September 1960; *Milwaukee Star,* 15 August 1962; Vorlop, "Equal Opportunity," 95; Great Cities School Improvement Program, "Project Proposal for Transient Pupils in Milwaukee," 1960, box 3, folder 6, Elizabeth Holmes Papers, Golda Meir Library, University of Wisconsin–Milwaukee, Milwaukee, Wis.; Callaway and Baruch, "Milwaukee Curriculum," 128; Nuhlicek, "Orientation Centers."

37. On the Vocational Opportunity Campaign, see box 10, folder 34, Milwaukee Urban League Papers, and also *Milwaukee Defender,* 15 March 1958 clipping in part 3, series C, box 166, "Milwaukee 1958" folder, National NAACP Papers. On Tomorrow's Scientists and Technicians (1958–59), see box 17, folder 25, Milwaukee Urban League Papers. On the League's policy shift, see Milwaukee Urban League board memo to Industrial Relations Committee Chair, 17 June 1960, and Milwaukee Urban League board minutes, 16 March 1960, page 3, microfilm reel 1, Milwaukee Urban League Papers (courtesy of Michael Grover).

38. *Milwaukee Journal,* 26 August 1962; Wesley Scott, interview with author, 1995. For William Kelley's recollections of poorly skilled job applicants, see *Milwaukee Star,* 11 September 1965.

39. Youth Incentive Project proposals and materials, 1962–63, box 17, folders 19, 39, and 40, Milwaukee Urban League Papers; *Milwaukee Star,* 1 September 1962; *Milwaukee Journal,* 26 August 1962; *Milwaukee Courier,* 3 December 1966; Wesley Scott, interview with author, 1995.

40. *New York Times,* 23 April 1962; *Milwaukee Journal,* 12 May 1964.

41. *New York Times,* 23 April 1962; *Milwaukee Journal,* 15 September 1965.

42. Milwaukee Commission on Community Relations, *Negro in Milwaukee.* See *Milwaukee Sentinel,* 20 August 1962, on Mayor Maier's selection of commission members. Glazer and Moynihan, *Beyond the Melting Pot;* W. Thompson, *History of Wisconsin,* 377.

43. For early national-level critics of compensatory education, see Baratz and Baratz, "Early Childhood Intervention," and Clark, "Cultural Deprivation Theories."

CHAPTER FOUR

1. *Milwaukee Journal,* 9 July 1963; *Milwaukee Sentinel,* 9 July 1963; Barbee to Rothwell, 8 July 1963, box 196, folder 12, Barbee Papers; Lloyd Barbee, interview with Clayborn Benson, 1990.

2. *Milwaukee Journal,* 9, 12 July 1963.

3. On "new guard" versus "old guard" in black Chicago politics, see Bates, "New Crowd." On the indigenous Southern movement, see Morris, *Origins of the Civil Rights Movement,* chapters 1–3. But see also Payne, *I've Got the Light of Freedom.*

4. Foster, "Constancy," 237, 239. See also Tyack, "Growing Up Black."

5. "Biographical Note," finding aid, Barbee Papers; *Milwaukee Journal Sentinel,* 30 December 2002, Barbee obituary.

6. *Milwaukee Sentinel,* 7 November 1959; Lloyd Barbee, interview with author, 1995; "Biographical Note," finding aid, Barbee Papers.

7. "Biographical Note," finding aid, Barbee Papers.

8. *Taylor v. New Rochelle* (24 January 1961); Maslow, "De Facto Public School Segregation," 358.

9. *Crisis*, August/September 1961, 403; August/September 1962, 384; October 1962, 481; December 1962, 610; February 1963, 93. See "Facts for Action—Public Schools in the North and West" and "NAACP Public School Desegregation Front in the North and West," memoranda by National NAACP special assistant June Shagaloff, 1962, box 95, folder 50, Barbee Papers; Lloyd Barbee, interview with Clayborn Benson, 1990.

10. National NAACP press release, 3 August 1962, part 3, section C, box 166, "Milwaukee 1961–62" folder, National NAACP Papers; *Milwaukee Sentinel*, 30 July 1962; *Milwaukee Journal*, 13 June 1961; *Crisis*, August/September 1962, 413; Smuckler, "Black Power and the NAACP," 37; Carter to Barbee, 7 March 1962, box 196, folder 12, Barbee Papers.

11. The 1954 redistricting split blacks into the First, Second, Sixth, Seventh, and Thirteenth Wards. See historical maps of city wards in Milwaukee Board of Election Commissioners, *Biennial Report*; W. Thompson, *History of Wisconsin*, 368; Milwaukee County Historical Society, *Negro in Milwaukee*, 30–32. On Golightly, see *Milwaukee Star*, 6 February 1971. On voting strength, see *Milwaukee Journal*, 21 February 1958; and Community-Relations Social Development Commission in Milwaukee County and the Milwaukee Urban League, *Black Powerlessness*.

12. *Milwaukee Journal*, 5 July 1960; *Milwaukee Defender*, 14 July 1960, which appears in part 3, section C, box 166, "Milwaukee 1959–60" folder, National NAACP Papers.

13. *Milwaukee Journal* 5 July 1960 editorial, italics in the original.

14. *Milwaukee Journal*, 11 July 1960.

15. Reuben Harpole Jr., interview with author, 1995; *Milwaukee Journal*, 6 December 1960.

16. Walker to Current, 7 December 1960, part 3, section C, box 166, "Milwaukee 1959–60" folder, National NAACP Papers; Smuckler, "Black Power and the NAACP," 37.

17. *Milwaukee Star*, 25 August, 8 September 1962.

18. Parrish to Hill, 16 January 1962, "Annual Report, Milwaukee Branch NAACP," 13 December 1961, both in part 3, section C, box 166, "Milwaukee 1961–62" folder, National NAACP Papers.

19. *Milwaukee Star*, 25 August, 6 October, 3, 24 November, 1 December 1962. Note that the Milwaukee NAACP lent their endorsement to the NALC fight. For a similar clash between styles of black protest in Cleveland, see L. Moore, "School Desegregation Crisis of Cleveland," 137.

20. *Milwaukee Journal*, 15 March 1962, 23 January 1963, cited in Vorlop, "Equal Opportunity," 107.

21. Lloyd Barbee, "Milwaukee School Desegregation: A History," *Milwaukee Community Journal*, 20 December 1978. See earlier draft in box 195, folder 5, Barbee Papers. See also Dahlk, "Black Education Reform Movement," 37–39.

22. Dialogue reconstructed from the perspective of Lloyd Barbee, interview with author, 1995; and Barbee, interview with Kay Shannon, 1968.

23. *Milwaukee Sentinel*, 15 December 1962; *Milwaukee Star*, 15 December 1962.

24. *Milwaukee Journal*, 4 May 1960, notes that eighty-six black families lived in private housing outside of central city boundaries: Capitol Drive, National Avenue, 27th Street, and Lake Michigan. See also "Negro Teachers in the Milwaukee School System," 1965, box 8, folder 21, p. 34, Milwaukee Urban League Papers, which notes that many black teachers "lived on the periphery of the central city and also in the suburbs." Grant and Lucinda Gordon, interview with author, 1995. On Jackson and Wauwatosa, see *Milwaukee Sentinel*, 24 March 1959.

25. "Statement III: Negro Teachers," 1965, box 97, folder 35, Barbee Papers; *Milwaukee Journal*, 15 October 1963, interview with the president of the Wisconsin Federation of Teachers; "Racial Isolation in the Milwaukee Public Schools," box 203, folder 1, Barbee Papers.

26. Barbee, interview with author, 1995, italics added; Cornelius Golightly, interview with Racial Isolation in Milwaukee researchers, 22 August 1966, box 95, folder 36, Barbee Papers.

27. "Biographical Note," finding aid, Barbee Papers; *Milwaukee Courier*, 27 March 1976, Golightly obituary.

28. Barbee italicized "inherently" in the "inherently unequal" passage in "Report of the Wisconsin NAACP," 1963, box 96, folder 9, p. 18, Barbee Papers. Wesley Scott, interview with author, 1995.

29. Rothwell to Barbee, 5 September 1963, box 196, folder 12, Barbee Papers; quotation from board member Harold Story, *Milwaukee Journal*, 11 May 1964.

30. *Milwaukee Sentinel*, 27 August 1963, 11 June 1964; teacher transfer applications in box 132, folder 25, Barbee Papers.

31. On corporal punishment, see *Milwaukee Journal*, 28 April 1962; *Milwaukee Sentinel*, 28 April 1962; Flahive, "Milwaukee's Change"; "Are Your Teachers Handcuffed on Discipline?" [interview with Superintendent Harold Vincent]. On origins of the Milwaukee Teachers' Education Association, see *Milwaukee Sentinel*, 14 March 1963; *MTEA* Newsletter [later titled *TEAM*], October 1963, and Delbert K. Clear, "Milwaukee Teachers' Education Association," unpublished manuscript, 1990, both in Milwaukee Teachers' Education Association Papers, Milwaukee Teachers Education Association, Milwaukee, Wis.; and Kritek and Clear, "Teachers and Principals," 177–79.

32. See various student transfer requests from the late 1950s and early 1960s in box 204, folder 2, Barbee Papers. *Milwaukee Sentinel*, 27 August 1963.

33. Cited in "Report of the Education Committee of the Wisconsin NAACP," 1963, box 96, folder 9, p. 18, Barbee Papers. For the original 1961–62 reports from the state superintendent, see box 203, folder 10, Barbee Papers, and *Milwaukee Journal*, 29 July 1962.

34. *Milwaukee Sentinel*, 12 July 1961; Meyer, *"Stalin over Wisconsin,"* 12.

35. *Bell v. Gary, Indiana* (29 January 1963); Story to Barbee, 7 August, 10 September 1963; Special Committee on Equality of Educational Opportunity minutes, 20 August 1963, p. 24; all in box 196, folder 12, Barbee Papers.

36. Barbee to Story, 16 September 1963, box 196, folder 12, Barbee Papers; *Milwaukee Weekly Post*, 2 October 1963; Lloyd Barbee, interview with Kay Shannon, 1968.

37. Milwaukee Urban League staff notes on conversation with Harold Story [undated, probably early September 1963], box 15, folder 5, Milwaukee Urban League Papers; Wesley Scott, interview with author, 1995.

38. Milwaukee Board of School Directors, Special Committee on Equality of Educational Opportunity minutes, 17 September 1963, 5–6; *Milwaukee Journal*, 18 September 1963.

39. Gwen Jackson, interview with author, 1995; see also biography in *Milwaukee Journal*, 10 February 1961. On the Marc's Big Boy pickets, see Milwaukee NAACP Youth Council, "Why We Demonstrate" [March 1963], and Gwen Jackson, "Youth Council Report for March, April, and May, 1963," both in box 5, folder 15, Milwaukee NAACP Papers.

40. Milwaukee Board of School Directors, Special Committee on Equality of Educational Opportunity minutes, 28 October 1963, 3, 5.

41. Wesley Scott, interview with author, 1995.

42. Meier and Rudwick, *Along the Color Line*, 382–84; Theoharis, "'We Saved the City,'" 69; L. Moore, "School Desegregation Crisis of Cleveland," 141; Anderson and

Pickering, *Confronting the Color Line*, 90; Orfield, *Reconstruction of Southern Education*, 162; C. Taylor, *Knocking at Our Own Door*, 129–30.

43. *Milwaukee Journal*, 15 October 1963, names the three black ministers. See *Milwaukee Star*, 6 July 1963, column by Larry Saunders, for criticism of black Milwaukee ministers for failing to lead the new movement.

44. *Milwaukee Weekly Post*, 23 October 1963.

45. Milwaukee Board of School Directors, Special Committee on Equality of Educational Opportunity minutes, 4 September 1963, 25.

46. On neighborhood school boundary changes, see Milwaukee Public Schools, Department of School Housing Research, "A Study of the Central Area of the City of Milwaukee," 1959, and "Report of School District Changes in Central Area of Milwaukee, 1943–1953–1963," 1964, both unpublished reports at the Milwaukee Public Library; Golightly, "De Facto Segregation in Milwaukee Schools," 28. See also Milwaukee Board of School Directors, Special Committee on Equality of Educational Opportunity minutes, 4 September 1963, 17. For later evidence of gerrymandering, see *Amos v. Board* (19 January 1976), 782–84.

47. "Busing policies" [research summary, c. 1967], box 73, folder 41; "History of Student Bussing Practices, 1949–1966," box 203, folder 8; and "Racial Isolation in Milwaukee Public Schools," box 203, folder 1, p. 117, all in Barbee Papers. Although some believed intact busing was unique to Milwaukee, compare with similar practices in L. Moore, "School Desegregation Crisis of Cleveland," 137.

48. *Amos v. Board* (19 January 1976), 790–91.

49. The first article appeared in the *Milwaukee Star*, 27 July 1963. See *Milwaukee Sentinel*, 18 May 1964, biography of Morheuser; personal resume in Morheuser Papers; Walter Jones, interview with author, 1995; and history of local black press in *Milwaukee Star*, 24 March 1977.

50. Meier and Rudwick, *CORE*, 197; "Report of Special Meeting, Milwaukee CORE Education Committee," 12 January 1964, box 1, folder 3, Milwaukee CORE Papers. Compare with *Milwaukee Star*, 18 January 1964, coverage of the same meeting. Although this particular meeting was held after CORE's December 1963 report to the Story Committee, similar communication with parents took place earlier to draft the report; see Milwaukee CORE, "Segregation in Milwaukee Public Schools," 10 December 1963, box 1, folder 3, Milwaukee CORE Papers. Years later, during the school desegregation trial, attorney Barbee asked one of his witnesses to recall her objections to intact busing. Delores Greene, the former president of the Brown Street Parent Teacher Association, gave testimony similar to that voiced by other black parents at the CORE meeting. "I objected to several things," she stated, "but primarily I objected to the fact that the students were losing so much academic instructional time via the busing." Delores Greene, testimony at *Armstrong* trial, 4 January 1978, box 147, folder 6, p. 5304, Barbee Papers.

51. The first report was titled "Position of the Near Northside Non-Partisan Conference of Milwaukee," 19 November 1963, box 1, folder 3, Milwaukee CORE Papers. Later, it was merged with a second report and retitled "Segregation in Milwaukee Public Schools: De Facto or De Jure? A Two-Phase Report," 19 November, 10 December 1963, box 1, folder 3, Milwaukee CORE Papers. On the origins of the NNNPC, see *Milwaukee Star*, 13 July 1963.

52. "Segregation in Milwaukee Public Schools," 19 November, 10 December 1963, box 1, folder 3, pp. 5, 6–12, Milwaukee CORE Papers.

53. "Report of the Education Committee of the Wisconsin NAACP," 1963, box 96, folder 9, pp. 18, 32, Barbee Papers. On the involvement of the national NAACP, see extensive correspondence with Barbee during November 1963 in box 196, folder 12, Barbee Papers.

54. Barbee to Shagaloff, 12 December 1963, box 196, folder 12, Barbee Papers;

Milwaukee Star, 18 January 1964; Meier and Rudwick, *CORE*, 248; McLeod to Chicago CORE, 8 January 1964, box 1, folder 1, and "Education Committee Workshop," 19 January 1964, box 1, folder 3, both in Milwaukee CORE Papers.

55. Milwaukee Board of School Directors, Special Committee on Equality of Educational Opportunity minutes, 21 January 1964, 2–3.

56. *Milwaukee Journal*, 22 January 1964; *Milwaukee Sentinel*, 22 January 1964; Milwaukee Board of School Directors, Special Committee on Equality of Educational Opportunity minutes, 21 January 1964, 21.

57. *Milwaukee Sentinel*, 22 January 1964.

58. Milwaukee Board of School Directors, Special Committee on Equality of Educational Opportunity minutes, 31 January 1964, 13–17.

59. *Milwaukee Star*, 1 February 1964.

60. Lloyd Barbee, interview with author, 1995; *Milwaukee Star*, 31 October 1964. Other recent historical accounts of Milwaukee's 1960s civil rights era have agreed with Barbee's assessment, commenting that black Milwaukeeans "had not been particularly militant in pressing their demands for an end to segregation and discrimination" (W. Thompson, *History of Wisconsin*, 368) and were "relatively quiescent concerning civil rights in the schools" (Vorlop, "Equal Opportunity," 103).

61. *Milwaukee Courier*, 12 May 1973. For related interpretations of the "forgotten years" of early civil rights activism, see Dalfiume, "'Forgotten Years'"; and Korstad and Lichtenstein, "Opportunities Found and Lost." Regarding the 1941 Milwaukee protest march, see biographical essay of James Dorsey, published by Virginia Williams as part of her "Negro History Makers in Milwaukee" series in the *Milwaukee Star*, 7 August 1965. Dorsey was later discredited by Barbee's supporters, and Williams was a long-standing black Milwaukee educator and independent publisher who did not identify strongly with the integration movement. See also a very brief mention by Dahlk, "Black Education Reform Movement," 49.

CHAPTER FIVE

1. On early protests, see *Milwaukee Star*, 8 February 1964. On MUSIC's official origin, see *Milwaukee Journal*, 2 March 1964; and Barbee to Sherard, 3 March 1964, box 2, folder 2, Milwaukee NAACP Papers.

2. On histories of black women activists that challenge conventional narratives of the 1960s, see Payne, "'Men Led, but Women Organized'"; Robnett, *How Long?*; Collier-Thomas and Franklin, *Sisters in the Struggle*; Perkins, *Autobiography as Activism*; and Gardner, "Coming of Age in the Movement." On black women activists in Northern school desegregation, see Kaufman, "Building a Constituency." On oral history of women activists and questions of historical periodization, see Nasstrom, "Beginnings and Endings."

3. For example, see Sitkoff, *Struggle for Black Equality*, 185. For other criticisms that the rise of black power has been misinterpreted, see Van Deburg, *New Day in Babylon*, 40–43 (about history textbooks); and Woodard, *Nation within a Nation*, 4–5.

4. Ravitch, *Great School Wars*, 247; Lowe and Kantor, "Creating Educational Opportunity," 197.

5. Joseph, "All Power to the People!," 147. For related criticisms of conventional civil rights narratives and periodizations, see Lowe and Kantor, "Considerations"; Chafe, *Civilities and Civil Rights*; Carson, "Civil Rights Reform"; Newby and Tyack, "Victims without 'Crimes'"; and Ladner, "What 'Black Power' Means to Negroes in Mississippi." On the influence of narratives on historical writing in general, see Cronon, "Place for Stories."

6. Carson, "Civil Rights Reform," 27–28.

7. Juanita Adams and Arlene Johnson, interview with author, 1995. On spiritual faith among activists, see Payne, *I've Got the Light of Freedom.*

8. Juanita Adams and Arlene Johnson, interview with author, 1995; *Milwaukee Star,* 31 August, 7 September 1963. On police harassment of interracial couples in the Milwaukee civil rights movement, see interviews with author of Arlene Johnson, Lloyd Barbee, Cecil and Loretta Brown, and Lawrence and Kathleen Saunders, 1995.

9. Juanita Adams and Arlene Johnson, interview with author, 1995; Lloyd Barbee, interview with Kay Shannon, 1968, 29–30; Meier and Rudwick, *CORE,* 248.

10. Juanita Adams and Arlene Johnson, interview with author, 1995; Lucius Walker, interview with author, 1996; Utz, "Northcott Neighborhood House."

11. Juanita Adams and Arlene Johnson, interview with author, 1995. For different interpretations of the size and scale of Milwaukee's July 1967 disturbance, see W. Thompson, *History of Wisconsin,* 386–89; and Wilde, "Milwaukee's National Media Riot."

12. Mildred Harpole, interview with author, 1995.

13. Ibid.; Harpole was assigned to teach senior high school students at the black-run Elks Club, the only Freedom School not located in a church, according to "Churches Available for Freedom Schools [1964]," p. 1, Morheuser Papers. On boycotts and Freedom Schools in other Northern cities, see C. Taylor, *Knocking at Our Own Door,* 129–31.

14. "Program of Activities—Primary Grades, Freedom Day School" and "Seventh to Twelfth Grade Schedules and Curriculum," 18 May 1964, both in box 1, folder 2, Milwaukee CORE Papers.

15. *Milwaukee Journal,* 18 May 1964; "Report from MUSIC on Disciplinary Action Taken against Students Who Attended Freedom Schools on May 18th [1964]," box 13, folder 11, Barbee Papers; Cecil Brown Jr., interview with author, 1995. The Milwaukee Police Department "Red Squad" also photographed activists at public meetings and protests, then cross-filed their names with information gathered from *Milwaukee Star* clippings and MUSIC leaflets. See *Milwaukee Journal,* 2 October 1965; *Milwaukee Courier,* 6 March, 8 May, 13 November 1976, for public pressure that led to the closure of the unit in the mid-1970s; and *Milwaukee Star,* 16 September 1976. According to the Milwaukee Police Department Open Records Section, the Red Squad files have been destroyed. On segregationists, see Carroll to Milwaukee School Board, 7 April 1964, in Morheuser Papers; and *Milwaukee Star,* 1 June 1964. On Radtke, see *Milwaukee Sentinel,* 22 October 1963; *Milwaukee Journal,* 1 June 1964; Radtke comments to Clements and Showalter [c. 1966] in box 132, folder 20, Barbee Papers; and *Armstrong v. O'Connell* (1 June 1978), 844.

16. WTMJ editorial No. 2/148, 25 February 1964, box 13, folder 10, Barbee Papers; *Milwaukee Journal,* 18, 20 May 1964; *Milwaukee Sentinel,* 20 May 1964; *Milwaukee Star,* 30 May 1964. On Dorsey's changing views over time, see folders 1–9, Dorsey Papers.

17. For debate over the number of boycott participants, see *Milwaukee Journal,* 19 May 1964; *Milwaukee Sentinel,* 19 May 1964. MUSIC claimed 16,000 boycott participants, while school officials reported 13,700 absent from inner-city schools, about 11,000 more than on the same day of the previous week.

18. Mildred Harpole, interview with author, 1995.

19. Ibid.

20. Ibid.; Holt, *Not Yet "Free at Last,"* 22–24. On the racial crisis at St. Elizabeth's, where Harambee was established, see *Milwaukee Courier,* 8 June, 28 October, 2 November 1968; and also "The St. Elizabeth Story (1902–1977)" and Sister Mary Jane Kreidler, "Of Kitchen Tables, Cigarettes, Coffee, and Other Things: Selected Memo-

ries of Austin Schlaefer, O.F.M. Cap.," in Father Matthew Gottschalk Papers, in possession of author. On racial change in Milwaukee's parochial schools, see Rauch, "Impact of Population Changes" and "Changing Status"; and in general, McGreevy, *Parish Boundaries*.

21. *Milwaukee Star*, 16 May 1970; *Milwaukee Courier*, 3 November 1973; Mildred Harpole, interview with author, 1995; Ronald Johnson, interview with author, 1995. On the Federation of Independent Community Schools, see "Federation of Independent Community Schools" brochure, box 7, folder 11, Barbee Papers; Modlinski and Zaret, *Federation of Independent Community Schools*; and Dahlk, "Black Education Reform Movement," 163–79. The federation included the Boniface, Francis, Harambee, Michael, Bruce-Guadalupe, Leo, and Martin Luther King Community Schools.

22. Urban Day grew from the roots of St. Benedict the Moor, a central-city parochial school operated by the Capuchin Fathers and the Dominican Sisters of Racine, which opened in 1912 to serve black Milwaukee and out-of-state boarder students. During its peak years from 1938 to 1963, enrollment reached 400. But pressures from rising costs, inadequate space, expressway construction, and the curricular demands of teaching an increasing number of poorly educated black Southern migrants led officials to close the high school in 1964 and the primary school in 1967. See "School of Saint Benedict the Moor Mission," *Crisis*, October 1926, 302; *Milwaukee Journal*, 25 February 1945, 22 December 1968; "St. Benedict Reunion Day 27 April 1969" [history of the school compiled by F. Sinclair] and "Dates Associated with the Building at 1004 West State Street" (November 1968), both in the Urban Day Papers, Urban Day Academy, Milwaukee, Wis.; and "Milwaukee's Urban Day School," *Milwaukee* (March 1969). On the 1970s voucher debate, see *Milwaukee Journal*, 6, 19, 26 October, 24 November 1970; Holt, *Not Yet "Free at Last,"* 25–29; and documents in box 69, folder 7, Barbee Papers. Bothwell's other contenders included Gary, San Diego, San Francisco, and Seattle. In the end, Alum Rock, a suburb of San Jose, was selected for the first federal school voucher experiment.

23. Mildred Harpole, interview with author, 1995. See related quote by Webster Harris, former education activist, who stated that "many of us were there for different reasons; not all of us were integrationists," in Holt, *Not Yet "Free at Last,"* 19.

24. Flo Seefeldt, interview with author, 1995; *Milwaukee Journal Sentinel*, 30 June 1998, Seefeldt obituary.

25. Flo Seefeldt, interview with author, 1995.

26. Wesley Scott, interview with author, 1995; Newby and Tyack, "Victims without 'Crimes,'" 201.

27. Flo Seefeldt, interview with author, 1995.

28. *Milwaukee Star*, 11 November 1967. See Seefeldt's role as co-founding member in Milwaukee County Welfare Rights Organization, *Welfare Mothers Speak Out*.

29. "A Proposal for an Inter-related Language Skills Center by the United Community Group," 18 December 1967, box 75, folder 35, Barbee Papers; UCAG "Community Position Paper" and related documents in "Evaluation of the Inter-related Language Skills Centers, December 1968," Office of State Superintendent, Department of Public Instruction Papers, Wisconsin Historical Society, Madison, Wis.

30. *Milwaukee Courier*, 17, 24 August 1968. For parallels between Milwaukee and the Ocean Hill–Brownsville crisis, see Byndloss, "Resistance, Confrontation, and Accommodation," and works focusing on New York City by Perlstein, *Justice, Justice*, and Podair, *Strike That Changed New York*.

31. UCAG itself was a coalition of members with multiple agendas, including some who opposed Chairperson Seefeldt. See author's interviews with Lauri Wynn and Cynthia Bryant Pitts in 1995 for different perspectives, and also Dahlk, "Black Education Reform Movement," 157–63. Even after school officials undermined UCAG,

Seefeldt continued to work with other women on public assistance to fight Milwaukee public schools for resources for their children, such as filing a lawsuit against "towel fees"; see *Milwaukee Courier*, 22 February 1969.

32. Vada Harris, interview with author, 1995. On racial identity and activism, see Tatum, *"Why Are All the Black Kids Sitting Together in the Cafeteria?,"* chapters 3–5; compare with Woodard, *Nation within a Nation*, 7.

33. Vada Harris, interview with author, 1995; *Milwaukee Star*, 6 May 1967.

34. Vada Harris, interview with author, 1995; NAACP Youth and College Division, *March on Milwaukee*; Aukofer, *City with a Chance*, chapters 7 and 8; Meyer, *As Long as They Don't Move Next Door*, 189–96; Wendelberger, "Open Housing Movement."

35. Aukofer, *City with a Chance*, 83–84, 138. For a critical analysis of Groppi in later years by black activist Carole Malone, see *Milwaukee Courier*, 28 December 1968. On Vada Harris and the Oshkosh demonstrations, see *Milwaukee Courier*, 30 November, 28 December 1968.

36. On the origins of the Clifford McKissick Community School (previously known as the Panthers' Den), see *Milwaukee Courier*, 13 July, 3 August, 14 December 1968, 2 August 1969, 22 August, 5 September 1970; Dahlk, "Black Education Reform Movement," 138–48; Beatrice Waiss, interview with author, 1995; and Milton Coleman, interview with Helen Hall, 1968.

37. *Milwaukee Courier*, 5 September 1970; Fred Hopkins, interview with author, 1996. For other interpretations of black Freedom Schools in this period, see Perlstein, "Minds Stayed on Freedom."

38. On black cultural education schools and groups, see *Milwaukee Star*, 13 July 1968; and *Milwaukee Courier*, 13, 27 July, 3 August, 14 December 1968. On Milwaukee's different black Muslim communities and their schools, see *Milwaukee Star*, 18, 25 May 1963, 26 July, 2 August, 8 November 1973; *Milwaukee Courier*, 30 December 1972; *Milwaukee Community Journal*, 18 January 1978; and Saleem El-Amin and colleagues, interview with author, 1996. On Howard Fuller/Owusu Sadaukai at the McKissick School, see *Milwaukee Star*, 23 May 1970; and *Milwaukee Courier*, 23 May 1970. On Black Panthers, see *Milwaukee Courier*, 14, 21 June, 12 July 1969, 17 January 1970; *Milwaukee Journal*, 26 November 1969; and Witt, "Self-Help and Self-Defense."

39. "Sounds of MUSIC," box 13, folder 7, and Milwaukee Urban League, "Negro Teachers in the Milwaukee School System," 1965, box 98, folder 4, p. 28, both in Barbee Papers; *Milwaukee Journal*, 21 February 1966.

40. See Barbee to NBC *Huntley-Brinkley Report*, 15 May 1965, box 12, folder 6, Barbee Papers; and *Milwaukee Journal*, 18 June 1965. The survey was conducted in October 1965 but reported in the *Milwaukee Journal* on 12 February 1966.

41. "The Second Boycott of the Milwaukee Public Schools [1965]," Morheuser Papers; *Milwaukee Journal*, 5 December 1965, 28 March 1966; MUSIC Board minutes, 7 April 1966, box 13, folder 6, and MUSIC financial records from 1965 to 1967, box 12, folder 9, both in Barbee Papers.

42. While Mack, *Our Children's Burden*, concluded that "protest pays," more persuasive research by Crain, *Politics of School Desegregation*, argued that protest tactics have little influence and that the ideological composition of the school board is more significant. Later, Kirby et al., *Political Strategies*, revised Crain's initial thesis by stating that protest tactics were influential only when joined by civic elites and elected leaders. On the numerous school desegregation reports generated by the Milwaukee controversy, see the Governor's Commission on Human Rights, *Racial Imbalance*; Academy for Educational Development, *Quality Education*; Greenleigh, *Plan to Reduce Prejudice*; and the Social Development Corporation, "Racial Isolation in Milwaukee Public Schools: A Final Report to the U.S. Commission on Civil Rights," 1967, in both Morheuser Papers and box 95, folder 51, Barbee Papers (fragment). Although

the latter report was contracted by the federal government, very little of it appeared in the final two-volume published report, U.S. Commission on Civil Rights, *Racial Isolation in the Public Schools*.

43. Carter to Barbee, 5 November 1964, box 196, folder 13, Barbee Papers; *Milwaukee Journal*, 22 January 1967; "The Future of MUSIC," 12 November 1966, Morheuser Papers. On the scope of the lawsuit research, see Morheuser to Cohen, 6 May 1966, box 196, folder 15, Barbee Papers.

44. *Milwaukee Star*, 11 August 1962; Cecil Brown Jr., interview with author, 1995; Reuben Harpole Jr., interview with author, 1995; Barbee 1964 campaign flyers, Morheuser Papers.

45. *Milwaukee Journal*, 9 October 1967; "The Basis for the Attack on School Segregation in the North [1966]," box 2, folder 14, Barbee Papers. Although the document is unsigned, Barbee confirmed authorship in an interview with author, 1995. On Barbee and the Black Panthers, see *Milwaukee Courier*, 8 April 1973; and *Capital Times*, 2 March 1972. For a similar interpretation of the merger of integration and black power in the 1966 documents of Chicago's Coordinating Council of Community Organizations (CCCO), see Anderson and Pickering, *Confronting the Color Line*, 199–200. See also their 1968 survey of CCCO participants, which confirms their interpretation that black power and integration were perceived by participants "as differences of emphasis rather than competing principles," 453. Compare Barbee's position in 1966 with New York City activist Milton Galamison in C. Taylor, *Knocking at Our Own Door*, chapters 6 and 7.

Chapter Six

1. Map of the City of Milwaukee Schools, 1972, box 226, folder 2, Barbee Papers; McEvilly, "Teacher and Student Images"; U.S. Census Bureau, *Census of Population and Housing*, Milwaukee, 1960 and 1970.

2. On spatial analysis in black freedom struggles, see Self, "'To Plan Our Liberation.'"

3. *Milwaukee Courier*, 3 August 1968; McEvilly, "Teacher and Student Images," 9–12; Milwaukee Public School racial enrollment data summarized in Washington and Oliver, *Identification of Strengths*, 66–70; *Amos v. Board* (19 January 1976), 790.

4. Washington and Oliver, *Identification of Strengths*, 66–70; *Milwaukee Star*, 28 September 1968. See related story about the struggle of Leona Reeves, the first black cheerleader at Washington High, in *Milwaukee Courier*, 18 May 1968.

5. *Milwaukee Star*, 28 September 1968. Perkins also graduated from the all-black Dunbar High School in Little Rock, the segregated school that Milwaukee educator Sarah Scott had attended. See F. Jones, *Traditional Model of Educational Excellence*; and Phyllis Perkins Banks and Teresa Greene, interview with author, 1995.

6. *Milwaukee Star*, 5 October 1968, 1 February, 22 March 1969. A similar controversy arose at nearby West Division High School, where black students (45 percent) walked out of the school to protest the principal's refusal to allow an all-black Afro-American club to exist. He objected on the grounds that it must be integrated. See *Milwaukee Courier*, 5 October 1968.

7. *Milwaukee Sentinel*, 22 November 1969; *Milwaukee Courier*, 29 November 1969. The observer is McEvilly, "Teacher and Student Images," 8.

8. *Milwaukee Sentinel*, 22 November 1969; *Milwaukee Journal*, 26 November 1969, letter to the editor, with excerpts reprinted in *Milwaukee Courier*, 6 December 1969.

9. *Milwaukee Journal*, 14, 17 April 1970; *Milwaukee Courier*, 20 May 1970; Milwaukee Board of School Directors, Committee on Appointments and Instruction, verbatim minutes, 28 April 1970, 25. See Grant, *World We Created at Hamilton High*, and also a critical review essay by Kantor and Lowe, "Reform or Reaction?"

10. *Milwaukee Journal*, 5 June 1970; *Milwaukee Courier*, 6 June 1970; *Amos v. Board* (19 January 1976), 784; Barndt, Janka, and Rose, "West and Midwest," 239.

11. *Milwaukee Journal*, 24 September 1972, 16 April 1973. On the Sherman Park neighborhood, see Beverstock and Stuckert, *Metropolitan Milwaukee Fact Book*.

12. Marian McEvilly, testimony in *Amos* school desegregation trial, 26 September 1973, box 107, folder 11, p. 1269, Barbee Papers; McEvilly, "Teacher and Student Images"; Dahlk, "Black Education Reform Movement," 184–85.

13. McEvilly, "Teacher and Student Images"; Marian McEvilly, testimony in *Amos* school desegregation trial, 26 September 1973, box 107, folder 11, p. 1267, Barbee Papers.

14. Washington and Oliver, *Identification of Strengths*, 66–70; *Milwaukee Courier*, 15 July 1972; *Milwaukee Journal*, 2 February 1972, 16 April, 13 June 1973; *Amos v. Board* (19 January 1976), 792.

15. *Milwaukee Journal*, 17 April 1973.

16. McEvilly, "Teacher and Student Images," 45; McEvilly memo to Washington cluster parents, and Audi flyer to Steuben parents, both 6 June 1973, box 74, folder 27, Barbee Papers.

17. McEvilly resignation letter, 29 June 1973, box 74, folder 27, Barbee Papers; McEvilly, testimony in *Amos* school desegregation trial, 26 September 1973, box 107, folder 11, pp. 1260, 1269, Barbee Papers.

18. McEvilly resignation letter, 29 June 1973, box 74, folder 27, Barbee Papers.

19. U.S. Census Bureau, *Census of Population and Housing*, Milwaukee, 1960 and 1970.

20. On black history protests at Rufus King, North Division, and Riverside High Schools, see *Milwaukee Courier*, 3, 10, 17 February 1968; Milwaukee Public Schools, Division of Curriculum and Instruction, "The Question of a Multi-Ethnic Approach to American History in the Milwaukee Public Schools" (1968), box 106, folder 14, Barbee Papers; and "The Negro in American Life: A Guide to Supplement the Study of United States History" (1967), Steve Baruch Papers, in possession of author. See also Baruch, "Factors Affecting the Process of Curriculum Formation," 244–48. Compare with a national perspective in Zimmerman, *Whose America?*

21. Beason, *Why We Lose*, 20–24; Jake Beason, interview with author, 1995; *Milwaukee Courier*, 5 October 1968.

22. *Milwaukee Courier*, 11 January, 16 August 1969, 29 August 1970; *Milwaukee Star*, 16 August, 13 September 1969, 8 August 1970; Beason, *Why We Lose*, 22; "Beckley's News Analysis," *Echo*, October 1969, 7.

23. Milwaukee Public Schools, "A Sub-System Approach to the Problems of a Large City School System: An Application for a Title III (ESEA) Grant," March 1968, box 74, folder 22, Barbee Papers. But note criticism of dependent subsystem programs as "more of the same" without the accountability of genuine community control in Fantini, Gittell, and Magat, *Community Control and the Urban School*, 43.

24. *Milwaukee Courier*, 18 May, 25 May, 1 June, 27 July 1968.

25. *Milwaukee Journal*, 18 March, 13 July 1971, 25 February 1972; "Beckley's News Analysis," *Echo*, September 1969, 17.

26. *Milwaukee Journal*, 23 April, 27 July 1972; *Milwaukee Courier*, 5 August 1972.

27. U.S. Census Bureau, *Census of Population and Housing*, Milwaukee 1960 and 1970.

28. *Milwaukee Star*, 8 July 1967; *Milwaukee Courier*, 16 January 1971; Rev. Joseph McNeil, interview with author, 1995.

29. *Milwaukee Courier*, 9 September, 28 October 1972, 28 April, 5 May 1973; *Echo*, May 1973, 12–14; Fred Hopkins, interview with author, 1996. On black unemployment in Milwaukee, see *New York Times*, 31 December 1977. On Busalacchi, see *Milwaukee Community Journal*, 12 July 1978.

30. *Milwaukee Courier,* 13 December 1975.

31. *Amos v. Board* (19 January 1976); *Milwaukee Journal,* 23 February 1970; *Milwaukee Journal,* 8 February 1964; "Details of Tour of School Administration Offices," 29 September 1965, and "Legal Research (Progress) Report," 31 July 1966, both in Morheuser Papers.

32. *Milwaukee Journal,* 8 September 1969; *Milwaukee Courier,* 2 December 1972.

33. *Milwaukee Journal,* 19 June 1970; *Milwaukee Courier,* 2 December 1972; Wilkins to Franklin, 20 June, 2 December 1969, part 5, section C, box 320, "Wisconsin Amos case January–September 1969" folder, National NAACP Papers.

34. *Armstrong v. O'Connell* (11 June 1976); *Milwaukee Journal,* 9 September 1973; Lloyd Barbee, interview with author, 1995; Rochelle and Roosevelt Savage, interview with author, 1995.

35. *Capital Times,* 2 March 1972; *Milwaukee Courier,* 17 August 1974; *Milwaukee Sentinel,* 3 July 1973; *Milwaukee Star,* 12 July 1973; *Milwaukee Journal Sentinel,* 30 December 2002, Barbee obituary.

36. *Milwaukee Journal,* 13 June, 9, 10 September 1973; *Milwaukee Courier,* 23 June, 15 September 1973. Morheuser later became director of the Education Law Center in Newark, New Jersey, where she served as the lead attorney who won the *Abbott v. Burke* school finance reform decision at the New Jersey State Supreme Court in 1990.

37. *Keyes v. Denver* (21 June 1973); Kluger, *Simple Justice,* 768–69; *Milwaukee Journal,* 5 September 1973; Stolee, "Milwaukee Desegregation Case."

38. *Milwaukee Journal,* 16 September, 7 October 1973, 13 January, 5 February 1974; *Milwaukee Star,* 20 September 1973, 17 January, 7 February 1974.

39. *Amos v. Board* (19 January 1976), 771, 812–13, 819; Stolee, "Milwaukee Desegregation Case"; *Milwaukee Courier,* 24 January 1976.

40. *Amos v. Board* (19 January 1976), 824; *Armstrong v. O'Connell* (11 June 1976); Stolee, "Milwaukee Desegregation Case," 246–47.

41. *Milwaukee Courier,* 18 January 1975, 29 May 1976; *Milwaukee Journal,* 8 May 1974, 30 March 1975.

42. On Black Community Caucus and Blac-a-Vention, see *Milwaukee Courier,* 23 December 1972, 10 March, 7 April, 6 October 1973, 25 May, 7 September 1974; and *Milwaukee Star,* 4 October 1973, 23 May 1974. Note that Blac-a-Vention did not endorse McEvilly, Todd, or New in 1973 or 1974 but did so in 1975 when the large number of open seats meant that black candidates did not compete against one another. See *Milwaukee Courier,* 1, 15 February 1975.

43. *Milwaukee Journal,* 4, 15 August 1971, 6 February, 8 May, 20 October 1974, 15 April 1975; *New York Times,* 5 September 1971.

44. *Milwaukee Journal,* 15, 21 October 1975. On school desegregation violence in other Northern cities, see Formisano, *Boston against Busing.* McMurrin obtained federal funding from the Emergency School Assistance Act.

45. Metz, *Different by Design,* chapter 2; Bennett, "Plan for Increasing Educational Opportunities," 86; Barndt, Janka, and Rose, "West and Midwest," 246.

46. *Milwaukee Courier,* 20 March 1976. According to this newspaper on 3 May 1975, 85 percent of North Division eleventh graders tested two years or more below reading level.

47. *Milwaukee Courier,* 20, 27 March 1976.

48. *Milwaukee Courier,* 20 March 1976.

49. *Milwaukee Journal,* 31 March 1976; *Milwaukee Courier,* 14 February, 20 March 1976; Barndt, Janka, and Rose, "West and Midwest," 254; Harris, "Towards an Understanding of Community Involvement in Desegregation: An Examination of Three Citizen Groups in Milwaukee, Wisconsin" (undated), unpublished manu-

script, in possession of author; Harris, "Citizens Committee of Milwaukee"; Harris, "Community Involvement in Desegregation."

50. *Armstrong v. O'Connell* (9 July 1976); *Milwaukee Courier*, 3, 10 July 1976; Blacks for Two-Way Integration, "Blacks Forced to 'Volunteer,'" box 49, folder 1, Zablocki Papers.

51. Stolee, "Milwaukee Desegregation Case," 256–58. On comparison of Milwaukee to Boston, see Willie, *School Desegregation Plans that Work*, 205.

52. Stolee, "Milwaukee Desegregation Case," 247–48; *Dayton v. Brinkman* (27 June 1977); *Brennan v. Armstrong* (29 June 1977).

53. *Milwaukee Courier*, 4 September 1976.

54. Dahlk, "Black Education Reform Movement," 189–202; *Milwaukee Courier*, 29 December 1973.

55. *Milwaukee Courier*, 7 May, 18 June 1977; "Blacks for Two-Way Integration Demands to the Milwaukee Board of School Directors," 1977, Peterson Papers. See also Larkin, "School Desegregation and Student Suspension."

56. *Milwaukee Community Journal*, 19 October 1977 (some grammar and punctuation have been modified to clarify McMurrin's rhetorical argument); *Milwaukee Journal*, 9 May 1978; *Milwaukee Journal Sentinel*, 19 October 1999. See also related story that questions the timing of these historical "revelations" and whether they were intended to politically support a retreat on school desegregation in *Capital Times*, 30 October 1999.

57. Milwaukee Board of School Directors, verbatim minutes, 27 July 1977, 44; "Coalition for Peaceful Schools," 2 September 1977, box 7, folder 9, Reuss Papers.

58. Blacks for Two-Way Integration, "Decision Day for Black Folks," 24 August 1977, box 49, folder 1, Zablocki Papers; *Milwaukee Courier*, 27 August 1977. Note that Polly Williams lived in the Rufus King district in 1977 and that she attempted to enroll her daughter in Riverside High. On the Blacks for Two-Way Integration boycott, which attracted some 3,000 participants on a Friday afternoon, see *Milwaukee Courier*, 8 October 1977.

59. *Milwaukee Courier*, 7 July 1980.

60. *Milwaukee Courier*, 10 June 1978; *Milwaukee Community Journal*, 10 June 1978; *Armstrong v. O'Connell* (1 June 1978).

61. Stolee, "Milwaukee Desegregation Case," 253–54; *Milliken v. Bradley* (25 July 1974). On the failed Conta plan, see *New York Times*, 3 April 1975; *Milwaukee Journal*, 8, 15 April, 30 June, 31 October 1975; and *Milwaukee Community Journal*, 4 April, 14 June 1978.

62. *Milwaukee Courier*, 10 July, 28 August 1976, 7 January, 10 June 1978; *Milwaukee Community Journal*, 7 June 1978.

63. *Milwaukee Sentinel*, 6 September 1978; *Milwaukee Community Journal*, 6 September 1978; *Milwaukee Journal*, 30 April 1979.

64. *Milwaukee Journal*, 3 May 1978; *Milwaukee Courier*, 5, 19 August 1978.

65. *Milwaukee Journal*, 15 April 1978; *Milwaukee Community Journal*, 26 July 1978. On North Division district closures and conversions, see "White Students Fleeing White Schools, Black Students Forced to White Schools," Organization of Organizations, Peterson Papers; Milwaukee Public Schools, "Facilities Removed from MPS, 1975–1978," 13 November 1978, Barndt Papers; and *Milwaukee Courier*, 5, 19 August 1978.

66. *Milwaukee Journal*, 26 February, 7 May 1979; *Milwaukee Courier*, 3 March 1979; Stolee, "Milwaukee Desegregation Case," 254–55.

67. *Milwaukee Journal*, 14 May 1979; *Milwaukee Community Journal*, 16 May 1979; *Armstrong v. Board* (4 May 1979).

CHAPTER SEVEN

1. Carter, "Reassessment of *Brown v. Board*," 27. Compare with his remarks over fifteen years later in Carter, "Unending Struggle." *Plessy v. Ferguson* (18 May 1896). See also Arnez, "Implementation of Desegregation"; Irvine and Irvine, "The Impact of the Desegregation Process"; Hochschild, *Thirty Years after Brown*; Monti, *Semblance of Justice*; and Wilkinson, *From Brown to Bakke*.

2. *Milwaukee Journal*, 30 April 1979; *Milwaukee Courier*, 26 May 1979; Marian McEvilly, "Remarks Prepared for the Milwaukee Urban League Guild," 21 August 1979, Barndt Papers; "The History of the Matter: North Division School Board Plan vs. Community Plan," Coalition for Peaceful Schools special newsletter, 1979, box 7, folder 9, Reuss Papers.

3. *Milwaukee Journal*, 4 May 1979; *Milwaukee Sentinel*, 5, 10 May 1979; *Milwaukee Community Journal*, 9 May 1979.

4. *Milwaukee Sentinel*, 10 May 1979; *Milwaukee Journal*, 10 May 1979; *Forced Choice* video, 1980.

5. *Forced Choice* video, 1980; *Milwaukee Sentinel*, 5 May 1979.

6. *Milwaukee Courier*, 5 July 1980; *Milwaukee Journal*, 10 July 1979; *Devil's Dispatch*, North Division student newspaper, February 1980, in Williams Papers; Rev. Joseph McNeil, and Evelyn and Ralph Williams, interviews with author, 1995; Pauline McKay, interview with author, 1996.

7. Anita Spencer, Tony and Zakiya Courtney, interviews with author, 1996.

8. Brian Verdin, interview with author, 1995; "The History of the Matter: North Division School Board Plan vs. Community Plan," Coalition for Peaceful Schools special newsletter, 1979, in box 7, folder 9, Reuss Papers.

9. Howard Fuller, interview with author, 1995; Davidson, *Best of Enemies*, 155–251; Bamberger, "Education of Howard Fuller"; Merida, "Howard Fuller"; Richardson, "Unexpected Superintendent."

10. Howard Fuller, interview with author, 1995; Davidson, *Best of Enemies*, 155–251; Bamberger, "Education of Howard Fuller."

11. Howard Fuller, interview with author, 1995; Davidson, *Best of Enemies*, 155–251; Bamberger, "Education of Howard Fuller"; *Milwaukee Courier*, 6 September 1969.

12. *Milwaukee Courier*, 26 April 1980, indirect quotations from Howard Fuller; *Forced Choice* video, 1980; Fuller, "Impact of the Milwaukee Public School System's Desegregation Plan," 156–57.

13. *Milwaukee Sentinel*, 24 March 1980; *Milwaukee Journal*, 10 July 1979; *Forced Choice* video, 1980; Holman to Monitoring Board, 4 October 1979, Williams Papers; Coalition to Save North Division, "Enough Is Enough" flyer, 1979, Wisconsin Historical Society periodicals microfilm collection.

14. *Milwaukee Community Journal*, 11 July 1979; *Milwaukee Sentinel*, 31 July 1979; *Milwaukee Journal*, "Plan's Foes Cheer Integration Appeal" [undated clipping, probably July 1979].

15. *Milwaukee Courier*, 29 March 1980; Bell, *Shades of Brown*; "Desegregation: A New Form of Discrimination?" conference program, 21–23 March 1980, Williams Papers.

16. Marian McEvilly, "Remarks Prepared for the Milwaukee Urban League Guild," 21 August 1979, Barndt Papers; *Milwaukee Journal*, 22 August 1979, 25 February 1980.

17. Marian McEvilly, "Remarks Prepared for the Milwaukee Urban League Guild," 21 August 1979, Barndt Papers.

18. Marian McEvilly, "Remarks Prepared for the Milwaukee Urban League Guild," 21 August 1979, Barndt Papers; *Milwaukee Journal*, 30 May 1979; *Milwaukee Courier*,

1 September 1979; *Forced Choice* video, 1980; Bamberger, "Education of Howard Fuller," 60. See also Leon Todd Jr. and Peg Kenner, interviews with author, 1996.

19. The month-long campaign for old classroom photos appeared in the *Milwaukee Courier*, 14 October, 11, 18 November 1972.

20. See publicity photos and articles for the "Fabulous Fifties Night" reunion in *Milwaukee Courier*, 15, 22 October, 5, 19 November 1977.

21. On nostalgia and school segregation, see Shircliffe, "'We Got the Best of That World.'"

22. Marian McEvilly, "Remarks Prepared for the Milwaukee Urban League Guild," 21 August 1979, Barndt Papers. For more on competing interpretations of the data, compare Fuller, "Impact of the Milwaukee Public School System's Desegregation Plan," to Archbald, "Magnet Schools," and Bennett, "Plan for Increasing Educational Opportunities," 103.

23. On editorials, see *Milwaukee Sentinel*, 31 August 1979, and *Milwaukee Journal*, 26 November 1979. On political support, see *Milwaukee Journal*, 31 August 1979, 25 April 1980; *Milwaukee Sentinel*, 24 April 1980; and *Milwaukee Courier*, 3 May 1980. On legal maneuvers, see Monitoring Board to LaFave, 16 November 1979, and *Armstrong v. Board, re: North Division* (4, 16 January 1980), all in Williams Papers.

24. *Milwaukee Courier*, 18 August 1979, 26 April 1980; *Milwaukee Journal*, 29 August 1979, 14 April 1980; *Milwaukee Community Journal*, 16 April 1980.

25. Lloyd Barbee, interview with Clayborn Benson, 1990.

26. Ibid.; "Milwaukee Schools: Separate, but Not Equal" videotape; W. Thompson, *History of Wisconsin*, 399.

27. *Milwaukee Courier*, 13 January, 1, 15 September 1979.

28. *Milwaukee Community Journal*, 30 April, 13 August 1980, 14 October 1981; *Milwaukee Journal*, 30 April 1980; Milwaukee Board of School Directors, Committee on Instruction, verbatim minutes, 9 February 1981, part 2, 85.

29. McMurrin to LaFave, certification regarding settlement, 15 October 1982, Barndt Papers; W. Thompson, *History of Wisconsin*, 396; Orum, *City-Building in America*, 134–40; Massey and Denton, *American Apartheid*, 76–77; Levine and Zipp, "City at Risk."

30. *Milwaukee Courier*, 23 February, 11 October 1980; *Armstrong and Jackson v. Board* (19 February 1980); *Milwaukee Community Journal*, 1 October 1980, 24 September 1986; Stolee, "Milwaukee Desegregation Case," 258–60; "Press Release" [from six former school board members protesting the limited terms of the metropolitan desegregation settlement], 27 January 1986, Barndt Papers; Rose and Stewart, *Milwaukee's City-Suburban Interdistrict Integration Program*.

31. Du Bois, "Does the Negro Need Separate Schools?," 335, quoted on front of "The New North Division District" brochure, 1987, and "A Manifesto for New Directions in the Education of Black Children in the City of Milwaukee," 1987, both in the Peter Murrell Jr. Papers, in possession of author; Bell, "Case for a Separate Black School System"; Smith, "Creation of an Inner City District"; Murrell, "North Division District Plan."

32. Witte, *Market Approach to Education*, 43–45, chapters 6, 7; Lowe and Whipp, "Examining the Milwaukee Parent Choice Program," 38; Peterson and Hassel, *Learning from School Choice*; Viadero, "Researcher at Center of Storm over Vouchers"; Lowe and Miner, *Selling Out Our Schools*; Wisconsin Department of Public Instruction, "Milwaukee Parental Choice Program," <www.dpi.state.wi.us/dpi/dfm/sms/choice.html> (14 April 2003).

33. See Carl, "Unusual Allies"; Wood, "Legislative Development"; Hess, *Revolution at the Margins*; and Holt, *Not Yet "Free at Last."* Compare with Farrell and Mathews, "School Choice"; Rigdon, "Business of Education Reform," chapter 4; Wortzel,

"Strange Bedfellows and Uncertain Futures"; McGroarty, *Break These Chains*; Witte, *Market Approach to Education*; and Lowe and Whipp, "Examining the Milwaukee Parent Choice Program."

34. Holt, *Not Yet "Free at Last,"* 72, 210; Byndloss, "Resistance, Confrontation, and Accommodation"; Lowe and Whipp, "Examining the Milwaukee Parent Choice Program," 38; African American Male Task Force, *Educating African American Males*; Leake and Leake, "Islands of Hope"; Leake and Faltz, "Do We Need to Desegregate All of Our Black Schools?"; Murrell, "Afrocentric Immersion"; Howard Fuller, interview with author, 1995; *Milwaukee Journal Sentinel,* 19 April 1995.

35. Wisconsin Advisory Committee to the U.S. Commission on Civil Rights, *Impact of School Desegregation in Milwaukee*; Murphy and Pawasarat, "Why It Failed"; Peterson, "Neighborhood Schools"; Peterson and Miller, "Forward to the Past?"; Barndt and McNally, *Return to Separate and Unequal; Milwaukee Journal Sentinel,* 30 December 2002, 27 February 2003.

CONCLUSION

1. Olson, "Black Community Is Frustrated"; Orfield and Eaton, *Dismantling Desegregation*; Orfield, *Schools More Separate*; Patterson, *Brown v. Board,* 212. See a similar interpretive taxonomy in Hochschild, *Thirty Years after Brown,* 17–22.

2. Patterson, *Brown v. Board,* xxi, 14–20; *Missouri ex rel. Gaines v. Canada* (12 December 1938); *Sweatt v. Painter* (5 June 1950); *McLaurin v. Oklahoma* (5 June 1950).

3. Patterson, *Brown v. Board,* 79, 142–46, 153–55, 171–72.

4. Ibid., 192–94, 210–11, 218–21. Compare with Carter, "Reassessment of *Brown v. Board,*" and Bell, *And We Are Not Saved,* chapter 4.

5. Ravitch, *Troubled Crusade,* 114, 127; *Briggs v. Elliott* (15 July 1955). See also Wolters, *Burden of Brown.*

6. Ravitch, *Troubled Crusade,* 165–66, 176, chapter 8; *Green v. New Kent County* (27 May 1968); *Swann v. Charlotte-Mecklenburg* (20 April 1971).

7. Hochschild, *Thirty Years after Brown,* 20. See also Lowe and Kantor, "Considerations."

8. Curry, *Silver Rights,* xix, 34, 172.

9. Cecelski, *Along Freedom Road,* 29, 33, 59, 60–64, 69, 92, 152–53.

10. For more on this example of contrasts, see Dougherty et al., "Teaching *Brown.*"

11. Neustadt and May, *Thinking in Time,* xv, 240.

12. Miner, "Splits Widen."

BIBLIOGRAPHY

See this book's website and related links at
<http://www.trincoll.edu/depts/educ/struggle>.

Manuscript Collections

Madison, Wis.
   Wisconsin Historical Society
      Department of Public Instruction Papers
   Wisconsin Legislative Reference Bureau
      Newspaper clippings
Milwaukee, Wis.
   Marquette University
      Clement J. Zablocki Papers
   Milwaukee County Historical Society
      James Dorsey Papers
      Wisconsin Civil Rights Congress Papers
   Milwaukee Legislative Reference Bureau
      Newspaper clippings
   Milwaukee Public Library
      Frank P. Zeidler Mayoral Administration Papers
   Milwaukee Teachers' Education Association
      Milwaukee Teachers' Education Association Papers

University of Wisconsin–Milwaukee, Golda Meir Library
  Lloyd A. Barbee Papers
  Helen I. Barnhill Papers
  Congress of Racial Equality, Milwaukee Chapter, Papers
  Kathleen Mary Hart Papers
  Elizabeth Holmes Papers
  Henry W. Maier Mayoral Administration Papers
  Milwaukee Citizens for Equal Opportunity Papers
  Milwaukee United School Integration Committee Papers
  Milwaukee Urban League Papers
  National Association for the Advancement of Colored People,
    Milwaukee Branch, Papers
  Lorraine M. Radtke Papers
  Henry S. Reuss Papers
Urban Day Academy
  Urban Day Papers
Washington, D.C.
  Library of Congress
    National Association for the Advancement of Colored People Papers
    National Urban League Papers
Author's collection
  Michael Barndt Papers
  Steve Baruch Papers
  Father Matthew Gottschalk Papers
  Marilyn Morheuser Papers
  Peter Murrell Jr. Papers
  Bob Peterson Papers
  Evelyn Williams Papers

BIBLIOGRAPHIES

Blessing, Matt, ed. "Bibliography on School Desegregation in Milwaukee, Wisconsin." Wisconsin Humanities Committee, unpublished, 1990.
Ford, Sarah Ann, and Lydia Brown, eds. *Black Heritage in Milwaukee: Preliminary Guide to Blacks in Milwaukee and Wisconsin.* Milwaukee: University of Wisconsin–Extension, 1981.

INTERVIEWS

Interviews with author, deposited at University of Wisconsin–Milwaukee, Golda Meir Library, and Wisconsin Black Historical Society/Museum, Milwaukee, Wis.
  Adams, Juanita, and Arlene Johnson, 15 June 1995
  Alexander, Ray, 19 July 1995
  Banks, Phyllis Perkins, and sister Teresa Greene, 28 June 1995
  Barbee, Lloyd, 12 July and 14 August 1995
  Beason, Jake, 11 July 1995
  Beckley, Maurice, 28 June 1995

Bell, Martha, 22 June 1995

Brown, Cecil, Jr., and Loretta, 9 August 1995

Caesar, Elsie, 7 August 1995

Champion, Rev. Leo, Inonia, and son Gene, 7 June 1995

Cheeks, Thomas, 22 June 1995

Courtney, Tony and Zakiya, 23 July 1996

Davis, Reginald, 4 July 1995

El-Amin, Saleem (formerly Jeff Crawford), and colleagues from the Sister Clara
    Muhammad School, 9 July 1996

Finlayson, Edith, 31 May 1995

Flowers, Allen L., 12 July 1996

Fuller, Howard, 28 December 1995

Goens, Geraldine Gilmer, and brother Jay Gilmer, 12 July 1996

Gordon, Grant and Lucinda, 9 June 1995

Gregg, Rev. B. S., 30 May 1995

Hannah, F. Marvin, Sr., 19 July 1996

Harper, Rev. Fred, 17 July 1995

Harpole, Mildred, 17 July 1995

Harpole, Reuben, Jr., 6 June 1995

Harris, Robert (Bob), Jr., 11 July 1995

Harris, Vada, 26 August 1995

Holt, Mikel, 16 July 1996

Hopkins, Fred, 2 July 1996

Jackson, Carolyn, 9 July 1996

Jackson, Gwen, 31 May 1995

Jackson, Harold B., Jr., 11 July 1996

Jeter, Maxine, 5 July 1995

Johnson, Ronald, 13 July 1995

Jones, Nellie, 6 June 1995

Jones, Walter, 19 June 1995

Kenner, Peg, 18 July 1996

Kirkendoll, Rev. Richard, 15 July 1996

Lucas, Reaber, 13 July 1996

McAlister, Mona, 19 July 1995

McKay, Pauline, 11 July 1996

McNeil, Rev. Joseph, 7 August 1995

Murrell, Peter, Sr., and Eva Ruth, 2 June 1995

Nicholas, Clarence, 2 July 1996

Pitts, Cynthia Bryant, 16 June 1995

Robertson, Helen, 24 July 1996

Robinson, Jeannetta, 31 May 1995

Rogers, Tazzalean, and daughter Cecelia, 25 July 1995

Saunders, Lawrence, and wife Kathleen, 6 July 1995

Savage, Rochelle and Rev. Roosevelt, 27 June 1995

Scott, Wesley, 25 July 1995

Seefeldt, Flo, 16 June 1995

Smith, Michael C., 12 July 1996
Spencer, Anita, 10 July 1996
Swan, Monroe, 17 July 1996
Todd, Leon, Jr., 15 July 1996
Verdin, Brian, 27 July 1995
Waiss, Beatrice, 28 June 1995
Walker, Rev. Lucius, 13 May 1996
Ward, Adolphus, 21 June 1995
Watkins, Ivory, and daughter Linda Watkins Jefferson, 12 June 1996
Williams, Evelyn and Ralph, Jr., 26 July 1995
Wray, Jessie, 15 June 1995
Wynn, Lauri, 9 June 1995
Young, Ruby, 17 July 1996

OTHER INTERVIEWS

Barbee, Lloyd, interview with Kay Shannon of the Civil Rights Documentation Project, 13 February 1968, Ralph J. Bunche Oral History Collection, Howard University, Washington, D.C.

Barbee, Lloyd, videotape interview with Clayborn Benson, 17 February 1990, Wisconsin Black Historical Society/Museum, Milwaukee, Wis.

Coleman, Milton, interview with Helen Hall of the Civil Rights Documentation Project, 14 February 1968, Ralph J. Bunche Oral History Collection, Howard University, Washington, D.C.

Halyard, Ardie Clark, interview with Marcia M. Greenlee, 24–25 August 1978. In *The Black Women Oral History Project: From the Arthur and Elizabeth Schlesinger Library on the History of Women in America, Radcliffe College*, vol. 5, edited by Ruth Edmonds Hill, 1–32. Westport, Conn.: Meckler Publishing, 1991.

Jackson, John H., interview with Michael Gordon, 26 July 1989, Milwaukee Public Schools Oral History Project Records, University of Wisconsin–Milwaukee, Golda Meir Library, Milwaukee, Wis.

FILM AND VIDEOTAPE

Decade of Discontent (1960–70). Written and produced by Charles Taylor for the Wisconsin Educational Television Network, 1981.

Eyes on the Prize: Awakenings, 1954–1956. Documentary. Blackside Productions, 1987.

Forced Choice: The Milwaukee Plan—A Model for Northern School Desegregation. Produced and directed by Jones Cullinan, 1980. University of Wisconsin–Milwaukee, Golda Meir Library, Milwaukee, Wis.

Milwaukee school desegregation protests, unedited television news footage, 1964. Wisconsin Black Historical Society/Museum, Milwaukee, Wis.

"Milwaukee Schools: Separate, but Not Equal." Videotape of public history panel discussion at Wisconsin Black Historical Society/Museum, Milwaukee, Wis., 5 May 1990.

Newspapers, Newsletters, and Magazines

Capital Times (Madison, Wis.)
Chicago Defender (national edition)
The Crisis
Echo (Milwaukee, Wis., edited by Virginia Williams)
Enough Is Enough (Coalition to Save North Division flyer)
The Freedom Call: Official Newsletter of the Milwaukee NAACP
Milwaukee
Milwaukee Community Journal
Milwaukee Courier
Milwaukee Defender
Milwaukee Globe
Milwaukee Journal
Milwaukee Journal Sentinel
Milwaukee Magazine
Milwaukee Sentinel
Milwaukee Star
Milwaukee Times
Milwaukee Weekly Post
Monthly Report (of the Milwaukee Urban League)
Opportunity
New York Times
The Socialist Call
Time
U.S. News and World Report
Wisconsin Enterprise-Blade
Wisconsin State Journal

Court Rulings

Plessy v. Ferguson, 163 U.S. 537 (18 May 1896).
Missouri ex rel. Gaines v. Canada, Registrar of the University of Missouri, et al., 305 U.S. 337 (12 December 1938).
Sweatt v. Painter et al., 339 U.S. 629 (5 June 1950).
McLaurin v. Oklahoma State Regents for Higher Education et al., 339 U.S. 637 (5 June 1950).
Brown v. Board of Education of Topeka, 347 U.S. 483 (17 May 1954).
Briggs et al. v. Elliott et al., 132 F. Supp. 776 (15 July 1955).
Taylor v. Board of Education of New Rochelle, 191 F. Supp. 181 (24 January 1961).
Bell v. School District of Gary, Indiana, 213 F. Supp. 819 (29 January 1963).
Green et al. v. County School Board of New Kent County et al., 391 U.S. 430 (27 May 1968).
Swann et al. v. Charlotte-Mecklenburg Board of Education et al., 402 U.S. 1 (20 April 1971).
Keyes et al. v. Denver School District No. 1 et al., 413 U.S. 189 (21 June 1973).
Milliken, Governor of Michigan, et al. v. Bradley et al., 418 U.S. 717 (25 July 1974).

Amos et al. v. Board of School Directors of the City of Milwaukee, 408 F. Supp. 765 (19 January 1976).

Armstrong et al. v. O'Connell et al., 416 F. Supp. 1344 (11 June 1976).

Armstrong et al. v. O'Connell et al., 416 F. Supp. 1347 (9 July 1976).

Dayton Board of Education et al. v. Brinkman et al., 433 U.S. 406 (27 June 1977).

Brennan et al. v. Armstrong et al., 433 U.S. 672 (29 June 1977).

Armstrong et al. v. O'Connell et al., 451 F. Supp. 817 (1 June 1978).

Armstrong et al. v. Board of School Directors of the City of Milwaukee, 471 F. Supp. 800 (4 May 1979).

Armstrong et al. v. Board of School Directors, re: North Division, United States District Court (4, 16 January 1980).

Armstrong et al. and Jackson et al. v. Board of School Directors of the City of Milwaukee, 616 F. 2d 305 (19 February 1980).

GOVERNMENT DOCUMENTS

Community-Relations Social Development Commission in Milwaukee County and the Milwaukee Urban League. *Black Powerlessness in Milwaukee Institutions and Decision-Making Structure.* Milwaukee: University of Wisconsin–Milwaukee, 1970.

Governor's Commission on Human Rights (Wisconsin). *Racial Imbalance in the Milwaukee Public Schools.* Madison: Governor's Commission on Human Rights, 1966.

Mayor's Study Committee on Social Problems in the Inner Core Area of the City. *Final Report to the Honorable Frank P. Zeidler, Mayor.* Milwaukee: City of Milwaukee, 1960.

Milwaukee Board of Election Commissioners. *Biennial Report.* Milwaukee: The Board, 1930–90.

Milwaukee Board of School Directors, Milwaukee Public Schools. *Annual Reports.* Milwaukee: The Board, 1930–90.

———. *Bibliographical Digest.* Milwaukee: The Board, 1964.

———. *Manual and Roster.* Milwaukee: The Board, 1930–90.

———. *Minutes.* Milwaukee: The Board, 1930–90.

———. *Proceedings.* Milwaukee: The Board, 1930–90.

———. Committee on Appointments. *Minutes.* Milwaukee: The Board, 1930–58.

———. Committee on Appointments and Instruction. *Minutes.* Milwaukee: The Board, 1959–80.

———. Committee on Instruction. *Minutes.* Milwaukee: The Board, 1981–90.

———. Special Committee on Equality of Educational Opportunity. *Minutes.* Milwaukee: The Board, 1963–66.

Milwaukee Commission on Community Relations. *The Negro in Milwaukee: Progress and Portent, 1863–1963.* Milwaukee: The Commission, 1963.

Milwaukee Commission on Human Rights. *Annual Report.* Milwaukee: The Commission, 1956.

New Jersey State Temporary Commission on the Condition of the Urban Colored Population. *Report to the Legislature of the State of New Jersey.* Trenton: The State, 1939.

U.S. Census Bureau. *Census of Population and Housing, Milwaukee, Wisconsin.* Washington, D.C.: Government Printing Office, 1930–2000.

U.S. Commission on Civil Rights. *Racial Isolation in the Public Schools: A Report.* Washington, D.C.: Government Printing Office, 1967.

Wisconsin Advisory Committee to the U.S. Commission on Civil Rights. *Impact of School Desegregation in Milwaukee Public Schools on Quality Education for Minorities, 15 Years Later.* Washington, D.C.: The Commission, 1992.

Wisconsin Department of Public Instruction, Study Commission on the Quality of Education in the Metropolitan Milwaukee Public Schools. *Better Public Schools.* Madison: The Commission, 1985.

Books, Articles, and Theses

Academy for Educational Development. *Quality Education in Milwaukee's Future.* New York: The Academy, 1967.

African American Male Task Force. *Educating African American Males: A Dream Deferred.* Milwaukee: Milwaukee Public Schools, 1990.

Anderson, Alan B., and George W. Pickering. *Confronting the Color Line: The Broken Promise of the Civil Rights Movement in Chicago.* Athens: University of Georgia Press, 1986.

Anderson, Harry, and Frederick Olson. *Milwaukee: At the Gathering of the Waters.* Tulsa: Continental Heritage Press, 1981.

Anderson, James D. *The Education of Blacks in the South, 1860–1935.* Chapel Hill: University of North Carolina Press, 1988.

Archbald, Douglas A. "Magnet Schools, Voluntary Desegregation, and Public Choice Theory: Limits and Possibilities in a Big City School System." Ph.D. diss., University of Wisconsin–Madison, 1989.

"Are Your Teachers Handcuffed on Discipline?" *School Management* 8 (April 1964): 107–15.

Armstrong, Julie Buckner, Susan Hult Edwards, Houston Bryan Roberson, and Rhonda Y. Williams, eds. *Teaching the American Civil Rights Movement: Freedom's Bittersweet Song.* New York: Routledge, 2002.

Arnez, Nancy. "Implementation of Desegregation as a Discriminatory Process." *Journal of Negro Education* 47 (1978): 28–45.

Aukofer, Frank. *City with a Chance.* Milwaukee: Bruce Publishing Company, 1968.

Back, Adina. "Up South in New York: The 1950s School Desegregation Struggles." Ph.D. diss., New York University, 1997.

Bamberger, Tom. "The Education of Howard Fuller." *Milwaukee Magazine,* July 1988, 39–62.

Banner, Warren M. *Study of Urban League Services, 1955–1959: Special Advisory Committee for the Board of Directors of the Milwaukee Urban League.* Milwaukee: Milwaukee Urban League, 1959.

Baratz, Stephen S., and Joan C. Baratz. "Early Childhood Intervention: The Social Science Basis of Institutional Racism." *Harvard Educational Review* 40 (Winter 1970): 31–50.

Barndt, Michael, Rick Janka, and Harold Rose. "The West and Midwest: Milwaukee, Wisconsin: Mobilization for School and Community Cooperation." In *Community Politics and Educational Change: Ten School Systems under Court Order*, edited by Charles V. Willie and Susan L. Greenblatt, 237–59. New York: Longman, 1981.

Barndt, Michael, and Joel McNally. *The Return to Separate and Unequal: Metropolitan Milwaukee School Funding through a Racial Lens*. Milwaukee: Rethinking Schools Report, 2001.

Baruch, Steven A. "Factors Affecting the Process of Curriculum Formation in the Milwaukee Public Schools, July 1955–June 1976." Ph.D. diss., University of Wisconsin–Milwaukee, 1982.

Bates, Beth Tompkins. "A New Crowd Challenges the Agenda of the Old Guard in the NAACP, 1933–1941." *American Historical Review* 102 (April 1997): 340–77.

Beason, Jake Patton. *Why We Lose: An Anthology for Black People's Cultural Survival*. Milwaukee: Col D'var Graphics, 1989.

Bell, Derrick. *And We Are Not Saved: The Elusive Quest for Racial Justice*. New York: Basic Books, 1987.

———. "The Case for a Separate Black School System." In *Black Education: A Quest for Equity and Excellence*, edited by Willy D. Smith and Eva W. Chunn, 136–45. New Brunswick: Transaction Press, 1989.

———, ed. *Shades of Brown: New Perspectives on School Desegregation*. New York: Teachers College Press, 1980.

Bennett, David A. "A Plan for Increasing Educational Opportunities and Improving Racial Balance in Milwaukee." In *School Desegregation Plans That Work*, by Charles V. Willie, 80–115. Westport, Conn.: Greenwood Press, 1984.

Beverstock, Frances, and Robert Stuckert, eds. *Metropolitan Milwaukee Fact Book: 1970*. Milwaukee: Milwaukee Urban Observatory, 1972.

Biondi, Martha. *To Stand and Fight: The Struggle for Civil Rights in Postwar New York City*. Cambridge, Mass.: Harvard University Press, 2003.

Blumberg, Rhoda Lois. *Civil Rights: The 1960s Freedom Struggle*. Rev. ed. Boston: Twayne Publishers, 1991.

Bolz, Robert Arthur. "A Descriptive Analysis of a Class for Educationally Underprivileged Children at Lloyd Street School, Milwaukee, Wisconsin." Master's thesis, University of Wisconsin–Milwaukee, 1958.

Bond, Horace Mann. *The Education of the Negro in the American Social Order*. 1934. Reprint, New York: Octagon Books, 1970.

Buchanan, Thomas P. "Black Milwaukee, 1890–1915." Master's thesis, University of Wisconsin–Milwaukee, 1974.

Bunche, Ralph J. *The Political Status of the Negro in the Age of FDR*. Chicago: University of Chicago Press, 1973.

Byndloss, Crystal. "Resistance, Confrontation, and Accommodation in Two Urban School Districts: Black-Led Reform Efforts in the 1960s and 1980s." Ph.D. diss., Harvard University, 1999.

Callaway, Rolland, and Steven Baruch. "The Milwaukee Curriculum." In *Seeds of Crisis: Public Schooling in Milwaukee since 1920*, edited by John L. Rury and Frank A. Cassell, 110–44. Madison: University of Wisconsin Press, 1993.

Carl, James. "The Politics of Education in a New Key: The 1988 Chicago School

Reform Act and the 1990 Milwaukee Parental Choice Program." Ph.D. diss., University of Wisconsin–Madison, 1995.

———. "Unusual Allies: Elite and Grass-Roots Origins of Parental Choice in Milwaukee." *Teachers College Record* 98 (Winter 1996): 266–85.

Carson, Clayborne. "Civil Rights Reform and the Black Freedom Struggle." In *The Civil Rights Movement in America*, edited by Charles W. Eagles, 19–32. Jackson: University of Mississippi Press, 1986.

Carter, Robert L. "A Reassessment of *Brown v. Board*." In *Shades of Brown: New Perspectives on School Desegregation*, edited by Derrick Bell, 21–28. New York: Teachers College Press, 1980.

———. "The Unending Struggle for Equal Educational Opportunity." In *Brown v. Board of Education: The Challenge for Today's Schools*, edited by Ellen Condliffe Lagemann and LaMar P. Miller, 19–26. New York: Teachers College Press, 1996.

Cecelski, David S. *Along Freedom Road: Hyde County, North Carolina, and the Fate of Black Schools in the South*. Chapel Hill: University of North Carolina Press, 1994.

Chafe, William. *Civilities and Civil Rights: Greensboro, North Carolina, and the Black Struggle for Freedom*. Oxford: Oxford University Press, 1980.

Chase, Phyllis McGruder. "African American Teachers in Buffalo: The First One Hundred Years." In *The Teacher's Voice: A Social History of Teaching in Twentieth-Century America*, edited by Richard Altenbaugh, 65–77. London: Falmer Press, 1992.

Citizens' Governmental Research Bureau. "Milwaukee's Negro Community." Unpublished report, compiled by Paula Lynagh, March 1946.

Clark, Kenneth, "Cultural Deprivation Theories." In *The Educationally Deprived: The Potential for Change*, edited by Kenneth Clark et al., 3–12. New York: MARC, 1972.

Clear, Delbert K. "Milwaukee Teachers' Education Association." Unpublished manuscript, MTEA, 1990.

Cohen, Lizabeth. *Making a New Deal: Industrial Workers in Chicago, 1919–1939*. Cambridge: Cambridge University Press, 1990.

Coleman, Jonathan. *Long Way to Go: Black and White in America*. New York: Atlantic Monthly Press, 1997.

Collier-Thomas, Bettye, and Vincent P. Franklin, eds. *Sisters in the Struggle: African American Women in the Civil Rights–Black Power Movement*. New York: New York University Press, 2001.

Conant, James Bryant. *Slums and Suburbs: A Commentary on Schools in Metropolitan Areas*. New York: McGraw Hill, 1961.

Countryman, Matthew J. "Civil Rights and Black Power in Philadelphia, 1940–1971." Ph.D. diss., Duke University, 1999.

Crain, Robert L. *The Politics of School Desegregation: Comparative Case Studies of Community Structure and Policy-Making*. Chicago: Aldine Publishing Company, 1968.

Crawford, Vicki L., Jacqueline Anne Rouse, and Barbara Woods, eds. *Women in the Civil Rights Movement: Trailblazers and Torchbearers, 1941–1965*. Brooklyn: Carlson Publishing, 1990.

Cronon, William. "A Place for Stories: Nature, History, and Narrative." *Journal of American History* 79 (March 1992): 1347–76.

Curry, Constance. *Silver Rights*. San Diego: Harcourt Brace and Company, 1995.

Cutler, Richard W. *Greater Milwaukee's Growing Pains, 1950–2000: An Insider's View.* Milwaukee: Milwaukee County Historical Society, 2001.

Dahlk, William John. "The Black Education Reform Movement in Milwaukee, 1963–1975." Master's thesis, University of Wisconsin–Milwaukee, 1990.

Dalfiume, Richard. "The 'Forgotten Years' of the Negro Revolution." *Journal of American History* 55 (June 1968): 90–106.

Danns, Dionne A. *Something Better for Our Children: Black Organization in the Chicago Public Schools, 1964–1971.* New York: Routledge, 2003.

Davidson, Osha Gray. *The Best of Enemies: Race and Redemption in the New South.* New York: Scribner, 1996.

Dempsey, Van, and George Noblit. "Cultural Ignorance and School Desegregation: Reconstructing a Silenced Narrative." *Educational Policy* 7 (1993): 318–39.

Donato, Ruben. *The Other Struggle for Equal Schools: Mexican Americans During the Civil Rights Movement.* Albany: State University of New York Press, 1997.

Dougherty, Jack. "From Anecdote to Analysis: Oral Interviews and New Scholarship in Educational History." *Journal of American History* 86 (September 1999): 712–23.

———. " 'That's When We Were Marching for Jobs': Black Teachers and the Early Civil Rights Movement in Milwaukee." *History of Education Quarterly* 38 (Summer 1998): 121–41.

Dougherty, Jack, et al. "Teaching *Brown*: Reflections on Pedagogical Challenges and Opportunities." *History of Education Quarterly* 44 (Spring 2004): forthcoming.

Douglas, Davison M. *Law and Culture: The Desegregation of Northern Schools, 1865–1954.* Unpublished manuscript, 2003.

———. "The Limits of Law in Accomplishing Racial Change: School Segregation in the Pre-*Brown* North." *UCLA Law Review* 44 (February 1997): 677–744.

Du Bois, W. E. B. "Does the Negro Need Separate Schools?" *Journal of Negro Education* 4 (1935): 328–35.

———. *The Philadelphia Negro: A Social Study.* Philadelphia: University of Pennsylvania, 1899.

———. "Postscript: Pechstein and Pecksniff." *Crisis,* September 1929, 313–14.

Edari, Ronald S. "The Life Cycle, Segregation and White Attitudes Towards Busing." Unpublished manuscript, University of Wisconsin–Milwaukee Urban Research Center, 1977.

Epstein, Terrie L. "Tales from Two Textbooks: A Comparison of the Civil Rights Movement in Two Secondary History Textbooks." *Social Studies* (May/June 1994): 121–26.

Ettenheim, Sarah C. *How Milwaukee Voted: 1848–1980.* Milwaukee: University of Wisconsin–Extension, Department of Governmental Affairs, 1980.

Fairclough, Adam. "Historians and the Civil Rights Movement." *Journal of American Studies* 24 (December 1990): 387–98.

Fantini, Mario, Marilyn Gittell, and Richard Magat. *Community Control and the Urban School.* New York: Praeger, 1970.

Farrell, Walter C., Jr., and Jackolyn E. Mathews. "School Choice and the Educational Opportunities of African American Children." *Journal of Negro Education* 59 (1990): 526–37.

Flahive, Robert. "Milwaukee's Change in School Discipline." *American School Board Journal* 147 (September 1963): 11–12.

Formisano, Ronald. *Boston against Busing: Race, Class, and Ethnicity in the 1960s and 1970s*. Chapel Hill: University of North Carolina Press, 1991.

Foster, Michele. "Constancy, Connectedness, and Constraints in the Lives of African-American Teachers." *NWSA Journal* 3 (Spring 1991): 233–61.

———. "The Politics of Race: Through the Eyes of African-American Teachers." *Journal of Education* 172 (1990): 123–41.

Franklin, Vincent P. *The Education of Black Philadelphia: The Social and Educational History of a Minority Community, 1900–1950*. Philadelphia: University of Pennsylvania Press, 1979.

Frazier, E. Franklin. *Black Bourgeoisie: The Rise of a New Middle Class*. New York: Free Press, 1957.

———. *The Negro in the United States*. Rev. ed. New York: Macmillan Company, 1957.

Fuller, Howard Lamar. "The Impact of the Milwaukee Public School System's Desegregation Plan on Black Students and the Black Community (1976–1982)." Ph.D. diss., Marquette University, 1985.

Fultz, Michael. "African American Teachers in the South, 1890–1940: Powerlessness and the Ironies of Expectations and Protest." *History of Education Quarterly* 35 (Winter 1995): 401–22.

Fure-Slocum, Eric. "The Challenge of the Working-Class City: Recasting Growth Politics and Liberalism in Milwaukee, 1937–1952." Ph.D. diss., University of Iowa, 2001.

Gaines, Kevin. *Uplifting the Race: Black Leadership, Politics, and Culture in the Twentieth Century*. Chapel Hill: University of North Carolina Press, 1996.

Gardner, Sarah. "Coming of Age in the Movement: Teaching with Personal Narratives." In *Teaching the American Civil Rights Movement: Freedom's Bittersweet Song*, edited by Julie Buckner Armstrong, Susan Hult Edwards, Houston Bryan Roberson, and Rhonda Y. Williams, 97–110. New York: Routledge, 2002.

Geib, Paul Edward. "The Late Great Migration: A Case Study of Southern Black Migration to Milwaukee, 1940–1970." Master's thesis, University of Wisconsin–Milwaukee, 1993.

Giddings, Paula. *When and Where I Enter: The Impact of Black Women on Race and Sex in America*. New York: Bantam Books, 1985.

Glazer, Nathan, and Daniel Patrick Moynihan. *Beyond the Melting Pot: The Negroes, Puerto Ricans, Jews, Italians, and Irish of New York City*. Cambridge: MIT Press, 1963.

Goddard, Caroline Katie. "Lloyd Barbee and the Fight for Desegregation in the Milwaukee Public School System." Master's thesis, University of Wisconsin–Milwaukee, 1985.

Goings, Kenneth W., and Raymond A. Mohl. "Toward a New African American Urban History." *Journal of Urban History* 21 (March 1995): 283–95.

Goldaber, Irving. "The Treatment by the New York City Board of Education of Problems Affecting the Negro, 1954–1963." Ph.D. diss., New York University, 1965.

Golightly, Cornelius. "De Facto Segregation in Milwaukee Schools." *Integrated Education* 1 (December 1963): 27–30.

Gosnell, Harold F. *Negro Politicians: The Rise of Negro Politics in Chicago.* Chicago: University of Chicago Press, 1935.

Grace, Alonzo Gaskell. "The Effect of Negro Migration on the Cleveland Public School System." Doctoral diss., Western Reserve University, 1932.

Granger, Lester. "Does the Negro Want Integration?" *Crisis*, February 1951, 73–79.

———. "Race Relations and the School System." *Opportunity*, November 1925, 327–29.

Grant, Gerald. *The World We Created at Hamilton High.* Cambridge, Mass.: Harvard University Press, 1988.

Greenleigh, Arthur. *A Plan to Reduce Prejudice and Discrimination in the Greater Milwaukee Area.* New York: Greenleigh Associates, 1967.

Grim, Valerie. "History Shared through Memory: The Establishment and Implementation of Education in the Brooks Farm Community, 1920–1957." *Oral History Review* 23 (Summer 1996): 1–17.

Grossman, James R. *Land of Hope: Chicago, Black Southerners, and the Great Migration.* Chicago: University of Chicago Press, 1989.

Grover, Michael Ross. "'All Things to Black Folks': A History of the Milwaukee Urban League, 1919 to 1980." Master's thesis, University of Wisconsin–Milwaukee, 1994.

Gurda, John. *The Making of Milwaukee.* Milwaukee: Milwaukee County Historical Society, 1999.

Hamilton, Roy L. "Expectations and Realities of a Migrant Group: Black Migration from the South to Milwaukee, 1946–1958." Master's thesis, University of Wisconsin–Milwaukee, 1981.

Handlin, Oscar. *The Newcomers: Negroes and Puerto Ricans in a Changing Metropolis.* Cambridge: Harvard University Press, 1959.

Harding, Vincent. *Hope and History: Why We Must Share the Story of the Movement.* Maryknoll: Orbis Books, 1990.

Harris, Ian M. "The Citizens Committee of Milwaukee." *Integrated Education* 15 (July/August 1978): 35–41.

———. "Community Involvement in Desegregation: The Milwaukee Experience." In *Strategies of Community Organization: Macro Practice*, edited by Fred M. Cox et al., 373–83. Itasca, Ill.: F. E. Peacock Publishers, 1987.

———. "Criteria for Evaluating School Desegregation in Milwaukee." *Journal of Negro Education* 52 (1983): 423–35.

———. "The Inequities of Milwaukee's Plan." *Integrated Education* 21 (July 1984): 173–77.

Hess, Frederick M. *Revolution at the Margins: The Impact of Competition on Urban School Systems.* Washington, D.C.: Brookings Institution Press, 2002.

Herrick, Mary J. "Negro Employees of the Chicago Board of Education." Master's thesis, University of Chicago, 1931.

Hill, Robert A., ed. *The FBI's RACON: Racial Conditions in the United States during World War II.* Boston: Northeastern University Press, 1995.

Hochschild, Jennifer L. *The New American Dilemma: Liberal Democracy and School Desegregation.* New Haven: Yale University Press, 1984.

———. *Thirty Years after Brown.* Washington, D.C.: Joint Center for Policy Studies, 1985.

Holt, Mikel. *Not Yet "Free at Last": The Unfinished Business of the Civil Rights Movement—Our Battle for School Choice.* Oakland: Institute for Contemporary Studies Press, 2000.

Homel, Michael W. *Down from Equality: Black Chicagoans and the Public Schools, 1920–1941.* Urbana: University of Illinois Press, 1984.

Imse, Thomas P. "The Negro Community in Milwaukee." Master's thesis, Marquette University, 1942.

Irvine, Russell W., and Jacqueline Jordan Irvine. "The Impact of the Desegregation Process on the Education of Black Students: Key Variables." *Journal of Negro Education* 52 (1983): 410–22.

Jacobs, Gregory S. *Getting around Brown: Desegregation, Development, and the Columbus Public Schools.* Columbus: Ohio State University Press, 1998.

Jeffrey, Julie Roy. *Education for Children of the Poor: A Study of the Origins and Implementation of the Elementary and Secondary Education Act of 1965.* Columbus: Ohio State University Press, 1978.

Jensen, Noma. "A Survey of Segregation Practices in the New Jersey School System." *Journal of Negro Education* 17 (Winter 1948): 84–88.

Jones, Faustine Childress. *A Traditional Model of Educational Excellence: Dunbar High School of Little Rock, Arkansas.* Washington, D.C.: Howard University, 1981.

Jones, Patrick D. "'The Selma of the North': Race Relations and Civil Rights Insurgency in Milwaukee, 1958–1970." Ph.D. diss., University of Wisconsin–Madison, 2002.

Joseph, Peniel E. "All Power to the People! Teaching Black Nationalism in the Post–Civil Rights Era." In *Teaching the American Civil Rights Movement: Freedom's Bittersweet Song,* edited by Julie Buckner Armstrong, Susan Hult Edwards, Houston Bryan Roberson, and Rhonda Y. Williams, 147–58. New York: Routledge, 2002.

Kantor, Harvey, and Robert Lowe. "Reform or Reaction? [Review Essay on *The World We Created at Hamilton High*]." *Harvard Educational Review* 59 (February 1989): 127–38.

Katz, Michael B. *Improving Poor People: The Welfare State, the "Underclass," and Urban Schools as History.* Princeton: Princeton University Press, 1995.

Kaufman, Polly Welts. "Building a Constituency for School Desegregation: African-American Women in Boston, 1962–1972." *Teachers College Record* 92 (Summer 1991): 619–31.

Kelley, Robin D. G. *Race Rebels: Culture, Politics, and the Black Working Class.* New York: Free Press, 1994.

Kersten, Andrew Edmund. *Race, Jobs, and the War: The FEPC in the Midwest, 1941–1946.* Urbana: University of Illinois Press, 2000.

Kirby, David J., T. Robert Harris, Robert Crain, and Christine H. Rossell. *Political Strategies in Northern School Desegregation.* Lexington, Mass.: D. C. Heath & Co., 1973.

Kirp, David. *Just Schools: The Idea of Racial Equality in American Education.* Berkeley: University of California Press, 1982.

Kluger, Richard. *Simple Justice: The History of Brown v. Board of Education and Black America's Struggle for Equality.* New York: Vintage Books, 1975.

Korstad, Robert, and Nelson Lichtenstein. "Opportunities Found and Lost: Labor,

Radicals, and the Early Civil Rights Movement." *Journal of American History* 75 (December 1988): 786–811.

Kritek, William J., and Delbert K. Clear. "Teachers and Principals in the Milwaukee Public Schools." In *Seeds of Crisis: Public Schooling in Milwaukee since 1920*, edited by John L. Rury and Frank A. Cassell, 145–92. Madison: University of Wisconsin Press, 1993.

Kuntz, Kathy. "A Lost Legacy: Head Start's Origins in Community Action." In *Critical Perspectives on Project Head Start*, edited by Jeanne Ellsworth and Lynda J. Ames, 1–48. Albany: State University of New York Press, 1998.

Ladner, Joyce. "What 'Black Power' Means to Negroes in Mississippi." *Transaction* 5 (November 1967): 7–15.

Lagemann, Ellen Condliffe, and LaMar P. Miller, eds. *Brown v. Board of Education: The Challenge for Today's Schools*. New York: Teachers College Press, 1996.

Lamers, W. *Our Roots Grow Deep: Second Edition, 1836–1967*. Milwaukee: Milwaukee Public Schools, 1974.

Larkin, Joe. "School Desegregation and Student Suspension: A Look at One School System." *Education and Urban Society* 11 (1979): 485–95.

Lawson, Steven F. "Freedom Then, Freedom Now: The Historiography of the Civil Rights Movement." *American Historical Review* 96 (1991): 456–71.

Lawson, Steven F., and Charles M. Payne. *Debating the Civil Rights Movement, 1945–1968*. Lanham, Md.: Rowman and Littlefield, 1998.

Leake, Donald O., and Christine J. Faltz. "Do We Need to Desegregate All of Our Black Schools?" *Educational Policy* 7 (1993): 370–87.

Leake, Donald O., and Brenda L. Leake. "Islands of Hope: Milwaukee's African American Immersion Schools." *Journal of Negro Education* 61 (1992): 24–29.

Levine, Marc V., and John F. Zipp. "A City at Risk: The Changing Social and Economic Context of Public Schooling in Milwaukee." In *Seeds of Crisis: Public Schooling in Milwaukee since 1920*, edited by John L. Rury and Frank A. Cassell, 42–72. Madison: University of Wisconsin Press, 1993.

Link, William A. "Film Review: *The Road to Brown*." *History of Education Quarterly* 31 (Winter 1991): 523–26.

Lowe, Robert, and Harvey Kantor. "Considerations on Writing the History of Educational Reform in the 1960s." *Educational Theory* 39 (1989): 1–9.

———. "Creating Educational Opportunity for African Americans without Upsetting the Status Quo." In *Changing Populations, Changing Schools: Ninety-fourth Yearbook of the National Society for the Study of Education*, edited by Erwin Flaxman and A. Harry Passow, 186–208. Chicago: University of Chicago Press, 1995.

Lowe, Robert, and Barbara Miner, eds. *Selling Out Our Schools: Vouchers, Markets, and the Future of Public Education*. Milwaukee: Rethinking Schools Publications, 1996.

Lowe, Robert, and Joan Whipp. "Examining the Milwaukee Parent Choice Program: Options or Opportunities?" *Educational Researcher* 31 (January/February 2002): 33–39.

Lukas, J. Anthony. *Common Ground: A Turbulent Decade in the Lives of Three American Families*. New York: Knopf, 1985.

Mabee, Carleton. *Black Education in New York State: From Colonial to Modern Times*. Syracuse: Syracuse University Press, 1979.

Mack, Raymond M. *Our Children's Burden: Studies of Desegregation in Nine American Communities.* New York: Random House, 1968.

Marable, Manning. *Race, Reform, and Rebellion: The Second Reconstruction in Black America, 1945–1990.* 2d ed. Jackson: University of Mississippi Press, 1990.

Maslow, Will. "De Facto Public School Segregation." *Villanova Law Review* 6 (Spring 1961): 353–76.

Massey, Douglas S., and Nancy A. Denton. *American Apartheid: Segregation and the Making of the Underclass.* Cambridge, Mass.: Harvard University Press, 1993.

McEvilly, Marian L. "Teacher and Student Images of Education, Safety and Integration in Three Racially Changing High Schools in Milwaukee." Master's thesis, University of Wisconsin–Milwaukee, 1973.

McGreevy, John T. *Parish Boundaries: The Catholic Encounter with Race in the Twentieth-Century Urban North.* Chicago: University of Chicago Press, 1995.

McGroarty, Daniel. *Break These Chains: The Battle for School Choice.* Rocklin, Calif.: Forum, 1996.

Meier, August, and Elliott Rudwick. *Along the Color Line: Explorations in the Black Experience.* Urbana: University of Illinois Press, 1976.

———. *CORE: A Study in the Civil Rights Movement, 1942–1968.* New York: Oxford University Press, 1983.

Ment, David. "Patterns of Public School Segregation, 1900–1940: A Comparative Study of New York City, New Rochelle and New Haven." In *Schools in Cities,* edited by Ronald K. Goodenow and Diane Ravitch, 67–110. New York: Holmes and Meier, 1983.

Merida, Kevin. "Howard Fuller: '60s Activist Still Active." *Milwaukee Journal Insight Magazine,* 21 March 1982, 5–9.

Metz, Mary Haywood. *Different by Design: Context and Character of Three Magnet Schools.* 1985. Reprint, New York: Routledge, 1992.

Meyer, Stephen. *"Stalin over Wisconsin": The Making and Unmaking of Militant Unionism, 1900–1950.* New Brunswick: Rutgers University Press, 1992.

Meyer, Stephen Grant. *As Long as They Don't Move Next Door: Segregation and Racial Conflict in American Neighborhoods.* Lanham, Md.: Rowman and Littlefield, 2000.

Milwaukee County Historical Society. *The Negro in Milwaukee: A Historical Survey.* Milwaukee: Milwaukee County Historical Society, 1968.

Milwaukee County Welfare Rights Organization. *Welfare Mothers Speak Out: We Ain't Gonna Shuffle Anymore.* New York: Norton, 1972.

Miner, Barbara. "Splits Widen within Wisconsin Voucher Movement." *Rethinking Schools* (Summer 1997): 10.

Mirel, Jeffrey. *The Rise and Fall of an Urban School System: Detroit, 1907–1981.* Ann Arbor: University of Michigan Press, 1993.

Modlinski, Jules, and Esther Zaret. *The Federation of Independent Community Schools: An Alternative Urban School System.* Milwaukee: The Federation, 1970.

Mohraz, Judy Jolley. *The Separate Problem: Case Studies of Black Education in the North, 1900–1930.* Westport, Conn.: Greenwood Press, 1979.

Montgomery, Theodore V., Jr. *School Desegregation Planning, Milwaukee 1976 Chronology, Plans, and Participants.* Milwaukee: Division of Urban Outreach, University of Wisconsin–Milwaukee, 1979.

Monti, Daniel J. *A Semblance of Justice: School Desegregation and the Pursuit of Order in Urban America.* Columbia: University of Missouri Press, 1985.

Moore, Jesse Thomas. *A Search for Equality: The National Urban League, 1910–1961.* University Park: Pennsylvania State University Press, 1981.

Moore, Leonard N. *Carl B. Stokes and the Rise of Black Political Power.* Urbana: University of Illinois Press, 2002.

———. "The School Desegregation Crisis of Cleveland, Ohio, 1963–64." *Journal of Urban History* 28 (January 2002): 135–57.

Morris, Aldon D. *The Origins of the Civil Rights Movement: Black Communities Organizing for Change.* New York: Free Press, 1984.

Murphy, Bruce, and John Pawasarat. "Why It Failed: School Desegregation Ten Years Later." *Milwaukee Magazine*, September 1986, 34–50.

Murrell, Peter, Jr. "Afrocentric Immersion: Academic and Personal Development of African American Males in Public Schools." In *Freedom's Plow: Teaching in the Multicultural Classroom,* edited by Teresa Perry and James Fraser, 231–60. New York: Routledge, 1993.

———. "North Division District Plan." *Rethinking Schools* 2 (December 1987): 1.

Myrdal, Gunnar. *An American Dilemma: The Negro Problem and Modern Democracy.* New York: Harper, 1944.

NAACP Youth and College Division. *March on Milwaukee: NAACP Milwaukee Youth Council Demonstrations for Fair Housing.* New York: NAACP, 1968.

Nasstrom, Kathryn L. "Beginnings and Endings: Life Stories and the Periodization of the Civil Rights Movement." *Journal of American History* 86 (September 1999): 700–711.

Nelsen, James K. "Racial Integration in the Milwaukee Public Schools, 1963–2003." Master's thesis, University of Wisconsin-Milwaukee, 2003.

Neustadt, Richard E., and Ernest R. May. *Thinking in Time: The Uses of History for Decision-Makers.* New York: Free Press, 1986.

Newby, Robert G., and David B. Tyack. "Victims without 'Crimes': Some Historical Perspectives on Black Education." *Journal of Negro Education* 40 (1971): 192–206.

Norrell, Robert J. "One Thing We Did Right: Reflections on the Movement." In *New Directions in Civil Rights Studies,* edited by Armistead L. Robinson and Patricia Sullivan, 65–80. Charlottesville: University Press of Virginia, 1991.

Nuhlicek, Allan L. "Orientation Centers for In-migrants and Transients." *National Elementary Principal* 46 (January 1967): 34–38.

Olson, Lynn. "Black Community Is Frustrated over Lack of Results from Desegregation." *Education Week* (17 October 1990): 1, 12–13.

O'Reilly, Charles T., Steven I. Pflanczer, and Willard E. Downing. *The People of the Inner Core-North.* New York: LePlay Research, 1965.

Orfield, Gary. *The Reconstruction of Southern Education: The Schools and the 1964 Civil Rights Act.* New York: Wiley, 1969.

———. *Schools More Separate: Consequences of a Decade of Resegregation.* Cambridge, Mass.: The Civil Rights Project, Harvard University, July 2001.

Orfield, Gary, and Susan E. Eaton. *Dismantling Desegregation: The Quiet Reversal of Brown v. Board of Education.* New York: New Press, 1996.

Orum, Anthony M. *City-Building in America.* Boulder: Westview Press, 1995.

Parris, Guichard, and Lester Brooks. *Blacks in the City: A History of the National Urban League.* Boston: Little, Brown, 1971.

Patterson, James T. *Brown v. Board of Education: A Civil Rights Milestone and Its Troubled Legacy.* New York: Oxford Press, 2001.

Payne, Charles M. *I've Got the Light of Freedom: The Organizing Tradition and the Mississippi Freedom Struggle.* Berkeley: University of California Press, 1995.

———. "'Men Led, but Women Organized': Movement Participation of Women in the Mississippi Delta." In *Women and Social Protest,* edited by Guida West and Rhoda L. Blumberg, 156–65. New York: Oxford University Press, 1990.

Pechstein, L. A. "The Problem of Negro Education in Northern and Border Cities." *Elementary School Journal* 30 (November 1929): 192–99.

Perkins, Margo. *Autobiography as Activism: Three Black Women of the Sixties.* Jackson: University of Mississippi Press, 2000.

Perlstein, Daniel. *Justice, Justice: School Politics and the Eclipse of Liberalism.* New York: Peter Lang, 2003.

———. "Minds Stayed on Freedom: Politics, Pedagogy, and the African American Freedom Struggle." *American Educational Research Journal* 39 (2002): 249–78.

Peterson, Bob. "Neighborhood Schools, Busing, and the Struggle for Equality." *Rethinking Schools* (Spring 1998): 20–22.

Peterson, Bob, and Larry Miller. "Forward to the Past?" *Rethinking Schools* (Fall 2000): 18–20.

Peterson, Paul E., and Bryan C. Hassel, eds. *Learning from School Choice.* Washington, D.C.: Brookings Institution Press, 1998.

Philipsen, Maike. *Values Spoken and Values Lived: Race and the Cultural Consequences of a School Closing.* Cresskill, N.J.: Hampton Press, 1999.

Phillips, Kimberley L. *AlabamaNorth: African-American Migrants, Community, and Working-Class Activism in Cleveland, 1915–1945.* Urbana: University of Chicago Press, 1999.

Pierce, Richard B., II. "Beneath the Surface: African-American Community Life in Indianapolis, 1945–1970." Ph.D. diss., Indiana University, 1996.

Podair, Jerald E. *The Strike That Changed New York: Blacks, Whites, and the Ocean Hill–Brownsville Crisis.* New Haven, Conn.: Yale University Press, 2002.

Porter, Jennie D. "The Problem of Negro Education in Northern and Border Cities." Doctoral diss., University of Cincinnati, 1928.

Pride, Richard A., and J. David Woodard. *The Burden of Busing: The Politics of Desegregation in Nashville, Tennessee.* Knoxville: University of Tennessee Press, 1985.

Proctor, Ralph, Jr. "Racial Discrimination against Black Teachers and Black Professionals in the Pittsburgh Public School System, 1834–1973." Doctoral diss., University of Pittsburgh, 1979.

Rauch, Sister Dolores. "The Changing Status of Urban Catholic Parochial Schools: An Explanatory Model Illustrating Demand for Catholic Elementary Education in Milwaukee County." Ph.D. diss., University of Wisconsin–Milwaukee, 1971.

———. "Impact of Population Changes in the Central Area of Milwaukee upon Catholic Parochial Schools, 1940–1970." Master's thesis, University of Wisconsin–Milwaukee, 1967.

Ravitch, Diane. *The Great School Wars, New York City, 1805–1973: A History of the Public Schools as Battlefield of Social Change.* New York: Basic Books, 1974.

———. *The Troubled Crusade: American Education, 1945–1980.* New York: Basic Books, 1983.

Reese, William J. *Power and the Promise of School Reform: Grass-Roots Movements during the Progressive Era.* Boston: Routledge and Kegan Paul, 1986.

Reid, Ira De A. *Social Conditions of the Negro in the Hill District of Pittsburgh.* Pittsburgh: General Committee on the Hill Survey, 1930.

Reid, John B. "Race, Class, Gender and the Teaching Profession: African American Schoolteachers of the Urban Midwest, 1865–1950." Ph.D. diss., Michigan State University, 1996.

Richardson, Joanna. "The Unexpected Superintendent." *Education Week,* 25 May 1994, 20–26.

Rigdon, Mark E. "The Business of Education Reform: An Analysis of Corporate Involvement in Education Reform Movements in Kentucky, Milwaukee, and Chicago." Ph.D. diss., University of Wisconsin–Madison, 1995.

Robnett, Belinda. *How Long? How Long? African-American Women in the Struggle for Civil Rights.* New York: Oxford University Press, 1997.

Rose, Harold M., and Linda Stewart. *Milwaukee's City-Suburban Interdistrict Integration Program: A Review of the Student Application and Assignment Process.* Milwaukee: Compact for Educational Opportunity, 1990.

Rury, John L., and Frank Cassell, eds. *Seeds of Crisis: Public Schooling in Milwaukee since 1920.* Madison: University of Wisconsin Press, 1993.

San Miguel, Guadalupe, Jr. *Brown, Not White: School Integration and the Chicano Movement in Houston.* College Station: Texas A&M University Press, 2001.

Schmitz, Keith Robert. "Milwaukee and Its Black Community, 1930–1942." Master's thesis, University of Wisconsin–Milwaukee, 1979.

Self, Robert. *American Babylon: Race and the Struggle for Postwar Oakland.* Princeton: Princeton University Press, 2003.

———. "'To Plan Our Liberation': Black Power and the Politics of Place in Oakland, California, 1965–1977." *Journal of Urban History* 26 (2000): 759–92.

Shircliffe, Barbara. "'We Got the Best of That World': A Case for the Study of Nostalgia in the Oral History of School Segregation." *Oral History Review* 28 (Summer/Fall 2001): 59–84.

Sitkoff, Harvard. *The Struggle for Black Equality, 1954–1992.* Rev. ed. New York: Hill and Wang, 1993.

Smith, Michael C. "The Creation of an Inner City District for Inner City Students: A Commentary." *Metropolitan Education* 5 (1987): 1–6.

Smuckler, Richard Charles. "Black Power and the NAACP: Milwaukee, 1969, A Case Study." Master's thesis, University of Wisconsin–Madison, 1970.

Smythe, Hugh H., and Rufus Smith. "Race Policies and Practices in Selected Public School Systems of Pennsylvania." *Journal of Negro Education* 17 (Fall 1948): 549–55.

Still, Bayrd. *Milwaukee: The History of a City.* Madison: State Historical Society of Wisconsin, 1948.

Stolee, Michael. "The Milwaukee Desegregation Case." In *Seeds of Crisis: Public School-*

ing in Milwaukee since 1920, edited by John L. Rury and Frank A. Cassell, 229–68. Madison: University of Wisconsin Press, 1993.

Stulberg, Lisa. "Teach a New Day: African American Alternative Institution-Building and the Politics of Race and Schooling since Brown." Ph.D. diss., University of California–Berkeley, 2001.

Sugrue, Thomas F. *The Origins of the Urban Crisis: Race and Inequality in Postwar Detroit.* Princeton: Princeton University Press, 1996.

Sullivan, Patricia, and Waldo E. Martin, Jr. "Introduction." In *Teaching the American Civil Rights Movement: Freedom's Bittersweet Song*, edited by Julie Buckner Armstrong, Susan Hult Edwards, Houston Bryan Roberson, and Rhonda Y. Williams, xi–xvi. New York: Routledge, 2002.

Tatum, Beverly Daniel. *"Why Are All the Black Kids Sitting Together in the Cafeteria?" and Other Conversations about Race.* New York: Basic Books, 1999.

Tatum, Elbert Lee. *The Changed Political Thought of the Negro, 1915–1940.* 1951. Reprint, Westport, Conn.: Greenwood Press, 1974.

Taylor, Clarence. *Knocking at Our Own Door: Milton A. Galamison and the Struggle to Integrate New York City Schools.* New York: Columbia University Press, 1997.

Taylor, Steven J. L. *Desegregation in Boston and Buffalo: The Influence of Local Leaders.* Albany: State University of New York Press, 1998.

Theoharis, Jeanne. "'We Saved the City': Black Struggles for Educational Equality in Boston, 1960–1976." *Radical History Review* 81 (Fall 2001): 61–83.

Theoharis, Jeanne F., and Komozi Woodard, eds. *Freedom North: Black Freedom Struggles Outside the South, 1940–1980.* New York: Palgrave Macmillan, 2003.

Thompson, Heather Ann. *Whose Detroit? Politics, Labor, and Race in a Modern American City.* Ithaca: Cornell University Press, 2001.

Thompson, William F. *The History of Wisconsin.* Vol. 6, *Continuity and Change, 1940–1965.* Madison: State Historical Society, 1988.

Thornbrough, Emma Lou. *Indiana Blacks in the Twentieth Century.* Bloomington: Indiana University Press, 2000.

———. *The Negro in Indiana: Study of a Minority.* Indianapolis: Indiana Historical Society, 1957.

Tien, H. Yuan. *Milwaukee Metropolitan Area Fact Book: 1940, 1950, and 1960.* Madison: University of Wisconsin Press, 1962.

Trotter, Joe William. *Black Milwaukee: The Making of an Industrial Proletariat, 1915–1945.* Urbana: University of Illinois Press, 1985.

Tyack, David B. "Growing Up Black: Perspectives on the History of Education in Northern Ghettos." *History of Education Quarterly* 9 (1969): 287–97.

———. *The One Best System: A History of American Urban Education.* Cambridge: Harvard University Press, 1974.

Tyack, David B., Robert Lowe, and Elizabeth Hansot. *Public Schools in Hard Times: The Great Depression and Recent Years.* Cambridge: Harvard University Press, 1984.

Tyson, Timothy B. *Radio Free Dixie: Robert F. Williams and the Roots of Black Power.* Chapel Hill: University of North Carolina Press, 1999.

Utz, Fielding Eric. "Northcott Neighborhood House." *Milwaukee History* 6 (Winter 1983): 115–24.

Vaeth, C. "Milwaukee Negro Residential Segregation." Unpublished report, Milwaukee Public Library, c. 1948.

Van Deburg, William L. *New Day in Babylon: The Black Power Movement and American Culture, 1965–1975*. Chicago: University of Chicago Press, 1992.

Viadero, Debra. "Researcher at Center of Storm over Vouchers." *Education Week*, 5 August 1998.

Vorlop, Frederic Clayton. "Equal Opportunity and the Politics of Education in Milwaukee." Ph.D. diss., University of Wisconsin–Madison, 1970.

Walker, Vanessa Siddle. *Their Highest Potential: An African American School Community in the Segregated South*. Chapel Hill: University of North Carolina Press, 1996.

Washington, Robert O., and John Oliver. *The Identification of Strengths in the Black Community of Metropolitan Milwaukee*. Milwaukee: Milwaukee Urban Observatory, 1976.

Watkins, Ralph Richard. "Black Buffalo, 1920–1927." Ph.D. diss., State University of New York at Buffalo, 1978.

Weems, Robert E., Jr. "Black Working Class, 1915–1925." *Milwaukee History* 6 (Winter 1983): 107–14.

———. "From the Great Migration to the Great Depression: Black Milwaukee, 1915–1929." Master's thesis, University of Wisconsin–Milwaukee, 1982.

Weiss, Nancy J. *The National Urban League, 1910–1940*. New York: Oxford University Press, 1974.

———. *Whitney M. Young, Jr., and the Struggle for Civil Rights*. Princeton: Princeton University Press, 1989.

Wells, Robert W. *This Is Milwaukee*. Garden City: Doubleday, 1970.

Wendelberger, Jay. "The Open Housing Movement in Milwaukee: Hidden Transcripts of the Urban Poor." Master's thesis, University of Wisconsin–Milwaukee, 1996.

West, Guida, and Rhoda L. Blumberg. "Reconstructing Social Protest from a Feminist Perspective." In *Women and Social Protest*, edited by Guida West and Rhoda L. Blumberg, 3–35. New York: Oxford University Press, 1990.

Wilde, H. R. "Milwaukee's National Media Riot." In *Urban Government*, edited by Edward Banfield, 682–88. New York: Free Press, 1969.

Wilkerson, Doxey. "The Negro in American Education: A Research Memorandum for the Carnegie-Myrdal Study, 'The Negro in America.'" Unpublished report in Schomburg Collection, New York Public Library, 1940.

Wilkinson, J. Harvie. *From Brown to Bakke: The Supreme Court and School Integration, 1954–1978*. New York: Oxford University Press, 1979.

Williams, Howard J. "The Educational Status of Colored Children in the Garfield Avenue, Ninth Street, and Fourth Street Public Elementary Schools of Milwaukee, Wisconsin." Master's thesis, Marquette University, 1935.

Williams, Lillian Serece. *Strangers in the Land of Paradise: The Creation of an African American Community, Buffalo, New York, 1900–1940*. Bloomington: Indiana University Press, 1999.

Williams, Virginia W. "Negro History Makers in Milwaukee [biography of William V. Kelley]." *Echo*, March 1967, 15–17.

———. "Negro History Makers in Milwaukee [biography of Vel Phillips]." *Echo*, November 1967, 8–10.

———. "Wisconsin Negro History Makers [biography of Grant Gordon]." *Echo*, June 1966, 10–11.

Willie, Charles V. *School Desegregation Plans That Work*. Westport, Conn.: Greenwood Press, 1984.

Wilson, Amy. "Exhibition Review: National Civil Rights Museum." *Journal of American History* 83 (December 1996): 971–76.

Witt, Andrew Richard. "Self-Help and Self-Defense: A Revaluation of the Black Panther Party with Emphasis on the Milwaukee Chapter." Master's thesis, University of Wisconsin–Milwaukee, 1999.

Witte, John F. *The Market Approach to Education: An Analysis of America's First Voucher Program*. Princeton: Princeton University Press, 2000.

Wolters, Raymond. *The Burden of Brown: Thirty Years of School Desegregation*. Knoxville: University of Tennessee Press, 1984.

Wood, Barbara Johnson. "The Legislative Development and Enactment of the Milwaukee Parental Choice Program." Ph.D. diss., University of Wisconsin–Madison, 1999.

Woodard, Komozi. *A Nation within a Nation: Amiri Baraka (Leroi Jones) and Black Power Politics*. Chapel Hill: University of North Carolina Press, 1999.

Wortzel, Dena. "Strange Bedfellows and Uncertain Futures: Racial and Class Politics in the Milwaukee School Voucher Debate." Master's thesis, University of Wisconsin–Madison, 1994.

Wye, Christopher G. "Midwest Ghetto: Patterns of Negro Life and Thought in Cleveland, Ohio, 1929–1945." Ph.D. diss., Kent State University, 1973.

Zimmerman, Jonathan. *Whose America? Culture Wars in the Public Schools*. Cambridge, Mass.: Harvard University Press, 2002.

INDEX